JAN BELL • ROGER GOWER

ficate

ert

OURSEBOOK

PEARSON
Longman

Contents

(Teacher's Book) **Paper 2 Part 2:** Writing (letter, article, composition, story). **Paper 4 Part 4:** Listening (multiple choice).

(Teacher's Book) **Paper 2 Part 2:** Writing (composition, report, article, letter). **Paper 4 Part 3:** Listening (multiple matching).

(Teacher's Book) **Paper 2 Part 1:** Writing (informal letter). **Paper 4 Part 2:** Listening (sentence completion).

Exam overview

▶ See page 188 for Exam reference

The Cambridge First Certificate in English has five papers. Each paper receives 20 per cent of the total marks and each has equal value. The pass mark is based on an overall mark (you do not need to pass every paper to pass the exam). There are three pass grades (A, B and C) and two fail grades (D and E). Normally, you need to get about 60 per cent to achieve a grade C.

Paper	Task type	Task description
Paper 1: Reading • 1 hour 15 minutes • Four parts • 35 reading comprehension questions in total	**Part 1:** multiple matching (6–7 questions). **Part 2:** multiple choice (7–8 questions). **Part 3:** gapped text (6–7 questions). **Part 4:** multiple matching (13–15 questions).	**Part 1:** matching headings or summary sentences to paragraphs in a text. **Part 2:** answering four-option multiple-choice questions on a text. **Part 3:** completing a gapped text with sentences or paragraphs which have been removed and placed in jumbled order. **Part 4:** matching information to 4–6 different texts (or different parts of a text).
Paper 2: Writing • 1 hour 30 minutes • Two tasks (one compulsory, the other a choice from five options) • 120–180 words for each task	**Part 1:** transactional letter (compulsory). **Part 2:** one writing task from a choice of five.	**Part 1:** using information provided to write a formal or informal letter. **Part 2:** carrying out a writing task, using appropriate format and style. Questions 2–4 may include an informal letter, a formal letter of application, an article, a report, a story. Question 5 is a two-option question based on the set books.
Paper 3: Use of English • 1 hour 15 minutes • Five parts • 65 questions in total	**Part 1:** multiple-choice cloze (15 questions). **Part 2:** open cloze (15 questions). **Part 3:** key word transformation (10 questions). **Part 4:** error correction (15 questions). **Part 5:** word formation (10 questions).	**Part 1:** choosing a word or phrase from four options to fill in gaps in a text. Vocabulary. **Part 2:** filling in gaps in a text with an appropriate word. Grammar. **Part 3:** using a given word to complete a sentence so that it means the same as a previous sentence. Grammar and vocabulary. **Part 4:** identifying extra, incorrect words in 15 lines of text. Grammar. **Part 5:** changing the form of a given word to make it fit the gaps in a text. Vocabulary.
Paper 4: Listening • Approximately 40 minutes • Four parts • 30 questions in total	**Part 1:** multiple choice (8 questions). **Part 2:** note-taking or sentence completion (10 questions). **Part 3:** multiple matching (5 questions). **Part 4:** choosing from 2 or 3 answers (7 questions).	**Part 1:** eight short unrelated extracts, each with a multiple-choice question with three options. **Part 2:** a longer text with note-taking or sentence completion questions. **Part 3:** five short related extracts to match to a list of six options. **Part 4:** a longer text with *True/False, Yes/No* or three-option multiple-choice questions.
Paper 5: Speaking • Approximately 14 minutes • Four parts	**Part 1:** interview, giving personal information (3 minutes). **Part 2:** individual long turn, giving information and expressing opinions (1 minute each candidate). **Part 3:** collaborative task, exchanging information and ideas (3–4 minutes). **Part 4:** discussion, developing the topic from Part 3 (4 minutes).	**Part 1:** examiner asks each candidate questions about themselves. **Part 2:** each candidate, individually, compares and contrasts two photos, and comments briefly on the other candidate's photo. **Part 3:** each candidate works with a partner to discuss a task, using pictures or diagrams. **Part 4:** the examiner leads a discussion between the two candidates, developing the topic of Part 3.

Lifestyles

Overview

- **Reading:** skills: skimming and scanning
- **Language development 1:** present and past habits
- **Writing:** an informal letter (Paper 2 Part 2)
- **Listening:** skills: listening for gist and specific information
- **Speaking:** comparing and contrasting photos (Paper 5 Part 2)
- **Language development 2:** comparatives and superlatives
- **Use of English 1:** key word transformation (Paper 3 Part 3)
- **Use of English 2:** lexical cloze (Paper 3 Part 1)
- **Language development 3:** collocations: adjectives and nouns

Living independently in a student hostel

A busy social life

Studying in groups

Lead-in

- Look at the extract from the Longman *Dictionary of Contemporary English*. Mark the key points that define *lifestyle*.

    life·style /ˈlaɪfstaɪl/ *n* [C] the way someone lives, including the place they live in, the things they own, the kind of job they do, and the activities they enjoy: *a luxurious lifestyle*

- The photos show typical aspects of a student's lifestyle in the UK. Which would you most/least enjoy? Why?

- Think of one adjective that describes your lifestyle best.

Reading

Before you read

1 a Look at the title of the article opposite and the introduction. What are you going to read about?

   b Look at the photos of the three families.
   1 What country do you think they live in?
   2 What kind of lifestyle do you think they have? Choose words from the list.
   traditional   modern   luxurious   hard   busy   well-organised
   3 What do you think they want for the future?

Skimming

2 a Skim the text to find the answers to the questions in Exercise 1b. In section A, the main ideas have been underlined for you.

   b Compare and discuss your answers. Were you right? Were there any surprises?

   c Which parts of sections B and C contain the main ideas?

Scanning

3 You are going to scan the text to answer the questions below.

   a Look at the example (0). The highlighted words in section B of the text link to the key words in the question.

   b Answer questions 1–10. The key words are highlighted for you.

Which section or sections mention(s) the following?		
Other relatives live with the family.	0 B	
The husband is self-employed.	1	
The family would like a different place to live.	2	3
The husband helps with domestic duties.	4	5
The husband likes to relax by singing.	6	
Both husband and wife have a job.	7	
The family has a pet.	8	
The couple has only one child.	9	

   c Compare and justify your answers. Which words and phrases in the text link to the key words in the questions?
   EXAMPLE: *Question 1–A: self-employed – has his own workshop*

Discussion

4 Discuss these questions.
   1 Which family's lifestyle is most similar to/different from yours?
   EXAMPLE: *In some ways, my family is quite similar to the de Frutos family. For example, …*
   2 What is your/your family's *greatest wish for the future?*

DIFFERENT WORLDS, SAME DREAMS

For the book Material World*, photo-journalists travelled to 30 nations around the world to live with an average family for a week. The extracts below describe the everyday lives of three of these families and their wishes and hopes for the future.*

A THE DE FRUTOS FAMILY

José Maria de Frutos, 25, and his wife Paloma, 23, represent a new generation of Spaniards who are doing things 'the European way'. The couple met when they were teenagers and didn't marry until their daughter was two. They do not want
5 to have any more children for the time being, a change from the days when Spanish families were 'as big as God wanted them'. They do not go to church unless there is a wedding or a christening. And, far from avoiding the household chores, José Maria is comfortable cooking for the family.
10 Of course their lives are not totally different from those of their parents. José Maria believes that the man of the household should be the provider and that the woman should stay at home with the children, and to a large extent this is what happens. José has his own workshop in the basement of
15 their apartment building, and when he leaves the flat for work, Paloma gives 5-year-old Sheila her morning bath and takes her to kindergarten. Returning home, Paloma cleans the house to the accompaniment of televised soap operas.
Wishes for the future include a new four-wheel drive
20 vehicle and clothes. Sheila would like a brother.

B THE REGZEN FAMILY

The Regzen family moved from the countryside to the outskirts of Mongolia's capital city, Ulaanbaatar five years ago, but in many ways, they still follow a traditional way of life. Their home is a *ger*, a tent-like house developed to be
25 portable when Mongols lived as nomads. Regzen Batsuury

and his wife, Lkhamsuren Oyuntsetseg, who have two children, share the *ger* with Batsuury's sister and her daughter. Nine-year-old Khorloo, the older of their children, walks the two kilometres to school with her cousin,
30 Yeruultzul.
But although they still live like country dwellers, Batsuury and Oyuntsetseg commute each day to city jobs in Mongolia's super-crowded buses. Batsuury is a truck driver and construction worker, and Oyuntsetseg works in the
35 dispensary of the downtown hospital. Dividing household chores is a necessity – Batsuury works 50-60 hours a week and Oyuntsetseg puts in a full 40-hour week at the hospital. She is occasionally able to take an afternoon off to get her hair done at a nearby salon.
40 The Regzens value the old ways and Lkhamsuren's most prized possession is the statue of Buddha which they inherited from her grandmother. Batsuury prizes their television, a benefit of 21st-century progress.
The couple want a better life for their children by giving
45 them an education. Their greatest wish is for a permanent home made of wood and cement.

C THE UKITA FAMILY

The Ukita family of Tokyo have the morning down to a science. The supremely organised Sayo rises half an hour before anyone else in the family. After waking her husband
50 Kazuo and the children, she prepares the meal, dresses the kids, collects the homework and gathers the family at the morning table. After a quick breakfast, Kazuo leaves for work at exactly 7.28, arriving at the station 45 seconds before the train – as this is Japan, it is exactly on time.
55 Several times a week, after an exhausting day at work, he'll stop in at a karaoke bar to have a drink, a cigarette and a turn at the microphone.
For the Ukita children, the schedule is equally hectic. Nine-year-old Miyo is at school, but, like most Japanese
60 children, she also attends extra classes on Saturday mornings to prepare for the national exams. It is essential to pass these exams in Japan if you want a good career. Maya is in kindergarten and therefore too young to worry about exams. Rather than study, she uses the time before school to
65 skip rope and play with the family dog.
The family's wish for the future is to have a larger house and a second apartment or house for rental income.

Language development 1

Situations and habits in the present

1 a Which person in the picture does each sentence describe?

1 She *lives* in a small house with her husband and children.

2 His children *are growing up* fast!

3 He*'ll sit and doze* in an armchair all evening.

4 She*'s always making* long calls on the phone.

5 He*'s staying* with the family at the moment.

6 She usually *goes out* in the evening.

b Match the meanings in the list a–f to the sentences in Exercise 1a. Look carefully at the context. Then complete the table below.

a a habit

b an annoying or surprising habit

c characteristic behaviour

d a long-term situation

e a changing situation

f a temporary situation

2 a Complete the dialogues with appropriate verb forms from Exercise 1b.

1 A: .... *(you/live)* in a house or a flat?

   B: We .... *(live)* in a flat for now, but we .... *(look for)* a house.

2 A: Who .... *(you/get on)* best with in your family?

   B: My father. He .... *(tell)* us endless funny stories.

3 A: .... *(anyone/annoy)* you in your family?

   B: Yes, my brother. He .... *(always/take)* my CDs without asking me.

4 A: How often .... *(you/go out)*?

   B: I usually .... *(go out)* every night, but I .... *(study)* a lot at the moment, so I .... *(only/go out)* at weekends until my exams are finished.

5 A: .... *(you/like)* learning English?

   B: Yes, I do. It was difficult at first, but it .... *(get)* easier now.

b In pairs, ask each other the questions in Exercise 2a, and give answers which are true for you.

Form	Meaning	Examples
A Present continuous (two meanings)	1	....
	2	....
B Present continuous + *always*	....	....
C Present simple (two meanings)	1	....
	2	....
D *will* + infinitive	....	....

▶ Grammar reference page 197

State verbs

3 a Look at these sentences. Does each one describe a state (S) or an action (A)?

1 I don't understand.   ..S..
2 Do you know Peter?   ....
3 We don't have a big house.   ....
4 Sorry, I'm having lunch.   ....

b Read the information in the box and complete it with the verbs from Exercise 3a.

A Some verbs are not used in the continuous because they describe states, not actions, e.g.
believe, like, seem, want, own, ..., ...

B Some verbs are not used in the continuous when they describe states, but can be used in the continuous when they describe actions, e.g.
look, appear, see, think, feel, ...

▶ Grammar reference page 197

4 Correct the mistakes in these sentences.

1 I'm having two brothers.
2 Jan has a shower – can you call back later?
3 I don't understand this word. What is it meaning?
4 Marina thinks about getting a car. Do you think it's a good idea?
5 We are not owning our house, we rent it.
6 The house look old, but it's quite modern inside.
7 What do you look at? Oh yes, I can see it now.
8 Phil sees a client at the moment. He won't be long.

Past habit

5 a Read the extract below by the ex-England footballer Alan Shearer. Mark two past habits and one past state.

My first memory

I used to like our garden. My father and I used to put jackets down to act as goals and we would play football for hours.

b Answer the questions.

1 Did they put jackets down once or many times?
2 Did they play football once or many times?
3 What verb forms are used to describe these past habits?
4 What verb form is used to describe the past state?

c Complete the information in the box with *used to* or *would* or past simple tense.

A To talk about past habits, use .... (*I* .... *put jackets down*) or .... (*We* .... *play football*).

B To talk about past states, use .... (*I* .... *like our garden*).

C The past simple can also be used for past habits and states. (*I* .... *our garden. I often* .... *football there.*)

▶ Grammar reference page 199

6 Complete the sentences using the correct form of the past simple, *would* or *used to* and the words in brackets. There may be more than one possibility.

1 Sorry I .... (*forget*) to write to you last week.

2 I .... (*live*) in France when I was a child. We .... (*have*) two beautiful cats.

3 When I was younger, my family .... (*always/go*) to the beach in summer. We .... (*have*) some great beach parties!

4 My father .... (*be*) a businessman. Often he .... (*work*) six or seven days a week, until he .... (*retire*) in 1995.

7 a Complete these sentences about yourself.

1 My … is always … .
2 I used to live … , but now I … in … .
3 At school I would often … .

b Now compare your experiences with other students.

8 Match the sentence halves from an informal letter.

1 I'm writing to tell you
2 I live in Poznan,
3 I live in a flat with
4 We don't look like each other,
5 When I'm not surfing the Internet,
6 When I was a child,

a but we have very similar personalities.
b we used to visit your country every summer.
c something about myself.
d I like going to clubs with my friends.
e a city in the west of Poland.
f my parents and my brother.

Writing   Informal letter (Paper 2 Part 2)

Lead-in   1   Discuss these questions.
1   Who do you write informal letters to?
2   What kind of things would you write in a letter to a new pen friend?

Understand the task   2   Read the task below and answer the question.
What is the PURPOSE of the letter?
a   to ask for information
b   to give information
c   to entertain the reader

> You have been given the address of an English-speaking person who is looking for a pen friend in your country. Write a letter about you and your family, and suggest meeting at some time in the future.
>
> Write your **letter** in **120–180** words in an appropriate style. Do not write any postal addresses.

Plan your letter   3   a   What information do you need to include in the letter? Make a list.
EXAMPLE: job, hobbies ...

b   Copy and complete the paragraph plan with the information you have listed.
Paragraph 1:   Why you are writing.
Paragraph 2:   About you.
Paragraphs 3/4: About your family.
Paragraph 5:   Suggesting meeting.

Language and content   4   a   These extracts from a student's letter are inappropriate. Rewrite them using informal language from the table on page 13.

1   It would be a pleasure to become acquainted with you.

2   I am an inhabitant of a small town in Spain.

3   We have a very good relationship.

4   At the next opportunity to write, I will despatch a photograph of us all.

5   When I was a child, it was customary for us to spend our vacations by the sea.

6   She has a similar appearance to me. However, she can seem rather talkative.

7   I understand you are in search of a pen friend.

8   Does the possibility ever arise for you to visit my country?

9   The reason for my writing is that ...

10   I should like to take this opportunity to inform you of my family situation.

Giving a reason for writing	Just a short note to let you know … .
	I thought I'd drop you a line because … .
	I'm writing because … .
	I hear you're looking for a pen friend.
Introducing yourself	My name's … .
	I live in … .
Talking about people	Let me tell you about my family.
	He likes … .
	She looks like me, but she can be a bit … .
	We get on (well) … .

Lifestyles	We like to … .
	We would always go on holiday … .
	I often used to … .
Talking about the future	Do you ever get the chance to …?
	It would be great to meet you sometime.
	Next time I write, I'll send a photo.

b Look at these statements giving advice about informal letters. Do you think they are *True* or *False*?

1 Use a personal, conversational style.
2 Avoid simple words.
3 Avoid phrasal verbs.
4 Avoid direct questions to the reader.
5 Use short simple sentences.
6 Use contractions.

c Find examples in the table above to justify your answers.

d Which of the expressions below would be appropriate to open and close the letter? Which ones would not be appropriate, and why?

A

Dear Mrs Watson

I hope to hear from you at your earliest convenience.

Lots of love

B

Dear Sue

Looking forward to hearing from you.

Best wishes

C

Dear pen friend

Well, that's all for now. Do write back soon.

Yours sincerely

Write your letter

5 Now write your letter, using some of the language above. You must answer all parts of the question. Do not include any postal addresses. Write your answer in 120–180 words.

Check and improve your letter

6 Edit your work using this list. Check your:
- paragraph plan (Have you included all the points?)
- use of present and past tenses
- use of time expressions
- style
- spelling
- number of words.

Note: There is a full checklist in the Writing reference.

▶ Writing reference page 206

LANGUAGE SPOT: sentence word order

Put these groups of words in the correct order to make sentences.

1 very well always English I speak don't
2 always my mother and father on Fridays fish eat
3 having great right now in Paris my sister's time a
4 usually her all gave help her friends a lot of
5 in bed music would my grandmother listen to always
6 at the party very much everyone themselves enjoyed
7 you I'll next week an email send on Tuesday
8 as soon as write please back can you

Festivals and traditions

A

B

C

Listening

Before you listen

1 a Look at the photos of festivals. Where do you think they are taking place?

b Match these words and expressions to the photos. Can you add any more?

parade   lamps   flag   river   statue
traditional costumes   religious procession

Listening for gist

2 a ▭ You are going to hear three different people talking about the festivals. Listen and match each speaker (1–3) to one of the photos (A–C).

b Which words and expressions helped you? Did you hear any of the language you predicted in Exercise 1b?

Listening for specific information

3 a ▭ Listen again and choose from the list A–D which festival each statement refers to. There is one extra statement which does not refer to any of them. Mark the most important words in each statement first. (The first one has been done for you.)

A Live animals play a part in the celebrations.

B Everyone dresses in a similar way.

C Traditional tales are acted out.

D Everyone tends to eat the same thing.

Speaker 1 [1]

Speaker 2 [2]

Speaker 3 [3]

b Did you hear the words you marked or similar words?

Discussion

4 You are going to describe an important festival in your country. Before you start, make some notes to prepare what you are going to say. Think about:
   • the reason for the festival
   • how people prepare
   • what people wear, do, etc.

Speaking

Lead-in

1 Look at the photos. What are the people celebrating in each one?

Comparing and contrasting photos

2 a You are going to talk for one minute about two of the photos. Choose two that you would like to compare, and make notes about them under these headings:
   - similarities between the two photos
   - differences between the two photos
   - what you would like/dislike about each celebration
   - which celebration you would prefer to be at and why.

Speaking strategy

If you have to speak for an extended period such as a minute, divide the time into smaller sections and think about what to say in each section. Don't try to say everything at once!

b 🔲 Listen to someone talking about two of the photos and answer the questions.
   1 Which two photos is she talking about?
   2 Which celebration would she prefer to be at, and why?

c 🔲 Listen again and tick (✓) the expressions she uses from the table below.

Similarities	Both of … are … . They both seem to be … . Neither of them … . In this one … and this one … .
Differences	One thing which is different in this one … . The main difference between … and … is … . This one is … whereas … is … .
Likes, dislikes, preferences	I would like … but … . I wouldn't mind … but on the other hand … . Although … I'd like … because … . I think I'd prefer … as … .

▶ Functions reference page 224

d Take turns to speak for a minute about the two photos you have chosen. Use your notes and expressions from the table.

Discussion

3 Has your family celebrated any of the occasions in the photos? What happened?

Language development 2

Comparatives and superlatives

1 **a** Correct the mistakes in these students' sentences.

1   Notting Hill Carnival in London is more popular one I know.

2   It is most large street carnival of Europe.

3   But more big it gets, more friendly it becomes.

4   The costumes are prettyest I have seen.

5   But the goodest thing is the music.

6   Each year it seems more loud that the last time!

7   Luckily, the weather is usually as good than the music.

8   Next year I will go more early, to see everything.

   b Check your answers in the Grammar reference on page 195.

   c Complete the text with comparative or superlative forms of the words in brackets.

The Mexican holiday Cinco de Mayo (5 May), which remembers the Mexican defeat of the French army in 1862, is celebrated **(1)**.............. (*enthusiastically*) in the state of Puebla than in other parts of Mexico. It is not **(2)**.............. (*popular*) holiday in Mexico. In fact, it is celebrated **(3)**............ (*widely*) by Mexicans in the USA than in Mexico, and the holiday is **(4)**.............. (*well-known*) in the USA than Mexican Independence Day. In recent years, Cinco de Mayo has become **(5)**.............. (*big*) than ever and is promoted as a celebration of Mexican culture, food and music. Participation is now **(6)**.............. (*wide*) than before, and non-Mexican Americans are **(7)**............ (*enthusiastic*) about it as Mexicans. In California, the **(8)**............ (*lively*) and **(9)**............ (*sensational*) parties take place in Los Angeles. Celebrations have become **(10)**.............. (*commercialised*) in recent years, but Cinco de Mayo is still a great festival.

Modifying adjectives and adverbs

A To express a big difference:
- *far/a lot/(very) much* + comparative
  He is **far better** than the other singers in the band. (~~very better~~)
  The food is **a lot nicer** in this café. (~~very nicer~~)
  The carnival is (**very**) **much more popular** this year. (~~very more popular~~)

- *by far/easily* + superlative
  He is **by far the best** singer in the band.
  The carnival is **easily the most popular** in the country.

- *not nearly as … as*
  This party is **not nearly as** good **as** last year's.
  This is **not nearly as** good **a** party **as** last year's.

B To express a small difference:
- *slightly/a bit/a little* + comparative
  The music is (only) **slightly better** than before.
  The concert was **a bit/a little better** than I expected.

- *just about* + superlative
  It was **just about the longest** carnival procession ever.

- *nearly/not quite as … as*
  The first show was **nearly as good as** the second one.
  The weather **isn't quite as hot as** it was last time.

2 Look at the information in the box above and complete the sentences with comparative or superlative forms.

1   Fiesta Broadway in Los Angeles is .... (*by far/large*) Cinco de Mayo celebration in the USA.

2   This year it was .... (*much/crowded*) than it was last year.

3   This year's parade was .... (*not quite/long*) as last time.

4   The costumes were .... (*a lot/colourful*) than before.

5   The food is .... (*far/spicy*) than I remembered.

6   I tried .... (*easily/mild*) dish, and it made my mouth burn!

7   And I'm sure I was .... (*just about/bad*) dancer there.

3 **a** Choose one of these topics and write four sentences about it. Compare:
- three types of dance you know (e.g. salsa, tango, ballet – *fast/slow, easy/hard, cheap/expensive…?*)
- three types of music (e.g. rap, jazz, opera – *interesting/boring, noisy/quiet…?*)
- three types of food (e.g. Italian, French, Chinese – *spicy/mild, light/heavy, tasty/bland…?*)

   b Discuss your ideas. Give reasons for your opinions.

Use of English 1 (Paper 3 Part 3)

Key word transformation

▶ page 190

1 a Look at the example and follow the instructions in the task strategy box.
EXAMPLE: Peter is a lot older than Martin.
as
Martin .... Peter.

b Do the first half of the task below. Use the Help clues if necessary.

Complete the second sentence so that it has a similar meaning to the first sentence, using the word given. **Do not change the word given.** You must use between **two** and **five** words, including the word given. Write **only** the missing words.

1 Fewer people read Carlton's books these days.
widely
Carlton's books .... these days.

2 The only person Jane didn't like was her boss.
apart
Jane liked everyone .... her boss.

3 Lucy doesn't swim nearly as well as Kate.
swimmer
Kate is .... Lucy.

4 He was offered some work but he wasn't able to accept it because he was too busy.
turned
He was offered some work but he .... because he was too busy.

5 Rap music isn't nearly as popular as it was ten years ago.
less
Rap music is .... it was ten years ago.

2 Now do the second half of the task. This time there are no Help clues.

6 I find studying more difficult as I become older.
is
I find it .... as I become older.

7 My brother never asks when he borrows my things.
always
My brother is .... asking.

8 I've always found learning languages easy.
good
I've always .... learning languages.

9 The last time Sally saw Jane was five years ago.
for
Sally .... five years.

10 Traffic today doesn't move much faster than 100 years ago.
little
One hundred years ago, traffic moved .... than today.

3 Answer the questions about the task.

1 Which questions test:
• vocabulary?
• comparative or superlative structures?
• tense forms?

2 Which of the questions did you find the most difficult and why? Which of these areas of language do you need more practice in?

Use of English 2 (Paper 3 Part 1)

Lead-in

1 Look at the picture. What hospitality customs do you have in your country?

Lexical cloze ▶ page 189

Task strategy

- Read the title and whole text quickly, ignoring the spaces.
- Read the text again. Try to guess what kind of word fits each space.
- Choose which answer A–D fits the grammar and meaning.
- If you aren't sure, cross out answers which you know are incorrect.
- Read the text again to check.

2 a Read the title and text quickly and answer the questions. (Ignore the spaces at this stage.)
  1 What did servants do for travellers in ancient times?
  2 What might be given to a guest in Japan?
  3 Why might guests eat too much in a foreign country?

b Do the task. Follow the task strategy and use the Help clues if necessary.
Read the text below and decide which answer **A, B, C** or **D** best fits each space. There is an example at the beginning **(0)**.

0 A hoped   **B** considered   **C** expected   **D** intended

HOSPITALITY

Hospitality – looking after visitors – is universal, but in different cultures hosts are **(0)** _C_ to receive guests in different ways.

In much of the ancient **(1)** ...., it was the custom to provide passing travellers with food and water, and **(2)** .... after them well. Indeed in some regions, if visitors were in the middle of a long **(3)** ...., servants would wash their feet.

Today, some old customs have **(4)** .... In a traditional Japanese household, if a guest admires a **(5)** .... object in the house, the host will give it to the guest straightaway. And it is still **(6)** .... in parts of Russia to greet guests with bread and salt on a special cloth. The guest is **(7)** .... to kiss them and hand them back to the host. Sometimes the guest breaks **(8)** .... a small piece of bread, dips it in the salt and eats it.

In some countries, when **(9)** .... guests arrive from abroad they may feel they have been given a particularly **(10)** .... meal. But this is probably because the host politely **(11)** .... offering more food and drink, and the guest is too embarrassed to **(12)** .... anything down.

HELP
➤ Question 1
  Which word can mean *civilisation*?
➤ Question 2
  Which phrasal verb means *care for*?
➤ Question 6
  Which word means *customary*?
➤ Question 10
  Which word might express a feeling in your stomach?
➤ Question 12
  Which phrasal verb means *refuse*?

	A	B	C	D
1	globe	earth	world	planet
2	look	name	take	go
3	day	travel	term	journey
4	supported	survived	preserved	existed
5	usual	precise	distinct	particular
6	typical	everyday	ordinary	average
7	needed	wanted	required	desired
8	off	down	out	in
9	strange	foreign	alien	unfamiliar
10	strong	dense	wide	heavy
11	keeps on	takes up	comes off	puts in
12	slow	turn	keep	take

c Answer the questions about the task.
  1 Did you guess any words before looking at the options?
  2 Which questions test:
     - the correct word from a set with similar meanings?
     - phrasal verbs?
     - adjective + noun combinations?

d Make a note in your vocabulary book of any expressions, phrasal verbs or adjective + noun combinations you want to remember.

Language development 3

Collocations: adjectives and nouns

> Look at this adjective + noun collocation from the Use of English text opposite:
>
> *a **heavy** meal*   *a ~~strong~~ meal*
> **but:**
> *a **strong** drink*   *a **heavy** drink*
>
> When you learn an adjective, note which nouns it collocates with.
>
> (LOOK) **Find five more adjective + noun collocations in the Use of English text opposite.**

1 Complete the diagram with nouns from the dictionary extract below.

.... ────────────   ....
                     (**sour**)
.... ────────────   ....

> **sour** *adj* **1** having a sharp acid taste that stings your tongue like the taste of a lemon: *sour apples* **2** milk or other food that is sour is not fresh: *In warm weather, milk can go sour.* **3** unfriendly or looking bad-tempered: *Rob gave me a sour look.* **4 sour grapes** the attitude of someone who pretends to dislike something they really want

2 a Match the nouns in the list below to these adjectives.

(**strong**)   (**wide**)   (**plain**)   (**high**)

influence

    heels   possibility   English   variety
    number   ~~influence~~   grin   speed   feelings
    choice   argument   clothes   gap

b Complete these sentences with one of the adjective + noun combinations from Exercise 2a.
1 My grandparents have .... on the subject of hospitality.
2 Can you give me directions to your house in .... so that I can understand them?
3 Dan's face broke into a .... when I invited him in.
4 Everyone drives at such a .... today – it's so dangerous.
5 Four different types of tea – what a ....!
6 In more traditional cultures, grandparents have a .... on children.
7 Please take your shoes off in the gym. .... can damage the floor.
8 If you call Toni, there's a .... that he'll invite you to visit him.

Phrasal verbs with *up* and *down*

3 Look at these two sentences with the phrasal verb *pick up*. Which one has an obvious meaning, and which one an idiomatic meaning?
1 I *picked up* a cup that was lying on the floor.
2 She *picked* me *up* at the hotel and took me to the party.

4 a In these sentences the meaning is fairly obvious. Complete the sentences with *up* or *down*.
1 The dinner won't cook if you don't turn the heat ....
2 We can't afford a big party – we need to keep costs ....
3 The old bus station has gone – they've pulled it ....
4 When you see someone's glass is empty, go and fill it ....
5 He settled .... on the sofa to read his book.
6 The town's getting bigger – they've put .... a lot of new houses.

b Some of these phrasal verbs have an idiomatic meaning. Match the sentence halves to make the most likely sentences. Use a dictionary if necessary.
1 Please tidy up   a the apartment and sell it for a big profit.
2 I never turn down   b your best friend by breaking a promise.
3 Remember to wrap up   c the time of the next train on the website.
4 She took down   d the mess as soon as possible.
5 Look up   e the presents before going to the party.
6 They put up   f the offer of a lift home.
7 Never let down   g the decorations from the wall.
8 He decided to do up   h a tent in the garden.

c Match the phrasal verbs in Exercise 4b to these near synonyms.
a decorate   e refuse
b look for information   f put in special paper
c fail someone   g remove
d erect   h make neat and organised

5 Make a note of the phrasal verbs you want to remember in your vocabulary book. Write the <u>whole</u> sentence and mark the phrasal verb.

6 Discuss these questions.
1 Who tidies up in your house?
2 How often do you look up a word in English?
3 Has a friend ever let you down? What happened?

Module 1: Review

1 a Complete the text with the prepositions *after, at, for, in, on, to.*

We live **(1)**............ the outskirts of town, and my father works **(2)**............ the town centre. He works **(3)**............ a mail-order company. My mother stays **(4)**............ home and looks **(5)**............ my younger brother. I go **(6)**............ college in the centre every day. If the bus is **(7)**............ time, I get **(8)**............ college at about 8:30 in the morning. Classes finish at 4 p.m., then I usually meet some friends **(9)**............ the way home and we go **(10)**............ a coffee.

b In what way is your life similar/different to the person in Exercise 1a?

2 a Read the questionnaire. Tick (✓) sentences with correct verb forms, and correct the incorrect verb forms. Use the present continuous, present simple, past simple, *will/would* or *used to.*

In your country:

1 are many people speaking more than one language?
2 are families getting bigger or smaller these days?
3 would people be happier 20 years ago?
4 would people work harder nowadays?
5 do people spend a lot of time watching TV these days?
6 do women do less housework than they would?
7 what sort of things are people doing on national holidays?
8 how did people use to celebrate on 31 December 1999?

b Answer the questions in Exercise 2a about your country.

3 a Complete the comparisons with a word/phrase from the list and <u>one</u> of the adjectives in brackets, in the correct form. There is more than one possibility.

slightly   far   not (quite) as   (not) nearly as
nowhere near as   much

1 Going out is .... staying at home. (*nice/exciting*)
2 Living in a village is .... living in a city. (*boring/dangerous*)
3 Working in an office is .... working from home. (*relaxing/interesting*)
4 Keeping pets is .... looking after children. (*expensive/easy*)
5 Giving presents is .... receiving presents. (*satisfying/important*)
6 Men's cooking is .... women's cooking. (*good/imaginative*)

b Complete the questions with <u>one</u> of the adjectives in brackets in the superlative form. Then answer the questions about yourself.

1 What's .... room in your house or flat? (*comfortable/pretty/quiet*)
2 What's .... party you've been to? (*enjoyable/big/lively*)
3 What's .... way of travelling to college or work? (*healthy/quick/easy*)

4 Correct the mistakes in the text. Use *strong, wide, plain* or *high.*

When young people finish school today, they are presented with a **(1)** *plain* choice of things to do. At colleges, for example, there is a **(2)** *high* variety of courses to choose from, but there is a **(3)** *wide* possibility that information about the courses will not be written in **(4)** *strong* English. We shouldn't be surprised, then, by research showing that, at the age of 17, friends have a **(5)** *high* influence on what you choose to do. The same research has also shown that by the age of 30, there is often a **(6)** *strong* gap between the jobs people are doing and the jobs they would like to do, so there is a **(7)** *wide* argument for not being pressurised into making decisions at **(8)** *plain* speed when you are too young.

5 Complete the second sentence so that it has a similar meaning to the first sentence, using the word given and any other necessary words. <u>Do not change the word given.</u> You must use between <u>two</u> and <u>five</u> words, including the word given.

1 I can't reach that poster – can you remove it for me?
down
I can't reach that poster – can you .... for me?
2 We can find her number in the phone book. **up**
We can .... in the phone book.
3 I hope my parents decorate my room soon! **do**
I hope my parents .... soon!
4 I like to make myself comfortable in the armchair.
settle
I like to .... in the armchair.
5 We'll need to put things back in the right place after the party. **tidy**
We'll need to .... after the party.
6 My friends can always rely on me when they need me.
let
I never .... when they need me.

MODULE 2
Careers

Overview

- **Reading:** skills: reading for detail
- **Language development 1:** past simple and present perfect tenses
- **Writing:** formal letter of application (Paper 2 Part 2)
- **Listening:** skills: listening for gist and opinions
- **Speaking:** discussion: giving opinions, agreeing and disagreeing (Paper 5 Parts 3 and 4)
- **Use of English 1:** structural cloze (Paper 3 Part 2)
- **Language development 2:** articles; *some/any*; *something/anything*
- **Use of English 2:** word formation (Paper 3 Part 5)
- **Language development 3:** forming adjectives; phrasal verbs: education

Lead-in

- Which of the jobs in the photos do you think are most/least difficult and demanding? interesting?
- Some people 'work to live', and others 'live to work'? Which do you do? What about other people you know?

3 Work

Reading

Before you read

1 Look at the film stills.
1 Can you name a) the actor who appears in both photos   b) the films   c) the characters he is playing?
2 Have you seen any of his films? What did you think of them?

Skimming

Reading strategy

The first and last paragraph of a text (**introduction** and **conclusion**) and the first or last sentence of the other paragraphs (**topic sentence**) usually contain the main ideas. Use them to get a general understanding of the text.

2 The title of an article usually summarises the main message of the text. Skim the text opposite and choose the best title below.

A **The early life of Sean Connery**

B **THE MILKMAN'S BOY WHO BECAME JAMES BOND**

C **How a handsome Scot became Mr Universe!**

Reading for detail

Reading strategy

To understand the details in a text, read it slowly and carefully. You may need to read parts of the text more than once.

3 a Read questions 1–6 below the text. Don't look at the options A–C yet. Try to find the answers yourself in the text. Mark the relevant parts of the text.

b Now choose the answer A, B or C which you think fits best according to the text. The first one has been done for you. The highlighted words show how the answer was found.

c Compare and justify your answers.
1 Which part of the text answered each question?
2 Which parallel words or phrases helped you to identify the correct answer A, B or C?

Discussion

4 In the text, mark all the jobs Sean Connery did.
1 Do you think any of the jobs were useful experience for his acting career?
2 Which ones would you most/least like to do? Why?

Vocabulary: deducing meaning

Reading strategy

Use clues like these to help you guess words you don't understand – you can't use a dictionary in the exam.
• *Is it like a word in your language?*
• *Is it formed from a word you know?*
• *Is it repeated in another context later in the text?*
• *Is there an explanation, synonym, opposite, etc.?*

5 a Look at the text and find the words 1–7. If you don't know the meaning, follow the reading strategy and try to work it out.

b Check your guesses by matching the words 1–7 to the correct definitions below.
A to pay towards the cost of something
B difficult and strict
C when things keep changing and the future is not certain
D someone who has special advantages, e.g. money
E the things that will happen to someone in the future
F when it is starting to get dark at the end of the day
G a physical condition that makes it difficult to do what most people can do

c Discuss how you worked out the meanings. What clues helped you?
EXAMPLE: *privileged–D (clue: the contrast with Connery's actual situation – his family was poor).*

d Make a note of the words in your vocabulary book. Write an example to show the meaning.

Sean Connery has made over 70 films and is one of the top five movie actors in the world. But the well-known star was not born into a privileged[1] theatrical family. On the contrary, he grew up in a working-class district of
5 Edinburgh in Scotland during the Great Depression of the 1930s. At that time, unemployment was high and most families were poor, so Sean and his parents were not unusual in living in a two-roomed flat with no bathroom. When his father was unemployed, young
10 Sean, glad to help, would get up at dawn to earn some money delivering milk before he went to school. By the age of ten, he already had the determination to control his own destiny[2], something that he continued to do throughout his life.
15 Sean left school at thirteen and worked from dawn to dusk[3] doing any jobs he could find. The milk round provided most of his income, though it was like a hobby for him, because he loved looking after Titch, the horse that pulled his milk cart. But as Sean approached his
20 seventeenth birthday, he was keen to extend his experience of life beyond his work, football and local dances. Despite his parents' objections, he signed on for seven years with the Royal Navy, boasting to his friends that he was off to see the world.

25 But this was not to be. After a thorough and rigorous[4] training programme, Sean was sent no further than the south coast of England. By then, he was already doubting whether the Navy was really the right thing for him. For such an independent young man, it
30 was hard not to be allowed to think for himself. Although in the end he had to leave the Navy for medical reasons, he must have had mixed feelings about it. On the one hand, it was a lucky escape; on the other hand, it meant returning home **with his tail
35 between his legs** and with only a small disability[5] pension to live on.

After the Navy, there followed an unsettled[6] period where he took on a variety of jobs in his home city. He delivered coal, and worked as a labourer and as a
40 French polisher in a furniture business. In fact, he didn't mind what he did as long as the job paid him enough to subsidise[7] his leisure pursuits, which now included bodybuilding. He even turned down the offer of a job with Manchester United Football Club on the
45 grounds that it wouldn't leave him enough time or money for his other interests.

Gradually, thanks perhaps to those trips to the gym, his attractive appearance was opening up other areas of work. He became a lifeguard, did a bit of acting and
50 worked as a fashion model for a magazine. The turning point, however, came when he entered the 'male beauty' competition known as Mr Universe. Although he didn't win, he was noticed and, on the strength of his looks alone, got a small part in the musical show *South
55 Pacific*. Here he began to attract crowds of female admirers. His destiny was finally unfolding. Television plays followed, which then led on to films, both in Britain and the USA. A few years later, Sean would meet the man who was writing the screenplay for the
60 first James Bond film *Dr No*. He saw in Sean Connery the perfect 007, a role that was to make the actor a household name the world over.

1 As a young child, Sean Connery's life was hard because
   A he came from an unhappy family background.
   B he was forced to do things he did not enjoy.
   C he grew up at a time of economic problems.

2 Why did Sean decide to join the Navy?
   A He wanted to get away from his life in Edinburgh.
   B His parents thought it would be good for him.
   C He couldn't find any other sort of work.

3 Why did Sean leave the Navy?
   A He found it difficult to accept orders.
   B He was no longer well enough to continue.
   C He was disappointed not to be sent abroad.

4 What does the expression *with his tail between his legs* (line 34–35) suggest about Sean?
   A He was pleased to be going home to his friends and family.
   B He realised he had made a mistake in joining the Navy.
   C He was ashamed of the way he had behaved whilst away.

5 What was Sean's attitude to work in the period after he left the Navy?
   A He was only interested in the money he could earn.
   B He was only willing to do work that he enjoyed.
   C He wanted to do jobs connected with his leisure pursuits.

6 Why was Sean chosen for a part in the musical show *South Pacific*?
   A He came first in a competition.
   B He had previous acting experience.
   C His physical appearance impressed people.

Language development 1

Past simple and present perfect

Summer assistant in Krakow Tourist Office.

Good English and experience with computers essential.

1 a Read the advert and the extract from Anna's letter of application. Is she a good candidate? Why?

I have often been to the United States to visit relatives, so I have learned quite a lot of English over the years. A year ago I helped to organise a children's holiday club on an international camping site in Boston. Although I haven't had much experience in using computers, I attended a short training course last year, so I am able to use them reasonably well.

b Underline examples of the past simple and circle examples of the present perfect simple in Anna's letter.

c Answer these questions.
   1 Do we know exactly when she:
   • visited relatives in the USA?
   • learned English?
   • organised a holiday club?
   • attended a training course?
   2 What verb form does she use in each case?
   3 What time expressions does she use with:
   • the past simple?
   • the present perfect simple?

d Complete this box with examples from Anna's letter.

A The present perfect simple expresses **experience**; **actions and situations at an unspecified time** in the past.
EXAMPLES:
1 ....
2 ....
3 ....
B The past simple expresses **actions at a specified time** in the past.
EXAMPLES:
1 ....
2 ....
▶ Grammar reference page 198

2 a Complete these extracts from a job interview. Use the correct form of the past simple or the present perfect simple.
   1 A: (*you/live abroad?*) ....
      B: (*Yes*) ....
      A: (*Where/live?*) ....
      B: In Dublin.
      A: (*When/go there?*) ....
      B: In 2002.
   2 A: (*you/work in an office?*) ....
      B: (*No*) ....
   3 A: (*you/ever go to/the USA?*) ....
      B: (*Yes*) ....
      A: (*When/go there?*) ....
      B: Last year.
      A: (*Why/go there?*) ....
      B: To study English.
   4 A: (*you/use English in your work before?*)
      ....
      B: (*No*) ....

b Ask each other the questions in Exercise 2a, and give answers which are true for you.

Present perfect simple and continuous

3 a Read the next part of Anna's letter.

> I have lived in Krakow since 1990. I have been studying French at university for two years and I have just taken my second-year exams, though I haven't had the results yet. Recently I have been reading more about Krakow, as the city interests me very much.

b Underline examples of the present perfect simple and circle examples of the continuous in Anna's letter.

c Answer these questions.
1 Does Anna live in Krakow now?
2 Is she still studying French?
3 Which is more permanent, 1 or 2?
4 Has she finished her exams?
5 Has she finished reading about Krakow?

d Complete the box with examples from Anna's letter.

A The present perfect simple expresses more **permanent** actions or states which started in the past and continue to the present.
   EXAMPLE: ....

B The present perfect continuous expresses more **temporary** actions or states which started in the past and continue to the present.
   EXAMPLE: ....

C The present perfect simple expresses **recent finished actions** including repeated actions.
   EXAMPLES: ....
   ....

D The present perfect continuous expresses **recent longer activities**, which may not be finished.
   EXAMPLE: ....

▶ Grammar reference page 198

---

e Look at the box and complete the phrases with *for* or *since*.

---

for or *since*?

Use *for* with a period of time, and *since* with a point in time:
for two years   *since 1990*

1 .... ages   4 .... six o'clock
2 .... my birthday   5 .... half an hour
3 .... a long time   6 .... I was born

---

4 Tick (✓) the correct sentences. Correct the wrong ones.
1 Sorry we're late. We've been sitting in traffic.
2 I've been having some good news. I've got the job!
3 Marta's been taking exams all week. She's exhausted.
4 I've read that book. Do you want it back?
5 Emma's been falling over and hurt her knee.
6 The lift isn't working so we've used the stairs all day.

5 a Complete the extract from a letter with the correct form of the verbs in brackets: past simple, present perfect simple or continuous.

I **(1)**........................ (*be*) here for two months now and **(2)**........................ (*not write*) to you yet. Sorry! I hope you **(3)**........................ (*not wait*) for a letter. I **(4)**........................ (*work*) a lot and I **(5)**........................ (*not have*) much free time.
At first I **(6)**........................ (*feel*) a bit lonely, but recently I **(7)**........................ (*make*) some friends. I **(8)**........................ (*try*) to find somewhere to live for weeks and I think I **(9)**........................ (*find*) a flat at last. Up to now I **(10)**........................ (*stay*) with a colleague.

---

b Complete these sentences about yourself.
1 I've written … .
2 I've never … .
3 I've … since … .
4 I've been …ing … this year.
5 I haven't … this month.

6 Find and correct the eight mistakes in this piece of writing.

I have been born in Poland 26 years ago and I've lived here all my life. I am married for two years but we don't have any children yet. I've been studying at teacher training college since four years and I enjoy it a lot. In my spare time I'm learning the clarinet – I've played it since five years. I also love reading. Last year I have read a lot of novels in English. I go to the country for my holidays during six years because I love the mountains. I've also gone to the USA two years ago to work.

Writing   Formal letter (Paper 2 Part 2)

Lead-in   1   Look at the different types of letter in the list. Which ones would be formal, and which informal?

a introducing yourself to a pen friend   d asking for information from a bank
b asking for information from a friend   e applying for a job
c applying to go to university   f giving news to your family

Understand the task   2   Read the task below and answer the questions.

1 WHO are you writing to?
2 What is the PURPOSE of your letter?
3 What INFORMATION will you include in your letter? (Read the question carefully.)
4 What EFFECT do you want to have on the reader? (How do you want them to feel about you?)

You see this advertisement in a student newspaper. You are interested in applying for the job.

DALESIDE HOTEL

Do you need a summer job?

Do you enjoy working with people?

Can you speak English?

Then you might be the person for us!

We are looking for a hotel receptionist for our international hotel during the summer. Experience not essential.

If you are interested, write to the Manager saying why you think you are the right person.

Good prospects and salary.

Write your **letter** of application in **120–180** words in an appropriate style. Do not write any postal addresses.

Plan your letter   3   a   Tick (✓) the points you should include in each paragraph.

Paragraph 1: Reason for writing:
• Your name   • Where you heard about the job

Paragraph 2: About you:
• Age   • Where you come from   • Where you live
• Number of brothers and sisters   • Knowledge of the area
• Training/qualifications   • Previous experience   • Hobbies
• Languages   • Other skills (e.g. computers)
• Clothes you like wearing   • What kind of person you are

Paragraph 3: Your reason for applying:
• Present job   • What you hate about your present job
• Why you are suitable for the job

Paragraph 4: Conclusion:
• When you are available for interview
• Names and addresses of two people who can recommend you

b   **Make notes about yourself for each paragraph.**

Language and content   4   a   Look at this extract from a student's letter. Which sentences are appropriately formal, and which are too informal?

1   I noticed the hotel job in the student magazine and I want to have a go.

2   I am 22 years old and I live in Holland.

3   I'm studying at uni right now and I can speak English pretty well.

4   I've never done this kind of stuff before but I'm great with computers.

5   I suppose you could say I really like working with different people.

6   The job would give me valuable work experience during the summer holidays.

7   I'd do the job really well – you don't have to worry about that.

8   Let me know if you want references or if you want me to drop in for a chat.

9   I hope you'll have a good think about it and give me the job.

10   I look forward to hearing from you in the near future.

b   Rewrite the inappropriate sentences in a more formal style. Use phrases from the table below.

Saying why you're writing	*I would like to apply for the position of … which I saw advertised … . One of my reasons for applying is … .*	**Talking about the job**	*I feel I would be suitable for the job … . I think I would be a suitable candidate for … because … . The job would give me the opportunity to … (get work experience during the summer).*
Talking about yourself	*I am … years old and I … . At present I am …(working for/a student at) … . I have a reasonable command of … (English). I have a good … (knowledge of computers/telephone manner). I regret I have had no experience of … (this kind of work). For the last (three) years I have been … (studying/working) … . When I was at … I … . I very much enjoy … (working with people/travelling).*	**Offers**	*I would be happy/free/able to (attend an interview/provide references). I am available to attend an interview … .*
		Concluding	*I hope you will consider my application. I look forward to hearing from you in the near future.*

c   Which of these phrases could you use to open and close the letter?
   Dear Sue   Dear Sir or Madam   Hi!   Dear Ms Smith   Hello
   Regards   Yours faithfully   Yours   Yours sincerely   Yours truly

Write your letter   5   Now write your letter, using the ideas and some of the language above. Do not write any postal addresses. Write your answer in 120–180 words.

Check and improve your letter   6   Edit your work using this list. Check your:
   • paragraph plan (Have you included all the points?)
   • use of the past simple and the present perfect
   • style
   • number of words.

▶ Writing reference page 206

Note: There is a full checklist in the Writing reference.

4 Education

Listening

Before you listen

Listening strategy

Try to recall what you know about the topic. Any knowledge you already have will help you to understand the main points better.

1 You will hear a radio discussion comparing the educational achievements of boys and girls in school. First, discuss these questions.
   1 How is achievement assessed in schools in your country – by exams, continuous assessment, both?
   2 Do boys and girls do equally well at school or are there any differences?

Listening for gist

▶ Listening strategy Unit 2 page 14

2 ▭ Read these questions. Then listen to the discussion once to answer them.
   1 The presenter mentions a report. What does the report show?
   2 The following possible reasons are mentioned. Number them in the order they are mentioned.
   ☐ Girls are more intelligent than boys.
   ☐ Very few primary school teachers are men.
   ☐ Girls are studying harder than in the past.
   ☐ Girls and boys have different learning styles.
   ☐ Most boys think that studying hard is not masculine.
   3 What are some schools doing to help boys?

Listening for opinions

Listening strategy

To help identify different speakers' opinions, listen for expressions that introduce opinions and express agreement and disagreement, e.g.:
I (don't) think ... .
In my opinion ... .
Yes, absolutely ... .
I'm sorry, but ... .
Yes, that's true ... .

3 a Read the statements 1–7 below. Mark the main points (the first two have been done for you). Decide which ideas you agree with.

   b ▭ Listen again. Write T for *True* if this is the speaker's opinion and F for *False* if it isn't.
   1 The presenter thinks that a report published today will shock people who work in education.   ☐ 1
   2 Caroline believes that girls are more intelligent than boys of the same age.   ☐ 2
   3 Caroline suggests that the attitudes of their friends may influence boys more than girls.   ☐ 3
   4 Tim feels that current methods of assessing students may benefit girls more than boys.   ☐ 4
   5 Caroline says that better career prospects encourage girls to study harder.   ☐ 5
   6 Tim and Caroline agree that there are advantages if boys and girls study in separate classes.   ☐ 6
   7 Tim and Caroline both feel that parents must accept more responsibility for boys' attitudes towards studying.   ☐ 7

   c Compare and justify your answers. Correct the false statements.

Discussion

4 Read this quote from the discussion. Do you think this is true of your country?
   ❛Interestingly, boys are still getting better degrees at university. Girls tend not to follow through this early promise and don't end up with the best paid jobs.❜

Vocabulary: school subjects

5 Make a list of subjects available at schools in your country. Then decide which ones are the most/least useful in future life.

Speaking

Lead-in

1 What were the good and bad things about the schools you went to?

Discussion 1

Speaking strategy

In a discussion, it's important to give your opinion, but also to ask for other people's opinions and respond to them.

2 a Which three of these things do you think are the most important in a school for children under 11? Tick (✓) them. Which one do you think is the least important?
  - lots of equipment (e.g. computers, laboratories)
  - highly qualified teachers
  - good exam results
  - the size of the school
  - beautiful buildings
  - small classes
  - (not) having a uniform
  - being near home
  - clubs after school
  - good sports facilities

b ▭ Listen to two people discussing the list above. What do they think are the most and least important factors? Why?

c ▭ Listen again and complete the expressions they use in the table below.

Giving opinions	.... me, one of the most important .... is ... . I just .... it matters ... . The .... important factor for me is ... .
Strong agreement	That's .... So do I. I agree .... Neither do I. I think ... . I couldn't ....
Tentative agreement	I .... so.
Disagreement	I agree .... to a .... , but ... . Yes, but what about ...? Do you ....? But don't you agree that ...? Actually, I think it's ....

▶ Functions reference page 224

d Work in pairs or groups. Discuss the list in Exercise 2a. Try to agree on either the most or the least important thing in the list.

Discussion 2

3 a Look at the statements and decide whether you agree with them.
  1 Schooldays are the happiest days of your life.
  2 We can learn more from computers than from teachers.
  3 Schools don't prepare children for 'the real world'.
  4 Life experience is more useful than college or university.

b Discuss the statements and give reasons for your opinions.

Use of English 1 (Paper 3 Part 2)

Lead-in

Structural cloze
▶ page 189

▶ page 189

Task strategy
- Read the title and text quickly for a general understanding. Ignore the spaces.
- Decide what type of word is missing in each space – a noun, an article, a verb?
- Put only one word in each space and do not use contractions (*isn't*, *doesn't*, etc.).
- Always write something.
- Read the text again and check your answers make sense and are correctly spelt.

HELP
In this text some, but not all, of the gaps require *a/the* or a determiner (e.g. *all*, *both*, *most*, etc.) of some kind.
➤ **Question 1**
Choose between *a* and *the*. Think about the difference.
➤ **Question 2**
Choose a determiner that combines with *nearly*.
➤ **Question 4**
Which words can be used to add one negative statement to another?
➤ **Questions 6/8**
Choose a word which expresses contrast (e.g. *however*, *although*, *nevertheless*, *despite*)
➤ **Question 11**
Remember what is said about these subjects earlier!
➤ **Question 15**
Definite or indefinite article?

1 Look at the photo of Albert Einstein. What do you know about him?

2 a Read the text quickly and answer the questions. (Ignore the spaces at this stage.)
  1 In what field is Einstein famous?
  2 What problems did he have as a student?
  3 How did he get time to develop his ideas?

 b Do the task. Follow the task strategy and use the Help clues if necessary.

 Read the text below and think of the word which best fits each space. Use only **one** word in each space. There is an example at the beginning (**0**).

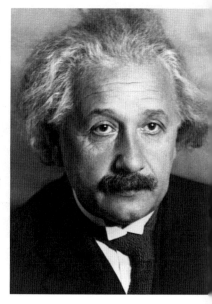

ALBERT EINSTEIN (1879–1955)

Albert Einstein is (**0**) **one** of the best-known scientists of the twentieth century. Yet he was not (**1**)............. particularly good student. At school in Munich, he got reasonable grades in nearly (**2**)............. subjects, and was outstanding in mathematics and physics, but he disliked doing (**3**)............. he was told. He didn't like exams and (**4**)............. did he like attending classes, so he left school early, only a (**5**)............. months after his family moved to Milan in 1894.

(**6**)............. failing the entrance exam, Einstein was eventually admitted to (**7**)............. Swiss Federal Institute of Technology in Zurich in 1896. (**8**)............. he did fairly well as a student in Zurich, after graduation he was unable to get a job in a university, mainly (**9**)............. he was thought to be extremely lazy. Instead, he worked in (**10**)............. secondary school, where he taught mathematics and physics, (**11**)............. of which he was good at.

Some two years later, in 1902, Einstein got a job at the Swiss patent office in Bern. (**12**)............. his life, Einstein had a huge appetite for books, and his new job gave him a (**13**)............. of time to read and think. In 1905, his special theory of relativity (**14**)............. published – one of the greatest intellectual achievements in (**15**)............. history of human thought.

 c Answer the questions about the task.
  1 Which questions test:
   • articles and determiners?
   • connecting expressions?
  2 Which one of these is also tested:
   • present perfect?
   • passives?
   • pronouns?
  3 Which questions did you find difficult and why?

Discussion

3 Was your school career similar to Einstein's? In what way was it different?

Language development 2

Articles

A *a/an*: before singular, countable nouns
- The first time we refer to something:
  *A man went into **a** café to ask for directions.*
- With jobs:
  *She's **an** airline pilot.*

B *the*
- To refer to something already known:
  ***The** man had seen **the** café from his car.*
- In certain expressions:
  *I play **the** piano.*
  *Are you going to **the** cinema tonight?*
- Before most seas, oceans, rivers, groups of islands/mountains, deserts, and nationalities:
  ***The** Pacific Ocean*
  ***The** British can be very reserved.*
- When there is only one of something:
  ***The** United Nations are meeting in New York.*
  ***The** sun rises very early in summer.*

C *No article*
- When talking about something in general:
  Schools are too big nowadays.
- Before subjects of study:
  I study physics.
- Before most countries, continents, towns and streets:
  I live in France.
- In certain expressions e.g.:
  at home, in summer/winter

LOOK **Find examples of articles in the Use of English text opposite and match them to the uses above.**

▶ Grammar reference page 192

1 a Correct these students' sentences.
   1 The best course was the one I did on the economics. The teacher was very good and I made a good progress.
   2 Nina's studying the German at evening classes in the London.
   3 My brother is 19. He's at the university in the Africa and wants to become English teacher because it would give him good opportunity to travel.
   4 When we were in Japan we noticed that most Japanese students work harder than the American students I met in USA.
   5 I go to college by the train. Unfortunately, the train is often late.

   b Complete the following text with the best form for each space – *a, an, the* or Ø (no article).

When **(1)**............. students in England were asked by **(2)**............. national newspaper what kind of **(3)**............. college they would like to go to, they agreed that one of **(4)**............. most important things was **(5)**............. location of **(6)**............. college and **(7)**............. other was **(8)**............. state of **(9)**............. buildings. **(10)**............. majority said they wanted **(11)**............. light, well-decorated college with **(12)**............. comfortable seats in the lecture rooms. They also wanted **(13)**............. college with **(14)**............. flexible timetable where they could spend **(15)**............. time on what they enjoy and where learning **(16)**............. new skills was fun and exciting. Interestingly, no one said they didn't want to go to **(17)**............. college at all.

some/any; something/anything

A *some/any (of)*
  *I got **some** good grades in my exams.* (countable)
  *The teacher gave me **some** good advice.* (uncountable)

  ***Some** (**of** the) grades were outstanding.* (= a limited number)
  ***Some of them** were excellent.* (*of* before pronouns)

  *Were **any** of them bad?* (it doesn't matter which ones)

  *It was **some** weeks/time before the exam results came out.* (a large number/amount of)

  *Take **any** books you want.* (it doesn't matter which ones)
  *Tell me if you have **any** problems.* (they may not exist)

B *something/anything*
  *I want to give you **something** to read.* (positive) (***a** thing*)
  *I don't want to give you **anything**.* (negative) (***a** thing*)
  *Have you got **anything** for me?* (I don't know if you have.)
  *Have you got **something** for me?* (I hope/think you have.)
  *There's **hardly anything** left to eat.* (= almost nothing)
  *Have you seen **anything** interesting lately?* (*something/anything* + adjective)

2 Read this extract from a student's email to her parents and mark the correct word in each pair.

It's been quite **(1)** *some / any* time since I've been in touch. Sorry about that. There never seems to be **(2)** *some / any* time to do **(3)** *something / anything* these days – except work of course. Anyway, I've decided to have **(4)** *some / any* time off in the next few weeks. I'm not promising **(5)** *something / anything* definite but I'm hoping to get home for at least a couple of days. But I'll need **(6)** *some / any* money for the train fare – I've got **(7)** *any / hardly any* left in the bank until my next cheque comes through. Could you lend me **(8)** *some / any*? I'll be able to get **(9)** *some / any* work in a restaurant in the holidays, so I'll pay you back then. Apart from that, what I'd like to do more than **(10)** *something / anything* else when I get home is just relax.

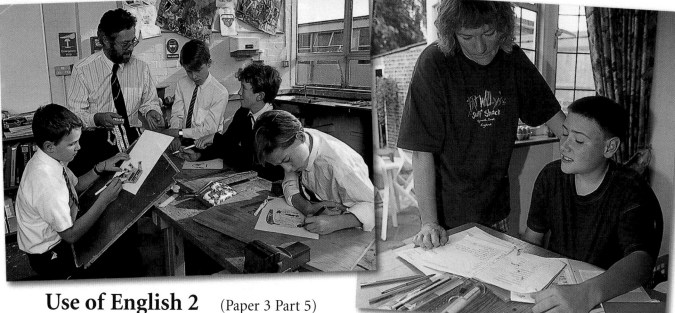

Use of English 2 (Paper 3 Part 5)

Lead-in

1 Discuss these questions.
 1 What do children learn at school, apart from what they are taught?
 2 Do you think you learn better on your own or in a class?

Word formation ▶ page 190

Task strategy

- Read the title and whole text first for general understanding. Ignore the spaces.
- Read each sentence. What kind of word is needed in each space – a noun, adjective, adverb or verb?
- Change the form of each word on the right to fit the space.
- Read the whole text again. Check it makes sense.
- Check your spelling. (It must be correct.)

HELP

Some words might need a prefix or a suffix and some might be negative.

➤ Question 1
 Is this a noun, *education*, or an adjective, *educational*?
➤ Question 2
 Choose from these suffixes which change an adjective into a noun: *-ness, -(i)ty, -ence.*
➤ Question 4
 This is a common word but it looks very different from the verb here. Be careful of the spelling!
➤ Question 6
 Is this a noun or an adjective?
➤ Question 7
 Choose from these negative prefixes for adjectives: *un-, il-, im-, in-.*
➤ Question 8
 Is this a comparative or a superlative?

2 a Read the title and text quickly and answer the questions. (Ignore the spaces at this stage.)
 1 Do children **have to** go to school by law in the UK?
 2 What problem is there sometimes with home tuition?

 b Do the task. Follow the task strategy and use the Help clues if necessary.

 Read the text below. Use the word given in capitals at the end of each line to form a word that fits in the space in the same line. There is an example at the beginning (0).

TEACHING CHILDREN AT HOME

In the UK there is no legal (0) obligation for children to go to school   OBLIGE
but they have to receive an effective full-time (1)............. . Nowadays,   EDUCATE
some parents are taking on the (2)............. of teaching their   RESPONSIBLE
children at home. Parents do not have to be (3)............. qualified   ACADEMIC
but it is (4)............. to have access to libraries and teaching   NEED
materials. They should also provide a (5)............. classroom-like   SUIT
environment in the home. The results are (6)............. , which   IMPRESS
surprises many people. Some children who were (7)............. in a   ATTENTIVE
large class change into model pupils. By far the (8)............. problem   BIG
for parent-teachers is the (9)............. attitude of other adults, who   SYMPATHY
say children don't socialise. But most of them seem (10)............. at   PERFECT
ease with other children.

---

 c Answer the questions about the task.
 1 Are there any answers you would like to check in a dictionary?
 2 Which answers required:
  • nouns? • adjectives? • adverbs?
 3 Which answers required a suffix?
 4 Which answers required a negative prefix?
 5 Which questions did you find difficult and why?

Discussion

3 What do you think are the advantages and disadvantages of home tuition?

Language development 3

Forming adjectives

A Suffixes
1 Sometimes we add a suffix to form an adjective:
   suit (verb) > *suitable* (adjective)
   health (noun) > *healthy* (adjective)
2 Sometimes the stem has to change:
   decide (verb) > *decisive* (adjective)
   beauty (noun) > *beautiful* (adjective)

B Sometimes we make internal changes:
   freeze (verb/noun) > *frozen* (adjective)
   heat (verb/noun) > *hot* (adjective)

C We can add a prefix to change the meaning of an
   adjective:
   regular > *irregular; honest* > *dishonest* (opposite)
   national > *international* (between)
   computer > *microcomputer* (small)

(LOOK) **Find examples of each type of adjective in the
   Use of English text opposite.**

▶ Grammar reference page 193

---

1 a **Complete each sentence with the word in brackets
   and one of the suffixes in the list.**

   -ible -ful -less -ic -al -ous -ate -ly -ish -y

   1 That boy is naughty but he's .... (*harm*).
   2 It's .... (*nature*) for a child to be like that
     sometimes.
   3 Despite his illness, Paul made the ....
     (*courage*) decision to sit his exams.
   4 Beth often behaves in a very silly and ....
     (*child*) way.
   5 Our teacher gave us some .... (*help*)
     suggestions about studying.
   6 Mr Turner has always been .... (*passion*)
     about science.
   7 Please clean any .... (*dirt*) equipment after
     you have done the experiment.
   8 The sports teacher at my old school was ....
     (*horror*)!
   9 There have been .... (*drama*) changes in the
     education system.
   10 I like my music teacher as she's very ....
     (*live*).

   b **Answer these questions about yourself.**
   1 Have you ever been *ir*responsible? What
     happened?
   2 Do you think everybody is *dis*honest on occasions?
   3 Is your handwriting the most *il*legible in the class?

Phrasal verbs: education

2 **Find a phrasal verb in the Use of English text. What
   noun does it collocate with?**

3 a **Match the phrasal verbs in italics in the sentences
   to the definitions a–j below.**
   1 The Principal *handed in* his resignation.
   2 The students *turned up* late for class.
   3 The teacher *got* her ideas *across* very well.
   4 We *worked out* the answers very easily.
   5 He *stayed on* at university another year.
   6 I *got down to* work as soon as I arrived.
   7 A taxi *picked* them *up* and took them to college.
   8 She *kept up with* the other students.
   9 We *carried out* a survey on staff attitudes.
   10 He *went over* the exercise with his students.

a arrived	f examined
b collected	g gave to a person in charge
c managed to understand	h communicated
d stayed level with	i started
e performed	j remained

   b **Complete these sentences with the phrasal verbs
   from Exercise 3a in the correct form.**
   1 Haven't your notes .... yet? Perhaps
     they're in your coat.
   2 Are you .... after class tonight or
     going home?
   3 Who's going to .... that experiment?
   4 It's time I .... marking the papers.
   5 .... your answers carefully.
   6 I haven't .... my homework yet. It's
     still in my bag.
   7 I can't .... all the latest technology.
   8 Come and .... your old coursework
     from my office.
   9 He didn't really .... his meaning .... to
     the students.
   10 We're trying to .... the best way to
     meet students' needs.

Exam practice 1

Paper 1: Reading

Part 4: multiple matching

You are going to read a magazine article about four people who travel to work by bicycle, motorbike or scooter. For questions 1–13, choose from the people (**A–D**). There is an example at the beginning (**0**).

Which of the people states the following?		
I like surprising the people I work with.	**0**	C
Going by bike gives me time to think.	**1**	
This form of transport helps me get more work done.	**2**	
I wanted to avoid being in large crowds.	**3**	
It's quite common to have bikes stolen.	**4**	
I dress so that drivers can see me.	**5**	
Buying a bike was a sudden decision.	**6**	
I feel I'm helping the environment.	**7**	
I can't carry very much on my bike.	**8**	
I don't care what people think of me.	**9**	
I bought the bike in order to save money.	**10**	
This way of travelling is reliable.	**11**	
I don't use the bike in freezing weather.	**12**	
It's easy to find somewhere to leave a bike.	**13**	

Me and my wheels

A WALTER, solicitor

'I've got a Kawasaki motorbike and I'm a passionate enthusiast. It all began 20 years ago when I was a student and I was looking for something cheaper to run than a car. Now, I use it every day. When it's windy or pouring down with rain it's not very pleasant, but only really low temperatures stop me going out on it. I am a very impatient person, so I really appreciate not being stuck in traffic jams. On the bike, you can get away from other traffic more easily – the journey to work would take twice as long by car. Also, when you have a demanding job like mine, it's useful to have an excuse to get away from work and the phone. The ride gives me a breathing space to go over things in my mind without being interrupted.'

B CLARE, project manager

'I cycle from my home to the office in north London every day. I started because I really couldn't bear being squashed in with all these other people on the underground in the rush hour. Another crucial thing for me is that I always know how long the journey's going to take; you can't always depend on public transport for that. In the six years I've been cycling around London, I've noticed that during commuting hours drivers are very careful when cyclists are around. Nevertheless, I make sure I wear a bright yellow jacket so that I can't be missed. I like to think that cycling is my contribution to making the air cleaner and saving the world's resources. However, I have to admit that I do go out in our car at weekends.'

C IVAN, insurance manager

'About four years ago, during a tube strike, I was in a taxi, running late for a meeting. As we passed a showroom, I saw this Piaggio scooter in the window. That's when I had my flash of inspiration. I jumped out of the cab, did the paperwork in 15 minutes, got on the bike and arrived at the meeting in time.

The bike can't go above 50 kilometres an hour, but because you can overtake lines of cars it doesn't seem slow. It has shrunk London for me and means I do extra business. I certainly couldn't fit in as many meetings without it.

I am aware that many colleagues and clients are astonished when I turn up for important meetings on my bike, but it's fun to challenge expectations. I also know that there are those who look down on this method of transport. But the opinions of others don't matter to me in the least; I would rather have the bike than a flash sports car!'

D ANGELA, financial consultant

'Although I have a full motorcycle licence, I prefer my scooter. It's not as powerful, obviously, but it's better in towns, as you can get through the traffic more easily. What is great is that there are loads of parking spots for bikes in London, so I don't get all the parking fines I did when I had a car.

I use the bike every day, not only to get to work but also to see clients. People in the streets sometimes stare at me as I ride along. I expect I look strange with my high heels, briefcase and work clothes. I also go shopping on the scooter, though space is limited and I need a car for my big monthly food shopping.

Like many bike owners round here, I've had two taken from outside my house. They were chained up, but the thieves lift the whole thing into a van and drive off.'

Paper 3: Use of English

Part 1: lexical cloze

Read the text below and decide which answer **A**, **B**, **C** or **D** best fits each space. There is an example at the beginning (**0**).

KNIFE-THROWING AT THE CIRCUS

Knife-throwing is a thrilling circus act, which is (**0**)....*B*.... for both the thrower and the assistant. Obviously, assistants need to be especially courageous, since they are (**1**)............ to stand in front of a board as knives land next to them at (**2**)............ speed. If a thrower's aim is not accurate, there is a (**3**)............ possibility that an accident might (**4**)............ . Such people need to feel (**5**)............ about the circus and enjoy the excitement of performing in front of hundreds of people. Not everyone is (**6**)............ for the work, particularly not nervous people!

Knife-throwers, on the other hand, need to be extremely (**7**)............ people. They can't (**8**)............ up for a performance feeling tired or having had an argument with their assistant because they have to be perfectly at (**9**)............ with what they are doing in order to be able to (**10**)............ the work their full concentration.

The knife-throwing tradition (**11**)............ partly because children follow their parents into the job. One (**12**)............ well-known knife-thrower, for example, has an assistant whose father was also a knife-thrower. She first had knives thrown at her when she was only 12 and has (**13**)............ doing the same job ever since. (**14**)............ , over the last 15 years she (**15**)............ that she has had about 300,000 knives thrown at her!

0	**A**	anxious	**B**	stressful	**C**	nervous	**D**	worried
1	**A**	insisted	**B**	considered	**C**	demanded	**D**	required
2	**A**	wide	**B**	great	**C**	plain	**D**	heavy
3	**A**	strong	**B**	tough	**C**	keen	**D**	deep
4	**A**	appear	**B**	develop	**C**	happen	**D**	exist
5	**A**	caring	**B**	devoted	**C**	loving	**D**	passionate
6	**A**	exact	**B**	suitable	**C**	proper	**D**	capable
7	**A**	reliable	**B**	doubtless	**C**	dependent	**D**	trusting
8	**A**	put	**B**	do	**C**	pick	**D**	turn
9	**A**	rest	**B**	ease	**C**	calm	**D**	quiet
10	**A**	take	**B**	hold	**C**	get	**D**	give
11	**A**	survives	**B**	stays	**C**	keeps	**D**	maintains
12	**A**	correctly	**B**	precisely	**C**	distinctly	**D**	particularly
13	**A**	taken up	**B**	come off	**C**	carried on	**D**	put in
14	**A**	Nevertheless	**B**	Despite that	**C**	In fact	**D**	Even so
15	**A**	totals	**B**	reckons	**C**	adds	**D**	counts

Part 2: structural cloze

Read the text below and think of the word which best fits each space. Use only **one** word in each space. There is an example at the beginning (**0**).

GREETINGS CARDS

British People have (**0**)..*been*.. sending greetings cards (**1**)............ over 600 years. On St Valentine's Day (14 February), medieval lovers (**2**)............ sing traditional romantic greetings to each other. (**3**)............ some point, a card was added to the song. In the British Museum there is (**4**)............ valentine card, made in the 1400s, which is (**5**)............ oldest known greetings card in existence.

These first cards (**6**)............ made by hand and consisted of a single sheet, not folded in (**7**)............ way, which had no envelope. The custom of exchanging cards remained popular throughout the middle ages, but not nearly as popular (**8**)............ it became later, in the 1800s, when factory-made cards were introduced.

In the factories, workers used (**9**)............ paint the black and white cards by hand, but these cards were not decorative enough for many people's tastes, (**10**)............ real lace and ribbons were added from the mid nineteenth century. However, the production process was much too slow to keep (**11**)............ with demand, and by the end of the century, nearly (**12**)............ cards were being produced by machine. This speeded up the process and (**13**)............ costs down.

Each year in the UK, people send even more greetings cards (**14**)............ they did the year before, and use them for many different occasions. But Christmas cards and Valentine cards remain the (**15**)............ popular of all.

Part 3: key word transformation

Complete the second sentence so that it has a similar meaning to the first sentence, using the word given. **Do not change the word given**. You must use between **two** and **five** words, including the word given. Write **only** the missing words.

EXAMPLE:

0 You must do exactly what the manager tells you.
   carry
   You must <u>carry out the manager's</u> instructions exactly.

1 I last saw Jane a week ago.
   since
   I have .... week.

2 Ann is the best chess player in our club.
   good
   Nobody in our club is .... at chess.

3 He usually falls asleep in the armchair in the evenings.
   will
   He .... in the armchair in the evenings.

4 John asked Caroline to marry him, but she didn't accept the offer because he was too old.
   turned
   John asked Caroline to marry him but she
   .... because he was too old.

5 I don't know many people taller than Mark.
   one
   Mark is .... I know.

6 I would prefer it if you said nothing to Tom about last night.
   want
   I don't .... to Tom about last night.

7 This car cost far less than my last one.
   expensive
   This car .... my last one.

8 It's three years since Nick started boxing.
   for
   Nick .... three years.

9 When I was 17, I rode my bike to college every day.
   used
   I .... to college every day when I was 17.

10 As the music got louder, it was more difficult to hear anyone speak.
   was
   The louder the music got, the .... to hear anyone speak.

Part 5: word formation

Read the text below. Use the word given in capitals below the text to form a word that fits the space in the text. There is an example at the beginning (0).

FAMILY BUSINESSES

In Europe, 85 per cent of companies are currently in private (0) <u>ownership</u> and amongst these (1)............ family businesses are often the most (2)............ . One problem that family-owned companies face, however, is finding (3)............ people to take over the running of the business when the (4)............ founder eventually dies or retires. The company may, for example, pass to children who don't share that person's (5)............ interest in the business. It often happens that such children are (6)............ to develop the business (7)............ , and sometimes they make bad decisions which result in the (8)............ of the company itself. However, there seems to be no (9)............ of enthusiastic people willing to set up new private companies, and hopefully these are just as (10)............ to do well as those they replace.

(0) OWNER   (6) ABLE
(1) TRADITION   (7) FAR
(2) SUCCESS   (8) FAIL
(3) SUIT   (9) SHORT
(4) ORIGIN   (10) LIKE
(5) ENTHUSIASM

MODULE 3
The world around us

Overview

- **Reading:** multiple matching: summary sentences (Paper 1 Part 1)
- **Language development 1:** adjectives and adverbs
- **Writing:** informal transactional letter (Paper 2 Part 1)
- **Listening skills:** listening for specific information
- **Speaking:** individual long turn (Paper 5 Part 2)
- **Use of English 1:** structural cloze (Paper 3 Part 2)
- **Language development 2:** *-ing* form and infinitives
- **Use of English 2:** lexical cloze (Paper 3 Part 1)
- **Language development 3:** nouns and adjectives: the weather

Red Square, Moscow

The Galapagos Islands, home of the land iguana

Lead-in

- The places in the photos are both World Heritage sites. Why do you think they were chosen?
- Why is it important to preserve our natural and cultural heritage?

5 Our cultural heritage

Venice●

Adriatic

Mediterranean

Reading (Paper 1 Part 1)

Before you read

1 a Look at the map of Italy and the pictures of Venice opposite. Discuss these questions.
   1 Where is Venice?
   2 What is special about it?
   3 How has the city changed over the years?

b Look at the title of the article and the introduction. What do you think the article will tell you about Venice?

Skimming

▶ Reading strategy
Unit 3 page 22

2 Skim the text. Match the parts 0–6 to these topics (a–g).
   a why Venice is very special **0**
   b falling population
   c growth of tourism
   d economic fall and rise
   e the need to change
   f location and its effects
   g environmental problems

Multiple matching:
summary sentences ▶ page 188

3 a Choose from the list A–G the sentence which best summarises each part (1–6) of the article. There is an example at the beginning (0). The highlighted words show how the answer was found. Read the task strategy before you start.

> A There is wide awareness of the dangers that Venice faces.
>
> B Venice's geographical position made it great.
>
> C The people of Venice have a will to succeed.
>
> D Venice needs more of its people to live in the city.
>
> E Venice has adapted to a new role.
>
> F A crucial decision must be taken.
>
> G Venice's location makes it different from other cities.

Task strategy

• Read the summary sentences. Each sentence expresses the main idea of one paragraph. Mark key words.

• For each sentence, look for the paragraph that contains the same idea.

• Read the paragraph carefully and check by marking the parts that express the same idea.

• Cross off the sentences as you use them.

b Compare and justify your answers.

Discussion

4 Discuss these questions.
   1 Would you like to live in Venice? Why/Why not?
   2 Do you think Venice should be 'preserved' or not? What are the pros and cons?

Vocabulary:
near synonyms

5 Find words in the text that mean:
   1 unusual, surprising (part 0)
   2 power, control (part 1)
   3 grand, important (part 3)
   4 weak, easily destroyed (part 4)
   5 got smaller, decreased (part 5)

City of change?

The City of Venice has enjoyed a thousand years of glory and power, but the pressures of modern life mean that Venetians now face a less secure future.

0	G

Venice is one of the few cities that can truly be described as unique. This is not just because of its remarkable buildings and long history, but because it is a city built on water. It was created in the fifth century by people who
5 were escaping from invaders on the mainland. They built their houses on low mud banks in the waters of the Adriatic Sea in order to protect themselves.

1	

Because it stood on the frontiers of east and west, the city state which developed was able to control important trade
10 routes. As a result, Venice became a strong commercial and naval force in the Mediterranean region. When the Venetian explorer Marco Polo reached China in 1275, he was able to extend his city's influence even further. Over the next three centuries, Venice became increasingly
15 richer and more powerful, and this economic success was matched by great cultural achievements. Venetian artists such as Bellini, Titian and Tintoretto played a decisive role in the development of Western art.

2	

However after 1600, a 200-year period of economic and
20 political decline followed as other sea powers grew in wealth and importance. From 1797, Venice came under foreign domination until, in 1866, it became part of Italy. However, one of the great qualities of the Venetians is their inner strength and ability to fight back. When they
25 realised that industrialisation was going to play an increasingly important role in the twentieth century, the Venetians turned their attention from trade to manufacturing. This led them back on the road to prosperity and economic growth.

3	

30 The appearance of the historic city itself has changed little in the last two hundred years. The Grand Canal, 'the most beautiful main road in the world', still carries most of the city's traffic. However, water buses and tourist gondolas have now replaced trading vessels. The impressive
35 churches and palaces which line both sides of the canal have become shops, hotels and flats, while former shipping warehouses have been turned into art museums. As a result, more than 12 million visitors a year pour into Venice, attracted by the dream-like romance of the city,
40 and at times they outnumber its residents.

4	

But Venice is not a dream. The development of industry and tourism has long threatened the city's fragile ecosystem, and floods have highlighted the fear that Venice really will sink unless something can be done to hold the sea back.
45 National and international efforts are now being made to protect Venice and its art treasures from the effects of air and water pollution, rising damp and flooding. But despite tremendous efforts, progress in finding a solution to the problem of high tides is still painfully slow.

5	

50 Many visitors to Venice dream of living there, but the reality is that around 1,500 Venetians a year leave the city. Many of them are young families unable to cope with the cost of living or find an affordable place to live. The resident population has shrunk by half over the past thirty
55 years, causing great concern that Venice is turning into a museum city for tourists, where nothing is real any more. In an effort to attract residents back, city developers have suggested re-introducing traditional industries such as glass and lace, filling in some canals to allow traffic in and
60 building underground roads to the mainland.

6	

But should Venice's heritage be preserved at all costs — so that it effectively remains a romantic city of art, frozen in time — or should it move with the rhythm of modern life, taking into account the needs of its residents? The
65 arguments between the conservers and the people of change continue.

Language development 1

Adjectives and adverbs

1 a Look at the photos in this extract from a magazine. Which of the sites do you recognise?

b Read the text. What do these sites have in common? (Don't worry about the words in italics at this stage.)

2 a In the context of the article, which of the words in italics are adjectives and which are adverbs? Write them in the correct place in the table.

Adjectives	Adverbs
natural	

b Answer these questions.
1 Most adverbs end in *-ly*. What exceptions are there in the text?
2 Which adjective in the text ends in *-ly*?
3 Some adverbs have two forms, depending on the meaning. What example is there of this?

c Check your answers in the Grammar reference on pages 193–194.

3 a Mark the correct word in each pair.
1 Usually it's *easy / easily* to know when you're looking at a World Heritage site.
2 Chartres Cathedral is *incredible / incredibly* well-preserved.
3 Our guide round the Summer Palace in Beijing spoke too *fast / quick*.
4 The Kremlin is a *classic / classically* Heritage site.
5 When we got to Glasgow it was very *late / lately* in the afternoon and it was snowing *hard / hardly*.
6 Some Heritage sites are quite *surprising / surprisingly*. For example, the city of Brasilia was *imaginative / imaginatively* created from nothing in 1956.

b Which place(s) in your country would you nominate as a Heritage site?

The world's *natural* and *cultural* heritage is disappearing *fast* but UNESCO, a United Nations organisation, is working *hard* to preserve it. UNESCO has created a list of 730 places, known as World Heritage sites. The sites on this list should be *actively* protected by all governments. Cultural sites on this list include the Taj Mahal, the *best-known* building in India, the *lively* Islamic centre of Marrakesh, and the Statue of Liberty, an *extremely impressive* gift from the people of France to the people of the United States. The World Heritage list also includes natural reserves, such as the Galapagos Islands, a place that at one time had *hardly* any tourists but is now in danger of being destroyed by them. UNESCO works *well* and without it the future of many *fascinating* Heritage sights would look *bleak*, so it is *worrying* that for *political* reasons some countries, like the USA and the UK, have withdrawn from *full* membership.

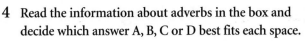

Adverbs of degree

A To make adjectives and other adverbs stronger.
- *extremely/very/really/remarkably*
  The castle is **really/remarkably** popular.
  It's a/an **very/extremely** popular attraction.

B To make adjectives and adverbs less strong.
- *rather/fairly/pretty* (positive and negative adjectives)
  The city wall is **rather/fairly/pretty** long.
  My town is **rather/fairly/pretty** small.
  It's **rather a/a rather/a fairly/a pretty** small town.
  (~~fairly a~~, ~~pretty a~~)
  It's **a fairly/a pretty small** town.

- *a bit/a little* (negative adjectives only)
  London's **a bit/a little** expensive.
  London's **a bit of an** expensive city. (before a noun phrase)

- *quite*
  The palace is **quite** interesting.
  It's **quite an** interesting palace. (~~a quite~~ interesting castle)

C To emphasise ungradable adjectives.
- *absolutely*
  The temperatures were **absolutely** freezing. (~~very freezing~~, ~~a bit freezing~~)
  There's an *absolutely* gorgeous view from the top. (~~very gorgeous~~).

▶ Grammar reference page 194

4 Read the information about adverbs in the box and decide which answer A, B, C or D best fits each space.
1 It was a .... simple idea.
   A bit   B little   C quite   D remarkably
2 Karl's got .... a fast car.
   A pretty   B very   C quite   D extremely
3 Everybody thinks he is .... crazy.
   A a little   B a little of   C a bit of   D quite a
4 Goya's paintings are .... well-known.
   A a bit   B absolutely C very   D rather a
5 This is .... an important day.
   A fairly   B rather   C extremely D pretty
6 Your new dress looks very ....
   A gorgeous B wonderful C marvellous D beautiful
7 The weather was .... wonderful.
   A very   B absolutely C extremely D remarkably

5 Use the adjectives in the list below, and adverbs of degree, to talk about:
- a place you have visited
- a person you know well
- a good film or book.

dull   interesting   lively   fantastic

6 Correct these students' sentences.

1
> It's easy to find my house. There's a very huge statue on the other side of the road.

2
> The park is really lovely, and the new theatre is very fantastic.

3
> You don't need to be smart dressed. People dress casually here in summer.

4
> Builders are working very hardly to restore the Town Hall before the President's visit next month.

5
> It's a fairly lively town, which I like, but the streets are sometimes bit noisy at night.

Writing Transactional letter (Paper 2 Part 1)

Lead-in 1 **Discuss these questions.**

1 Which city would you most like to spend a weekend in? Why?
2 What can a tourist see and do in your home town?

Understand the task 2 **Read the task below and answer the questions.**

1 WHO are you writing to?
2 What is the PURPOSE of your letter?
3 How many pieces of INFORMATION should you include in your letter?
4 What STYLE are you going to use? (Remember who you are writing to.)

An old friend, Sue Brown, has written to you saying she would like to come and visit your home town. She has asked you a list of questions.

Read the beginning of Sue's letter and your notes, which answer her questions. Then write a letter to her, recommending the city as a place to visit and suggesting she should come and stay with you.

I'm going to a conference at that big Conference Centre on the coast on the 18 July so I thought I might come down and stay the night and then have a weekend with Tom in your home town. It'd be really helpful if you could tell me:

Hourly train connections. —— • how to get to your home town from the Conference Centre

• about a good hotel —— *Stay with me.*

• what we can see there

• what kind of clothes we will need —— *Usually very hot weather in July. Shorts. T-shirts.*

Lovely park. Medieval castle.

Write a **letter** of between **120** and **180** words in an appropriate style. Do not write any postal addresses.

Plan your letter 3 a **How many paragraphs will you have?**

b **This is an example of a paragraph plan for the letter. What points would you include in each paragraph? Make notes. The first and last paragraph are done for you.**

Paragraph 1: Reacting to Sue's letter: Glad you're coming.
Inviting her to stay: You can stay at my house.

Paragraph 2: Travel instructions: ...

Paragraph 3: Places to go: 1 ...
  2 ...

Paragraph 4: Clothes: ...

Paragraph 5: Conclusion: More questions (email?) Look forward to ...

Language and content

4 a Which paragraph would be more appropriate to begin the letter? Why?

A Thank you very much for your letter of 10 July. I was delighted to hear about your visit to my home town. I am writing to invite you to stay with me at my house.

B It was great to hear from you and I'm thrilled you're coming to visit me. I hope you'll stay with me – I've got loads of room to put you up now I've unpacked!

b Can you find any specific examples of formal and informal language in A and B above?

c Complete some of the expressions in the table for the letter.

Getting there	It's about … away by train.
	You can easily get here by … .
	It probably only takes … .
Suggesting things to do	I hope you will … .
	You really must … ./You absolutely have to … .
	You could go to the … .
	How do you fancy …?
	What/How about …?
Suggesting what to bring	It'd probably be a good idea … .
	Don't bother … .

d Which sentence in each of the pairs below would be most appropriate in the last paragraph of the letter?

1 A Why don't you give me a ring when you get here?

   B May I suggest that you telephone me upon arrival?

2 A I look forward to meeting you.

   B I'm really looking forward to seeing you again.

3 A If you need further information please don't hesitate to contact me.

   B Let me know if there's anything else you'd like to know.

e How will you close the letter? (e.g. *Cheers, Love, Yours sincerely*)

Write your letter

5 Now write your letter using the ideas and some of the language above. You must include the most important information. Do not write any postal addresses. Write your answer in 120–180 words.

Check and improve your letter

6 When you edit your letter, what things will you check? Refer to the checklist in the Writing reference.

▶ Writing reference page 206

LANGUAGE SPOT: punctuation

Write this paragraph with appropriate capital letters and punctuation.

chester itself is a very pretty town it dates back to roman times so there are a lot of fascinating ruins and lovely architecture which im sure will interest you the roman amphitheatre is well worth a visit with its guides dressed up as roman soldiers there is also a cathedral and a church and there are red sandstone walls all round the town it takes about an hour and a half to walk around them but its a lovely walk henry james the american writer wrote about how much he loved the walls youll also find a river in chester where you can go for a boat trip or have a picnic if you have time to go shopping there are lots of wonderful shops

6 Our natural heritage

Listening

Before you listen

▶ Listening strategy Unit 2 page 14,
Unit 4 page 28

1 a You will hear an interview with Nick Gordon (in the photo above), who spent ten years in the rainforest. What do you think his job is? What do you think he liked and disliked about being in the rainforest?

b 🔊 Listen to the first part of the interview and check your guesses.

Listening for specific information

Listening strategy

Read the questions first so you know what you need to listen for.

2 a Decide what kind of information is missing in Exercise 2b.
EXAMPLE: *Question 1 – a time*

b 🔊 You will now hear the rest of the interview with Nick Gordon. For questions 1–10, complete the sentences. Listen to the recording twice.

1 Nick says that he first saw a jaguar at .... in the morning.

2 The jaguar's coat was a mixture of .... and .... in colour.

3 Nick was disappointed at not getting a .... of his first jaguar.

4 Most male jaguars have a territory of .... in size.

5 The fact that jaguars move around so much and so .... makes it easy to miss them.

6 On a trip in search of jaguars, Nick was once given a very large .... to eat.

7 Nick says that forest people have a feeling of .... for the jaguar.

8 To help them study jaguars, researchers have fixed .... on to some they have caught.

9 In some areas, jaguars are killed by .... because they are seen as a threat.

10 The health of jaguars may be in danger due to contact with animals such as .... and ....

c Compare and discuss your answers.

1 How many words did you write in each gap?

2 Were the words you needed on the recording?

Speaking (Paper 5 Part 2)

Lead-in

1 Look at the photos. What jobs do they illustrate?

Comparing and contrasting photos

2 Answer these questions.
1 What do the photos have in common?
They both show … .
2 What is different about them?
In the one on the left … , whereas in the other one … .

Sample answer

3 a 🔈 Listen to the examiner and complete her instructions.
EXAMINER: I'd like you to compare and contrast these photographs and say what you think ....

b 🔈 Listen to a student doing the task and answer the questions.
1 Did he mention the same similarities and differences as you?
2 Did he use the same language to compare and contrast?

c 🔈 Listen again and tick (✓) the expressions he uses for giving a personal opinion.

Personally, I … .	*It's very hard to say, but … .*
I'm not really very interested in … .	*If I had to choose … .*

▶ Functions reference page 224

d Which two words didn't the student know? How did he explain them?

Individual long turn ▶ page 191

Task strategy

- Listen carefully to the instructions.
- Say what is similar and different about the photos. Don't just describe each one.
- Give your personal opinion in the second part of the task.
- Keep talking!

4 Work in pairs. Follow the task strategy.
STUDENT A: Compare and contrast the photos above and say what you think is difficult about these jobs.
STUDENT B: Compare and contrast the photos on page 218 and say why you think dogs are useful for this kind of work.

5 Did you:
- compare and contrast the pictures?
- give your personal reaction?
- speak for a full minute?

Discussion

6 What other jobs involve working with animals? Which ones would you most/least like to do? Why?

6

Use of English 1 (Paper 3 Part 2)

Lead-in

1 a Do you think the following statements are *True* or *False*?
   1 Cats don't see colours as clearly as people do.
   2 A dog's sense of smell is much better than a person's.
   3 Elephants have long memories.
   4 Crickets can tell us the temperature.
   5 Cows lie down before a storm.

   b Check your answers on page 218.

Structural cloze ▶ page 189

   ▶ Task strategy Unit 4 page 30

2 a Read the title of the text below. What connection do you think it has with animals?

   b Read the text quickly and answer the questions. (Ignore the spaces at this stage.)
   1 How do some animals change their behaviour before an earthquake?
   2 What use have the Chinese made of animals?
   3 How can the animals' behaviour be explained scientifically?

   c Do the task. Follow the task strategy on page 30 and use the Help clues if necessary.

   Read the text below and think of the word which best fits each space. Use only **one** word in each space. There is an example at the beginning (**0**).

HELP

➤ **Question 1**
This question tests tenses. Which tense is correct here?

➤ **Question 7**
This is another question testing tenses. Were the animals restless before the reports were made or at the same time?

➤ **Question 9**
This city has been mentioned before. Which article is used to show this?

➤ **Question 13**
Which word is correct here, *it* or *there*?

PREDICTING EARTHQUAKES

It has long (**0**) .been.. known that animals, birds and insects behave differently before an earthquake. People (**1**)............. seen fish jump out of water on to dry land, and mice appear dazed before quakes, allowing (**2**)............. to be caught easily.

In December 1974, Chinese scientists began (**3**)............. receive reports of snakes coming out of hibernation and freezing to death on the cold ground. This was followed (**4**)............. a series of minor tremors at the end of the month. The following month they received even (**5**)............. reports of strange animal behaviour in the city of Haicheng. Many (**6**)............. these concerned cattle and horses which (**7**)............. become restless and were (**8**)............. frightened to enter buildings. As a result, city leaders evacuated (**9**)............. entire city. Soon after, a major earthquake struck; the city leaders had succeeded (**10**)............. saving countless lives.

(**11**)............. then China has suffered a number of major quakes, which they were not as prepared (**12**)............. . Nevertheless, the Chinese have demonstrated that earthquakes do not always strike without warning.

(**13**)............. is a fact that some animals are very sensitive to sound, temperature, touch, light and even magnetic fields. Therefore, they may be able to detect the seismic activity (**14**)............. comes before an earthquake. It would (**15**)............. a pity to ignore the signs.

   d Which questions in the task test:
   • articles? • auxiliary verbs? • verb + verb patterns? • verb + preposition?

Language development 2

-ing forms and infinitives

A After a main verb we can use:
- an -ing form: *I like walking. I heard a man shouting.*
- a to-infinitive: *I wanted to see her.*
- an infinitive (without to): *Let me help! That makes me feel better. Did anyone see John leave?*

B The -ing form is used after prepositions.
I'm thinking of getting a new job.
Nadia is keen on learning new things.

C The -ing form can also be used in some fixed expressions.
The family spent a lot of time arguing.
It's always worth asking for a discount.

D The infinitive can be used after:
- some adjectives: *She's eager to learn.*
- some nouns: *It was my decision to leave.*

(LOOK) **at the Use of English text opposite and find examples of the structures above.**

▶ Grammar reference pages 204–205

1 a Discuss these questions.
1 What causes a solar eclipse?
2 Have you ever seen a solar eclipse?

b Look at the notes made by a journalist about a solar eclipse. Put the verbs in brackets in the correct form.

Many creatures wanted (1)............ (settle) down to sleep.
Other animals, like owls, had problems (2)............ (sleep) and woke up.
I saw a bat suddenly (3)............ (fly) out of a tree.
I couldn't help (4)............ (notice) a strange, cold breeze.
Scientists were interested in (5)............ (solve) the mysteries of the sun.
Spectators saw the sky gradually (6)............ (go) dark.
I regretted (7)............ (not, bring) a video camera.
The experience was awesome – it made us (8)............ (feel) very small.
I found it hard (9)............ (talk) for a few minutes.
A lot of people made the decision (10)............ (not, drive) during the eclipse.

2 a The verbs *stop, try, remember* can be followed by -ing or a to-infinitive. Look at the sentence pairs below. What is the difference in meaning?
1 a He remembered to wear protective glasses.
  b He remembered wearing protective glasses.
2 a She tried using a camcorder to record the event.
  b She tried to use a camcorder to record the event.
3 a He stopped to look at the bright lights.
  b He stopped looking at the bright lights.

b Mark the correct form of the verb in each pair.
1 He stopped at the shop *to buy / buying* a pint of milk.
2 I tried *to get / getting* eggs but they didn't have any.
3 Lucy stopped *to drink / drinking* coffee ages ago.
4 Please remember *to post / posting* the letter.
5 I remember *to call / calling* Mike yesterday.
6 Try *to add / adding* some salt. It might taste better.

3 a Look at the photo. Have you heard of this natural phenomenon?

b Read about a couple's trip to see the Northern Lights. Then complete the spaces in the text. Use *to, on, from, for, of* or *in* and put the verb in brackets in the correct form.

Northern Lights in the skies above Scotland

The possibility (1)............ (see) the Northern Lights was Laura's main reason for visiting the Shetland Islands. She had been looking forward (2)............ (go) there for ages. I was more interested (3)............ (get) some rest and fresh air.

When we arrived, Laura had a headache, so I insisted (4)............ (put up) the tent myself. She apologised (5)............ (not, help) and decided (6)............ (go) for a walk. I didn't object (7)............ (her, go) as I'm not very keen (8)............ (walk) and I thought it might help her headache. And anyway, I can rarely prevent (9)............ (her, do) what she wants to do!

Soon, it got very dark. I decided to look for Laura. I was afraid (10)............ (get lost), but I needn't have worried – suddenly there were curtains of red, green and white light everywhere. It was the Northern Lights.

4 a Complete these sentences about yourself.
1 When I'm on holiday, I enjoy … .
2 My greatest ambition in life is … .
3 The country I'd most like … (visit) is … .

b Compare your answers with other students.

Use of English 2 (Paper 3 Part 1)

Lead-in 1 Read the title of the text below and look at the photo. Have you heard of Groundhog Day?

Lexical cloze ▶ page 189

▶ Task strategy Unit 2 page 18

2 a Read the title and text quickly and answer the questions. (Ignore the spaces at this stage.)

1 What happens on Groundhog Day?

2 Why has it become better-known in recent years?

b Do the task. Follow the task strategy on page 18 and use the Help clues if necessary.

Read the text below and decide which answer **A**, **B**, **C** or **D** best fits each space. There is an example at the beginning (**0**).

0 A eager   B enthusiastic   C optimistic   D interesting

GROUNDHOG DAY

According to an (**0**) ..D.. US popular tradition, the groundhog, a small furry animal, (**1**)............. of its winter sleep on 2 February. If the sky is (**2**)............., he sees his shadow. This means there's going to be six more weeks of (**3**)............. weather and he returns to his hole. If the day is cloudy and he can't see his shadow, it means there will be an (**4**)............. spring and he stays above ground. Each year reporters (**5**)............. in Punxsutawney at dawn and a large (**6**)............. of cameras are focused on the burrow of a groundhog named Punxsutawney Phil. Is spring just around the (**7**).............? That's what they want Phil to tell them. Or is it going to be a long, (**8**)............. winter with a risk of more (**9**)............. snow? Groundhog Day has become more popular in recent years, mainly because of the 1993 Hollywood film of the same (**10**)............., which made Punxsutawney famous and (**11**)............. Phil into a major celebrity. The following February, over 30,000 people (**12**)............. in Punxsutawney, Pennsylvania for Phil's big day. Unfortunately, (**13**)............. the large crowds were hoping (**14**)............. a prediction of good weather, Phil saw his shadow and returned to his hole, so everyone knew that winter was going to (**15**)............. for a few more weeks.

Punxsutawney Phil

HELP

➤ **Question 3**
Only one of these adjectives can combine with *weather* to mean *bad*.

➤ **Question 6**
Remember that cameras are countable.

➤ **Question 9**
Only one of these adjectives can combine with *snow*. The others combine with *fog* or *wind*.

	A	B	C	D
1	gets out	comes out	gets up	comes up
2	calm	apparent	clear	fair
3	low	severe	ill	rude
4	advanced	ahead	early	immature
5	gather	group	crowd	combine
6	quantity	number	total	sum
7	street	turn	bend	corner
8	stiff	hard	solid	forceful
9	strong	dense	heavy	warm
10	name	title	label	term
11	got	became	took	turned
12	turned up	called off	came on	looked over
13	despite	although	still	otherwise
14	for	to	by	on
15	exist	rest	last	hold

c Which questions test:

• words that go together?

• the correct word from a set with similar meanings?

• fixed expressions?

• phrasal verbs?

• linking words?

d Which adjective + noun combinations in the text link to either weather or the seasons? Make a note of the words you want to remember in your vocabulary book.

Language development 3

Nouns and adjectives: the weather

1 **Discuss these questions.**
   1 What's the weather like in your country at different times of the year?
   2 What kind of weather do you like best?

2 **a** **Write the nouns below in the appropriate place in the table. Use a dictionary if necessary.**
   breeze   drizzle   hail   shower   snow   gust
   hurricane   thunder   gale   lightning   downpour

Rain	Wind	Storm

   b **Read these statements about extreme weather. Mark the correct word in each pair.**

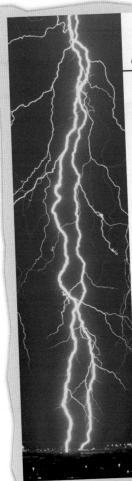

FASCINATING
WEATHER FACTS

1 When *thunder / lightning* strikes the earth, its temperature is hotter than the surface of the sun.

2 In the Antarctic, *gales / gusts* of wind can reach speeds of over 320 kilometres per hour.

3 In some parts of the world, *hail / drizzle* can damage crops and kill animals.

4 *Hurricanes / Downpours* are whirling storms that can create giant waves up to 8 metres high.

5 Snow and hail are both frozen water, but *snow / hail* doesn't fall in thunderstorms.

3 **a** **Match the adjectives in A with the nouns in B. There may be more than one possibility.**

A	B
1 torrential	a breeze
2 tropical	b shower
3 gentle	c downpour
4 heavy	d thunder
5 high	e rain
6 light	f wind
7 loud	g storm
8 strong	
9 hard	
10 pouring	
11 chilly	

   b **Which adjective in Exercise 3a best completes each sentence? There may be more than one possibility.**
   1 Because of the .... winds, all flights have been cancelled.
   2 We're soaked. We got caught in a .... shower.
   3 We sat in the garden and enjoyed the .... spring breeze.
   4 The storm's nearly over. The thunder's not as .... as it was.
   5 The rain's quite .... Let's stay indoors.
   6 The wind always turns a little .... in autumn.
   7 In the tropics you usually get .... rain during a storm.

4 **a** **Weather adjectives can also be used to describe people or things. Match the adjectives in A with nouns in B.**

A	B
1 stormy	a smile
2 heated	b manner
3 icy	c discussion
4 sunny	d relationship
5 breezy	e stare

   b **Can you guess what the phrases mean? Use a dictionary to help you.**

5 **What kind of weather do you think would be most appropriate for:**
   1 a romantic encounter?
   2 a quarrel with your best friend?
   3 a long car journey?
   4 a holiday in the mountains?
   5 a trip in a sailing boat?

Module 3: Review

1 Complete the extract from a newspaper report with words from the list. There are some extra words which you do not need to use.

cope falling affordable fragile achievement
increasingly remarkable commercial impressive
growth shrink

Until recently, the museum had never been run on a
(1).............. basis and visitor numbers had started to
(2)............ . For example, it had never organised
exhibitions abroad because it said its exhibits were too
(3).............. to be moved. Two years ago though, the
building was renovated and the fees reduced to make
them (4).............. for most people. As a result, there has
been a tremendous (5).............. in visitor numbers, and
staff sometimes find it difficult to (6).............. . Last year
there were a (7).............. two million visitors – a fantastic
(8).............. .

2 **a** Mark the correct word in each pair.
   1 Dolphins are *surprising / surprisingly* intelligent.
   2 *Interesting / Interestingly*, cats were first domesticated 4,000 years ago by the Egyptians.
   3 Ants are very *hard / hardly* workers.
   4 Many birds migrate from Britain *late / lately* in the summer.
   5 The sailfish swims very *quick / fast*. It can reach speeds of 109 km per hour.

   b Correct the mistakes in these sentences.
   1 There is a quite large number of foxes in Britain's cities.
   2 Camels can lose fairly a large amount of water without harming their bodies.
   3 Dogs are extreme faithful pets.
   4 The life of a performing animal in the circus can be a pretty miserable.
   5 When it's very freezing most animals try to find shelter.

3 Punctuate these sentences about a TV programme.
   1 im watching a programme called our disappearing world have you seen it
   2 according to the presenter many peoples lives have changed dramatically
   3 i think its a tragedy he said that so many languages are disappearing
   4 ongota an ethiopian language is only spoken by 78 people
   5 however some regional languages like catalan welsh and trentine are surviving

4 **a** Use a verb from both A and B to make five sentences about yourself. Four must be *True* and one must be *False*.
   EXAMPLE: *I've forgotten to bring my mobile phone today.*

A	B
forget	visit
want	ask
try	bring
stop	get
regret	think
make me	run
can't help	wait
remember	feel
see people	take
be worth	get out

   b Work in pairs. Tell each other your sentences. Can you guess which one is *False*?

5 Complete these extracts from a class survey on global issues with the correct prepositions.
   1 Everyone is interested .... protecting the environment.
   2 Most people are afraid .... what might happen to the rainforests.
   3 80 per cent of the class object .... governments dumping waste at sea.
   4 Some think there is little possibility .... world poverty being reduced.
   5 15 per cent think we should be prevented .... having large families.
   6 Everyone is keen .... equal opportunities for men and women.

6 Mark the correct word in each pair.

I'm a weather forecaster, and I hate boring days when the sky is (1) *apparent / clear* and there is nothing more interesting than a (2) *gentle / heavy* breeze to talk about. We end up having (3) *sunny / heated* discussions in the office about which is the hottest place in the country! I much prefer it when there are (4) *heavy / high* winds and (5) *heavy / high* rain. In fact, last night there was a (6) *pouring / torrential* downpour, with lightning and (7) *loud / strong* thunder.

MODULE 4
Challenges

Overview

- **Reading:** gapped text (Paper 1 Part 3)
- **Language development 1:** narrative tenses; time conjunctions
- **Writing:** story (Paper 2 Part 2)
- **Listening:** multiple matching (Paper 4 Part 3)
- **Speaking:** collaborative task (Paper 5 Part 3)
- **Use of English 1:** error correction (Paper 3 Part 4)
- **Language development 2:** quantity; determiners
- **Use of English 2:** lexical cloze (Paper 3 Part 1)
- **Language development 3:** adjectives often confused; phrasal verbs with *take*

Lead-in

- The photos show people in challenging situations. Which situations would, for you, be the hardest/easiest? the most satisfying? the most interesting?
- What's the most challenging situation you've faced in your school, college or working life?

Reading (Paper 1 Part 3)

Before you read

1 a Look at the photos opposite. Where is the man? What is he doing?

b Look at the title of the article and the introduction. Then write down at least three questions you would like to find the answer to in the text.
EXAMPLE: Which desert is it?

Skimming and scanning

▶ Reading strategy Unit 1 page 8, Unit 3 page 22

2 Skim and scan the text. (Ignore the gaps at this stage.) Does the text contain the answers to your questions?

Gapped text: sentences

▶ page 188

Task strategy

- Read the whole of the base text and example sentence carefully.
- Read the text before and after each gap and predict the missing information.
- Look for a sentence in the box that fits the topic.
- To check, look for grammatical links (e.g. pronouns and tenses); lexical links (e.g. synonyms).
- If you are not sure, go on to the next gap.
- Read the text again with your answers, to check it makes sense.

3 Eight sentences have been removed from the article. Choose from the sentences A–H the one which fits each gap (1–7). There is an example at the beginning (0).

a Look at the example. The highlighted words show why H fits here.
- *this cruel and unusual punishment* refers back to *Each day for 18 days …*
- *This* in the sentence after the gap refers back to *his ambition*.

b Do the task. Follow the task strategy. For gaps 1–3, the links have been highlighted for you.

c Compare and justify your answers. What links helped you?

Discussion

4 Discuss these questions.
1 What do you think of Ray Mouncey? Do you agree that he's a true hero?
2 Have you or your friends ever done anything to raise money for a good cause?

Vocabulary: phrasal verbs

5 Find phrasal verbs in the text that mean:
1 begin (a journey) (para. 1)
2 start, establish something (para. 1)
3 anticipate something with enthusiasm (paras. 2 and 6)
4 stop (doing) something (para. 3)
5 care for (para. 3)
6 tell someone something they did not know before (para. 5)
7 begin (a journey) (para. 6)
8 use up a large quantity of (para. 6)

Ray Mouncey is no ordinary runner. He's chosen to run through one of the world's most inhospitable deserts in order to raise money for a charity very dear to his heart. Malcolm Macalister Hall explains.

Next week, at the age of 50, Ray Mouncey will set out on the awful task he has set himself – to run 575 km through
5 Death Valley and the Mojave Desert in California. Each day for 18 days, he will run the same distance as a runner in a marathon race. **0 H** This is
10 to raise enough money through sponsorship to set up a special needs centre for disabled children and their families.

The World's Scariest Running Track

Not many people would want to do what Ray is going to do and he's not looking forward to it much either. 'The route's just hell,' he says, looking depressed. [1] 'The one thing you want is for the run to finish, and the only thing that keeps you going is the thought of the kids.'

Ten years ago, Ray's world collapsed when doctors discovered that his son, Luke, had a rare disease that meant he would soon be unable to move. Ray gave up his job and, at first, spent all his time looking after his son. [2] As Ray explains, 'Although these kids are in wheelchairs, they can still enjoy themselves if they are given the opportunity. I wanted to give them a place where they can make friends and have the chance to laugh again; a place which would offer an improved quality of life.'

The idea for his fund-raising runs came to him in California after an American consultant confirmed what doctors in England had already told him: Luke's condition was untreatable. 'I was sitting in the car, feeling depressed. I was looking out over a stretch of desert, thinking to myself, "That's it then, this is your precious child and you've just been told there's nothing anyone can do for him." [3] I was going to do something to help. I don't know where I heard about Death Valley. I must have read about it somewhere and the idea of it just stayed in my mind.'

Ray lives with his family in a bungalow in a tiny coastal village in the east of England. The cold wind-swept beaches nearby, where Ray has been training every day, are not ideal preparation for the roads in Death Valley, where temperatures reach over 50°C down on the salt flats at nearly 90 m below sea level. As Ray points out, [4] 'The mountains around it trap the heat so it's roasting there.'

[5] This involves him setting off at around 11 a.m. and running through the heat of the day. Last time he got through four sets of training shoes. 'One pair just split, so I took them off and buried them in the sand,' he recalls.

Ray admits that the desert run is a way of coping with Luke's condition. 'I feel that if he can suffer and be so brave, then so should I. But I'm also doing it so that he can have something to look forward to. [6] He's really excited about that already – so those 575 km have got to be done.'

The chairman of a television company which is filming Ray's latest run said, '[7] How else can you describe a man who is living proof that determination can win over hardship, who keeps punishing his own body in order to help others?'

A But soon he began to realise that more could be done for children like Luke.

B This time I'm using some of the money to take him round the theme parks in California.

C He's a true hero.

D Then suddenly my mood changed. I decided that I wasn't going to sit back and accept the situation.

E That part of the run goes through one of the most hostile environments on earth.

F Despite all these potential difficulties, Ray insists on doing the run the hard way.

G The feeling you have for it is absolute hatred really.

H From this cruel and unusual punishment, he hopes to raise enough money to achieve his ambition.

Language development 1

Narrative tenses

1 a Read the first sentence of this student's story. How do you think it continues?

> I was unlocking my front door when I heard a noise inside the flat.

b Read the next part of the story and compare. Does it continue the way you thought it would?

> I closed the door again quickly and ran out into the street. Then I tried to call the police but my mobile phone wasn't working, because I'd been talking to people all day and the battery had run down.

c Mark the different past verb forms in the story so far.

d Match the meanings in the list a–d to the sentences in the story. Then complete the table below.
  a an activity in progress at a point in the past
  b a single action which happened before a point in the past
  c an action or event at a point in the past
  d an activity which happened before a point in the past

2 Now complete the rest of the story with the correct forms of the verbs in brackets. Sometimes there may be more than one possible answer.

> I (1)......................... (run) down the street to a payphone, but someone (2)......................... (talk) on the phone. I think she (3)......................... (argue). After I (4)......................... (wait) for about ten minutes, she (5)......................... (come) out. I could see from her eyes that she (6)......................... (cry).
>
> I (7)......................... (tell) the police officer what (8)......................... (happen). But then, while I (9)......................... (talk) to him, a friend of mine (10)......................... (come) out of my house. He (11)......................... (carry) balloons. Then I realised what (12)......................... (go) on. Of course! It (13)......................... (be) my birthday, and my friends (14)......................... (wait) in the house to give me a surprise birthday party!
>
> I (15)......................... (explain) everything to the officer. When I (16)......................... (go) into the house, everyone (17)......................... (laugh), and they (18)......................... (start) to sing Happy Birthday. I (19)......................... (feel) very stupid about the way I (20)......................... (react) ...

Form	Meaning	Example
A Past simple	....	....
B Past continuous *was/were* + *-ing*	....	....
C Past perfect simple *had* + past participle	....	....
D Past perfect continuous *had been* + past participle	....	....

▶ Grammar reference pages 198–199

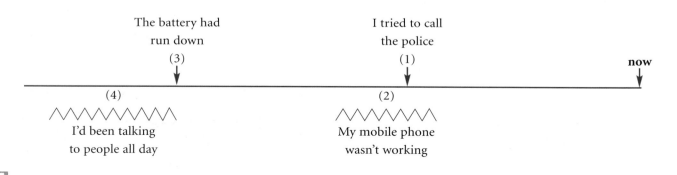

The battery had run down		I tried to call the police		
(3)		(1)		**now**
↓		↓		↓
(4)		(2)		
∿∿∿∿∿∿∿		∿∿∿∿∿∿		
I'd been talking to people all day		My mobile phone wasn't working		

Time conjunctions

A *As, while, when*
- A longer activity happening 'around' a short event:
  ***As/While/When** I was watching a horror movie, I heard a noise outside.*
- Two longer activities happening at the same time:
  ***As/While/When** I was working, my brother was sitting on the beach.*

B *When*
- A short event in the middle of a longer activity:
  *I was watching a horror movie **when** I heard a noise outside.*
- A short event immediately before another short event:
  ***When** he crossed the finish line, everybody cheered.*

C *Before, after*
- *Before* always goes with the **second** action in the sequence:
  ***Before** we left, I filled up/had filled up with petrol.*
  (= first: I filled up, second: we left)
  *I filled up/had filled up with petrol **before** we left.*

- *After* always goes with the **first** action in the sequence:
  ***After** I filled up/had filled up with petrol, we left.*
  (= first: I filled up, second: we left)
  *We left **after** I filled up/had filled up with petrol.*

D *As soon as*
- *(= immediately after)*
  ***As soon as** he went/had gone outside, it started raining.*
  *It started raining **as soon as** he went/had gone outside.*

E *By the time*
- *(= before)*
  ***By the time** the police arrived, the robbers had run away.*
  *The robbers had run away **by the time** the police arrived.*

3 Read the information about time conjunctions in the box and decide which answer A, B, C or D best fits each space.
1 .... Joe arrived at the cinema, the film had finished.
   A While   B As soon as   C By the time   D As
2 .... we were sitting in a traffic jam, our plane was taking off.
   A As soon as   B While   C After   D By the time
3 .... I phoned Sara, she said she had been ill.
   A While   B Before   C When   D By the time
4 She fell asleep .... she was reading her book.
   A as soon as   B before   C by the time   D while
5 .... I turned on the TV, the programme ended.
   A While   B As soon as   C By the time   D Before
6 Mechanics had checked the cars .... the race started.
   A before   B while   C as   D after
7 The police searched us .... we arrived.
   A as   B by the time C while   D before
8 I felt so relieved .... I found my missing purse.
   A while   B before   C by the time   D after

4 a Complete these sentences about yourself. Use the past simple, past continuous or past perfect.
   1 When I left school, I … .
   2 I was … when I saw … .
   3 I had been … when I … .
   4 I had … but I … .
   5 When I heard the news about …, I … .

b Compare your sentences with other students.

5 Join the sentence pairs. Use the time conjunctions in brackets and make any other changes necessary. You may need to change the order of the sentences.
   1 I heard the news. Then I phoned my sister. (*as soon as*)
   2 I went to see a friend. Then I went home. (*after*)
   3 I waited for around an hour. Then he eventually arrived. (*by the time*)
   4 The boss resigned. Then the business collapsed. (*when*)
   5 I was gardening for hours. Then she phoned me. (*when*)
   6 His owner was talking. At the same time, the dog ran into the road. (*while*)
   7 The plane left. Then we got to the airport. (*by the time*)
   8 I never ate caviar. Then I went to Russia. (*before*)

6 Think of a different ending for the story in Exercise 1. Continue your story from the opening sentence.

Writing   Story (Paper 2 Part 2)

Lead-in   1   a   What kind of stories do you like?

| love stories ☐ | ghost stories ☐ | adventure stories ☐ |
| crime stories ☐ | science fiction ☐ | |

b   What makes a good story for you?
EXAMPLE: *Interesting characters …*

Understand the task   2   Read the task below and answer the questions.
1   What KIND OF STORY from Exercise 1a above will your readers expect?
2   What will make it a GOOD story? A strong storyline? Interesting characters? Vivid language?
3   What EFFECT do you want to have on the readers? To make them laugh, move them emotionally or frighten them?

> You have been asked to write a **story** for a student magazine. Your story must begin with the words:
>
> *That day, my life changed forever.*
>
> Write your **story** in **120–180** words.

Plan your story   3   a   Brainstorm ideas for a story. Use these pictures to help you.

b   Now make notes under these headings.
Paragraph 1:   Set the scene (people and place)
Who? What? When? Where?
(What sort of people? How old?)
Paragraphs 2–4:   Say what happened (action)
What? When? Where? Why? How?
(How did it happen? How long did it last? How did they feel?)
Paragraph 5:   Bring it to a conclusion
What? How? Why?

Language and content

4 a Which of these opening paragraphs would have most impact on the readers? Why?

A That day, my life changed forever. I'd been a fashion model since I was 16 and had had my photograph taken for all the top fashion magazines. But I had grown tired of this way of life.

B That day, my life changed forever. I had taken up modelling when I was 16 and I was now tired of it.

b Which of these closing paragraphs would have most impact on the readers? Why?

A I went without sleep for 60 hours and my skin turned green but I was glad I did it.

B Although people in the fashion world thought I was mad, I had never had such a wonderful feeling of having achieved something.

c Look at the phrases in the table for sequencing events. How would you continue at least <u>one</u> of the phrases from each section for your story?

Beginning	*At the beginning … (I had been …).* *That was when … (I saw …).*
Middle	*Right from the start … (I was …).* *Before long … . Eventually … (I managed to …).* *To my amazement … . Luckily … .* *Naturally … (I was very pleased …).*
End	*After it was all over … . In the end … (when I got back …).* *Of course … (I was … but …).*

d Complete the sentences with an adverb.

1 I was .... fascinated by the sight of these people riding camels across the desert.
2 I wanted to send off my application ....
3 The race was .... organised.
4 I don't remember .... how many people took part.
5 We talked .... about the race.
6 Next year, I'm .... going to take part in the Raid Gauloises, the most difficult race in the world.

Write your story

5 Now write your story, using some of the language and ideas above. Write your answer in 120–180 words.

Check and improve your story

6 Edit your story using this list. Check your:
- plan (Is the story clear and interesting?)
- use of narrative tenses and linking expressions
- range of adjectives, adverbs and verbs (Is the story vivid?)
- number of words.

▶ Writing reference page 206

LANGUAGE SPOT: making a story vivid

Complete these extracts from a story with more vivid equivalents of the words in brackets.

1 Yesterday it was a .... (*nice*) sunny morning.
2 There had been a .... (*large*) snowfall the night before.
3 Zoe left her friends and .... (*went*) off on her own.
4 When she got to the top, she was .... (*very tired*).
5 People .... (*not often*) go to that part of the mountain.
6 .... (*finally*) she came to the frozen lake.

8 Sport

Listening (Paper 4 Part 3)

Before you listen

▶ Listening strategy Unit 2 page 14, Unit 4 page 28

1 a Look at the sports in the photos.

1 Can you name each sport?
2 Have you played any of these sports?
3 Why did you take the sport(s) up?

b Read the task in Exercise 2a.

1 How many speakers will you hear? What will they talk about?
2 Compare **your** reasons for taking up a sport with those in **A–F**. Which are the same?

Multiple matching ▶ page 191

Task strategy

- Read the task and mark key words in each option A–F.
- The first time you listen, focus on each speaker's main point.
- Match the main points with the closest options and note down your answers.
- During the second listening, check that the statement matches exactly what the speakers say.

2 a 🔈 You will hear five different people giving their reasons for taking up a sport. For questions 1–5 choose from the list A–F what each speaker says. Use the letters only once. There is one extra letter which you do not need to use. Listen to the recording twice. Follow the task strategy.

A I was persuaded by other people.

B I was advised to take more exercise.

C I did it to raise money for charity.

D I wanted to give my family a surprise.

E I needed to find a way to relax.

F I wanted to prove to someone that I could do it.

Speaker 1	1
Speaker 2	2
Speaker 3	3
Speaker 4	4
Speaker 5	5

b Compare and justify your answers. Listen to the recording again if necessary.

1 How was the main point in each extract expressed?
   EXAMPLE: 1C – *get people to give donations to a medical research organisation*
2 Did you need to change any answers the second time you listened?

Discussion

3 Discuss these questions.

1 Would you like to do a parachute jump or go scuba diving? Why/Why not?
2 What other risk sports can you think of? Have you tried any of them yourself?
3 Which do you think are most dangerous? Why?
4 Why do you think people take up risk sports?

Vocabulary: idiomatic expressions

4 In the sentences, replace the words in italics with an expression from the following list. (All the expressions were on the recording.) Make any other changes necessary.

fancy (something)   sign up (for something)   from the word go
give (something) a go   (be) into (something)

1 I really enjoyed playing tennis *from the moment I took it up.*
2 My cousin has always been *keen on* snooker.
3 Shall we *enrol* for the judo course on Fridays?
4 Do you *like the idea of* joining the netball team?
5 She has never tried diving but she is happy to *try it.*

Speaking (Paper 5 Part 3)

Lead-in

1 You are thinking about taking up a sport. Look at the different sports in the photos. Think of one advantage and one disadvantage of each one, in your situation.
EXAMPLE: *Tennis is good for meeting people, but it's very expensive in my town.*

Sample answer

2 a 📼 Listen to the examiner's instructions. What <u>two</u> things do the students have to do?
EXAMINER: *First* .... *Then* ....

b 📼 Now listen to the two students doing the task. Which sport do they choose, and why?

c 📼 Listen again and tick (✓) the expressions in the table that the students use.

Starting a discussion	*Why don't we start by …?* *Shall we … first?* *Let's begin with … .* *We could start by talking about … .*
Interrupting/Showing you want a turn	*Can I just say…?* *Sorry to interrupt, but … .* *Yes, and as well as that … .*
Involving the other person	*What do **you** think (about) …?* *Do you agree with that?* *What would you say?*
Bringing the discussion to an end	*So let's decide which … .* *Shall we make a decision?* *Anyway, we have to decide … .*

▶ Functions reference page 224

Collaborative task ▶ page 191

Task strategy

- Listen carefully to the examiner's instructions.
- Talk to your partner, not the examiner.
- Take an active part in the discussion, but involve your partner, too.
- Talk about more than one option before making a decision, or you will finish too quickly.

3 Work in groups of three.
STUDENT 1: You are the examiner. Give the instructions (look at page 218) and stop the discussion after three minutes.
STUDENTS 2 AND 3: You are Candidates A and B. Follow the examiner's instructions. Read the task strategy before you start.

4 Discuss the task you have done.
EXAMINER: Did Candidates A and B listen and respond to each other? Did they both put forward ideas?
CANDIDATES: Did you come to a conclusion? Did you run out of time or have too much time?

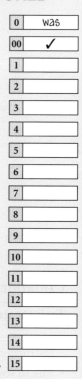

Use of English 1 (Paper 3 Part 4)

Lead-in

1 Discuss these questions.
1 Who is this sportsman?
2 What do you know about him?
3 Which famous sportspeople do you most admire?

Error correction ▶ page 190

2 a Read the title and text below quickly and answer the questions. (Ignore the mistakes at this stage).
1 What effect has Tiger Woods had on sport?
2 Is he an extrovert or an introvert?

b Look at this sentence from the text and mark one example of a pronoun, a preposition, an article, a determiner, an auxiliary verb and a linking word.

> *Tiger Woods ... has changed golf from a sport for the few to a sport for everyone, and has proved that every one of us can be successful in the life.*

c Which word should not be there?

d Do the task. Follow the task strategy and use the Help clues if necessary.

Read the text below and look carefully at each line. Some of the lines are correct, and some have a word which should not be there.
If a line is correct, put a tick (✓) by the number. If a line has a word which should **not** be there, write the word in the space. There are two examples at the beginning (**0** and **00**).

Task strategy

- Read the title and text quickly for general understanding. Ignore the mistakes.
- Read each sentence carefully and make sure you understand it.
- Go through each line and mark any word you think should not be there.
- Then read each sentence without the word to check it makes sense.
- Read the whole text again to check it makes sense.

HELP

➤ **Line 3**
Is there an article, determiner or pronoun that should not be here?
➤ **Line 7**
Is there an auxiliary, pronoun or determiner that should not be here?
➤ **Line 10**
What can come before an uncountable noun?
➤ **Line 12**
What construction should follow the verb *enjoy*? Look at the next line.
➤ **Line 15**
How many negatives are there in this line?

THE BEST-KNOWN SPORTSMAN IN THE WORLD

I have admired Tiger Woods since I was started playing golf	0	was
years ago. He has changed golf from a sport for the few to	00	✓
a sport for everyone, and has proved that every one of us can	1	
be successful in the life. Tiger's father is an Afro-American who	2	
served in the army for a number of some years, and his mother	3	
she is from Thailand. When he was two, Tiger appeared on TV	4	
hitting any golf balls, and at three he was already playing	5	
a very good golf. At 21, he was the youngest-ever world	6	
champion. One thing I like about which Tiger is that he always	7	
seems calm and has a great deal of much confidence. He is	8	
polite to his opponents, and he speaks and dresses well. Like many	9	
famous people, he rarely carries many cash. When he stays in	10	
hotels, he makes his bed and irons shirts that have already been	11	
pressed. Although a megastar, he is a private man who enjoys to	12	
watching lots movies, going fishing or scuba diving and playing	13	
video games. When he was young, he had speech problems and now	14	
he cannot speak not any foreign languages, although he reads Spanish.	15	

e Which questions test:
- articles?
- determiners with countable/uncountable nouns?
- subject + verb?
- verb + verb?

Language development 2

Quantity

> A Countable nouns have singular and plural forms:
> *Tiger Woods is a great **golfer**.*
> *He is one of the greatest **golfers** of all time.*
>
> B Uncountable nouns only have one form:
> *He has a lot of **confidence**.*
>
> C Some nouns can be countable or uncountable, depending on the meaning:
> *Golf has become a **sport** for everyone.* (countable – a particular sport)
> ***Sport** is big business these days.* (uncountable – sport in general)
>
> (LOOK) **at the Use of English text opposite and find examples of the three types of noun.**
>
> ▶ Grammar reference page 193

1 a **Decide whether each of these nouns is countable, uncountable or both. Use a dictionary if necessary. Which noun in each group is different from the other two? Why?**

1 spectator	fan	excitement
2 advice	fact	information
3 skiing	athletics	football
4 money	salary	coin
5 racket	equipment	glove
6 temperature	weather	sunshine
7 exercise	tracksuit	trainer

b **Which two words in Exercise 1a can be both countable and uncountable? What is the difference in meaning?**

2 **Correct the mistakes in these sentences.**
  1 Our trainer gives us good advices.
  2 I've heard the results. The news are very bad.
  3 People likes Tiger Woods.
  4 Some footballers have long hairs.
  5 It was a terrible weather so the match was cancelled.
  6 Beckham has very expensive furnitures in his house.
  7 My shorts was very dirty after the match.
  8 I had to do some hard works to beat the champion.
  9 The national team stayed in a luxury accommodation.
  10 I need informations about tickets.

Determiners

> A Plural countables
> - *(a) few/fewer*
> - *many; a great many; very many; not many*
>   *There were **a few** people at the match but **not many**.*
> - *Several*
>   ***Several** players were injured.*
> - *small/a good/a large/a great number of*
>   ***A large number** of fans watch matches on Saturdays, but only **a small number** go on Wednesday evenings.*
>
> B Uncountables
> - *(very) little/not much*
>   *There was**n't much** interest in the village cricket match.*
> - *a good/a great deal of; a small/a large amount of*
>   *The club spent **a great deal of** money on their star player, so they only had **a small amount** left to improve facilities for spectators.*
>
> C Uncountables and plural countables
> - *a lot of/lots of/plenty of*
>   *There's been **a lot of** improvement in her tennis.* (uncountable)
>   *She's got **a lot of** fans.* (countable)
> - *no … at all; none*
>   *He takes **no** pride **at all** in his appearance.*
> - *a lack of*
>   *There's **a lack of** honesty in sport these days.*

3 **Read the information about determiners in the box and mark the correct word(s) in each pair in the text.**

(1) *Many / Much* famous sportspeople get injured for unexpected reasons. For example, the English footballer Rio Ferdinand managed to injure himself by watching TV for (2) *a number of / a great deal of* hours with his leg on a coffee table. And after the cricketer Chris Lewis shaved his head he spent too (3) *many / much* time in the sun and got sunstroke.

But the worst accident occurred in 1913 when the racing driver Camille Jenatzy took (4) *several / a small amount of* friends hunting for boars. They didn't see (5) *no / any* boars, so the group went back to the house and had (6) *lots / too many* to eat and drink. Jenatzy was convinced they would soon have (7) *many / much* better luck and offered (8) *much / a lot of* money as a bet that they would be shooting in the next (9) *little / few* hours. After everyone had gone to bed, he crept outside, walked (10) *few / a few* metres away from the house and made (11) *a few / a little* sounds like a wild boar to wake up his friends. Unfortunately, his friends opened the window and shot him by mistake.

Use of English 2 (Paper 3 Part 1)

Lead-in

1 Discuss these questions.
  1 In what ways is tennis similar and different to other sports?
  2 Do you know much about the history of tennis?

Lexical cloze ▶ page 189

▶ Task strategy Unit 2 page 18

2 a Read the title and text quickly and answer the questions. (Ignore the spaces at this stage.)
  1 What did tennis players use before rackets and a net?
  2 In what way did a clockface influence the method of scoring?

b Do the exam task. Follow the task strategy and use the Help clues if necessary.

Read the text below and decide which answer **A**, **B**, **C** or **D** best fits each space. There is an example at the beginning (**0**).

0 **A** debut   **B** start   **C** origin   **D** birth

THE HISTORY OF TENNIS

Everyone agrees that tennis is a very old game but its actual (**0**) _C_ is unknown. Some people (**1**)............ it came from ball games played in ancient (**2**)............. However, most historians believe it was started in France in the twelfth century, by groups of men (**3**)............ a simple religious life. They played a very (**4**)............ game, where a ball was (**5**)............ against a wall or over a rope with the palm of the hand.

During the next century, the French upper classes became interested, and they (**6**)............ the sport. (**7**)............, in the sixteenth century, people started to (**8**)............ rackets of varying shapes and sizes. In those (**9**)............ days of tennis, balls were made (**10**)............ leather with wool or hair inside, and were hard enough to cause serious injury. The game soon spread to England and (**11**)............ in a big way. Even kings became (**12**)............ players.

The scoring system in tennis (15, 30, 40 – Game!) is interesting but it has often (**13**)............ great confusion. It probably comes from the time when the hand on a clock face was moved forward 15 minutes to show that a point had been (**14**)............ and when the hand reached 60 the game was over. Eventually, for reasons no one understands, the 45 minutes was abbreviated (**15**)............ 40.

HELP
➤ Question 6
  A phrasal verb which means *start to do something for pleasure.*
➤ Question 9
  An adjective that can mean *near the beginning of a period* and combines with *days.*
➤ Question 12
  Only one of these adjectives makes sense in context.
➤ Question 13
  Only one of these adjectives combines with *confusion.*

1	**A** demand	**B** claim	**C** request	**D** confess
2	**A** cultures	**B** backgrounds	**C** customs	**D** traditions
3	**A** holding	**B** running	**C** carrying	**D** leading
4	**A** similar	**B** same	**C** like	**D** alike
5	**A** punched	**B** hit	**C** kicked	**D** popped
6	**A** brought up	**B** set out	**C** took up	**D** put on
7	**A** Following	**B** Later	**C** Soon	**D** Shortly
8	**A** use	**B** wear	**C** exercise	**D** play
9	**A** previous	**B** beforehand	**C** preceding	**D** early
10	**A** by	**B** in	**C** of	**D** to
11	**A** got out	**B** took off	**C** turned on	**D** came out
12	**A** keen	**B** interested	**C** occupied	**D** busy
13	**A** influenced	**B** made	**C** resulted	**D** caused
14	**A** won	**B** beaten	**C** succeeded	**D** marked
15	**A** at	**B** with	**C** to	**D** on

c Make a note of the verbs, phrasal verbs and adjective + noun collocations you want to remember in your vocabulary book.

Language development 3

Adjectives often confused

> 1 The **actual** origin of tennis is unknown. ✓ (= real)
> The ~~current~~ origin of tennis is unknown. ✗ (= present)
> 2 It came from ball games played in **ancient** cultures. ✓
> (from many centuries ago)
> It came from ball games played in ~~old~~ cultures. ✗
> (= not young or new)
> 3 The scoring system has often caused **great** confusion. ✓
> (= large amount of)
> The scoring system has often caused ~~big~~ confusion. ✗
> (= large in size)

1 Match the words to the definitions. They are in pairs.

1 pleasant   a understanding other
people's problems

2 sympathetic   b friendly, easy to talk to

3 sensitive   c understanding other people's
feelings

4 sensible   d practical and able to judge
things well

5 nervous   e happy because something
good is happening

6 excited   f worried about something
that is happening

7 usual   g having the normal features
of a group

8 typical   h the same as what happens
most of the time

2 a Mark the most likely word(s) in each pair.

Buster Crabbe won the 400 m swimming at the 1932 Olympics, and then became a Hollywood film star. It is hard to imagine **(1)** *actual / current* athletes becoming actors! I always thought he had a friendly, **(2)** *pleasant / sympathetic* face, and although he was never a **(3)** *great / big* actor, I was always **(4)** *nervous / excited* to see his films. In some of his roles he gave a very **(5)** *sensitive / sensible* performance, but in those **(6)** *old / ancient* movies, it was **(7)** *usual / typical* for him to play an action hero even though he was not a **(8)** *usual / typical* tough guy.

b Answer these questions about yourself.
1 Are you sensitive or sensible? Or both?
2 When do you get nervous? Or excited?
3 Who's the most sympathetic person you know?

3 What is the difference between *-ing* and *-ed* adjectives? Look at these examples from the Use of English text opposite.
1 *The French upper classes became* **interested**.
2 *The scoring system in tennis is* **interesting**.

▶ Grammar reference page 193

4 a Complete the sentences with an adjective formed from the words in brackets.
1 Golf is so .... (*bore*)!
2 The team felt .... (*disappoint*) not to win the final.
3 Professional football looks glamorous, but it's .... (*tire*).
4 The crowd got .... (*annoy*) because the game was so bad.
5 I've never tried skiing. It looks .... (*terrify*) to me.
6 The team captain is .... (*depress*) about his injuries.
7 I'm not at all .... (*interest*) in sport.
8 It was very .... (*amuse*) when a dog ran onto the field!

b Answer these questions about yourself.
1 What do you find interesting/amusing?
2 When was the last time you felt annoyed/disappointed?
3 What's the most boring/terrifying thing you've ever done?

Phrasal verbs with *take*

5 Find an example of a phrasal verb with *take* in the Use of English text opposite.

6 Phrasal verbs sometimes have more than one meaning. Rewrite the phrases in italics in these sentences using *take* and the particles in the list.
after   to   up   over   off
1 The darts player Bobby George *started a new career in* acting after he was discovered by a film producer during the World Darts Championship.
2 Venus Williams' tennis career *began to be successful* after she won Wimbledon.
3 The England soccer team improved enormously after a foreign manager *became responsible*.
4 Damon Hill *did the same thing as* his father, Graham Hill, and became a racing driver.
5 Although Sonny Liston was a great boxer, the general public never really *felt a liking for* him as they did Mohammed Ali.

7 For you, which is the best way to keep a record of phrasal verbs – by topic, verb or particle? How do you record a phrasal verb with more than one meaning?

Exam practice 2

Paper 1: Reading

Part 1: multiple matching (summary sentences)

You are going to read a newspaper article about children who don't have any brothers and sisters. Choose from the list **A–H** the sentence which best summarises each part (**1–6**) of the article. There is one extra sentence which you do not need to use. There is an example at the beginning (**0**).

A A rise in the number of one-child families may have a negative effect on the way people behave.

B Children with no brothers or sisters have to learn from an early age how to enjoy their own company.

C In some places, there is official concern over falling family size.

D There is no evidence that children without brothers and sisters grow up differently to other children.

E The benefits of growing up with brothers and sisters may not always be obvious to a child.

F It is too early to link the growing number of one-child families to people's changing values.

G Smaller families are a logical result of the lives people now lead in some places.

H The idea of the one-child family may seem an attractive fantasy to some people.

The One and Only

With birth rates falling across the West, Rebecca Abrams wonders how families and society will be affected by the rise of the one-child family.

0	H

To those of us brought up with brothers and sisters, the prospect of the one-child family sounds wonderful. Imagine it – never having to wait for people to listen when you have something to say, always having new toys and clothes, never doubting that your parents love you best, and always feeling confident that your toys will be where you left them. Wouldn't that have been great?

1	

Parents may concentrate on the positive reasons for giving their first-born child a brother or sister, but for the child the reality is usually a mixture of good and bad. Brothers and sisters may teach you about sharing, but they can teach you less useful lessons too – that love isn't always shared out equally and that some people always get blamed more than others.

2	

Although in most parts of the world, people still believe that the ideal family size is two children or more, across Europe, the United States and parts of South America birth rates are falling. More and more couples have just one child or none at all, and governments in some countries are actively trying to encourage larger families; some are even considering giving couples money to have a baby.

3	

The rise of the one-child family in western society seems to be part of a much larger picture of changing family life. The increase in divorce rates in some cultures means that more children will be brought up as the only child in a family. As well as this, the difficulty of balancing a job and a family life means that an increasing number of women are choosing to have only one child, or leaving it too late to have any more.

4	

Child psychologist Dr Richard Woolfson insists that there are no benefits in having brothers and sisters in terms of an individual's personal development. 'Compared to the general population, the only child does well educationally and is no more self-centred than other children. And today's parents are very good at compensating for any possible problems. Many of the children from one-child families have incredibly active social lives, for example.'

5	

But, apart from economic factors such as a reduced workforce, does the trend towards one-child families pose a threat to society? Analyst Karen Stobart believes that there might be problems. 'Sharing is life, and with brothers and sisters you learn that you can fight and survive it. We may become a community of people who don't know much about turn-taking and cooperating, and respond to problems either by fighting or walking away.'

6	

30 years ago, the one-child family was unusual; now they're fast becoming normal and the implications of this trend are still uncertain. It may suggest that children and family life are not so important as they once were, or it may mean exactly the opposite – that this is the best way that couples can find to be both good parents and effective working adults. Only time, and the children, will tell.

Paper 3: Use of English

Part 1: lexical cloze

Read the text below and decide which answer **A**, **B**, **C** or **D** best fits each space. There is an example at the beginning (**0**).

KEW GARDENS

The Royal Botanic Gardens at Kew is home to the world's (**0**).....B...... collection of living plants. Situated (**1**)............. to the River Thames in south west London, the gardens are one of Britain's most (**2**)............. tourist attractions. The gardens are (**3**)............. 'royal' because, before the government (**4**)............. the area in 1841, members of the royal family used to live there.

Today, a large (**5**)............. of people come to visit Kew's three museums and see the 40,000 different kinds of plants (**6**)............. on display there. Every season is fascinating at Kew, but as long as the winter hasn't been too (**7**)............. , Easter is a good time to visit, as then it's possible to see beautiful springtime flowers in an area not usually (**8**)............. to the public.

In 2002, Kew was nominated as a possible UNESCO World Heritage site. This is (**9**)............. an impressive achievement because only one other botanic garden has been (**10**)............. in this way. The Orto Botanico, in Padova, Italy, is the world's oldest, and home to a (**11**)............. fine collection of rare herbs. Interestingly, since 2002, UNESCO will (**12**)............. only one nomination a year from countries which already have a World Heritage site. This is because the (**13**)............. list includes only a relatively (**14**)............. number of sites from outside Western Europe, and UNESCO wants more countries to be (**15**)............. on it.

0	**A**	longest	**B**	largest	**C**	thickest	**D**	fattest
1	**A**	close	**B**	handy	**C**	local	**D**	neighbouring
2	**A**	common	**B**	regular	**C**	major	**D**	popular
3	**A**	told	**B**	claimed	**C**	called	**D**	identified
4	**A**	brought up	**B**	took over	**C**	gave in	**D**	handed out
5	**A**	quantity	**B**	number	**C**	figure	**D**	lot
6	**A**	currently	**B**	shortly	**C**	mainly	**D**	finally
7	**A**	heavy	**B**	strong	**C**	deep	**D**	hard
8	**A**	open	**B**	allowed	**C**	vacant	**D**	permitted
9	**A**	due	**B**	quite	**C**	so	**D**	instead
10	**A**	granted	**B**	passed	**C**	wished	**D**	honoured
11	**A**	remarkably	**B**	clearly	**C**	greatly	**D**	readily
12	**A**	view	**B**	consider	**C**	regard	**D**	apply
13	**A**	nowadays	**B**	instant	**C**	present	**D**	meanwhile
14	**A**	short	**B**	small	**C**	slight	**D**	brief
15	**A**	associated	**B**	expressed	**C**	represented	**D**	accounted

Part 2: structural cloze

Read the text below and think of a word which best fits each space. Use only **one** word in each space. There is an example at the beginning (**0**).

THE LEGEND OF MANCHESTER UNITED

Manchester United, one of the world's greatest football clubs, was founded over 100 years (**0**)....ago.... . The club was originally called Newton Heath, named after the area (**1**)............. it started in 1878. Unfortunately, the club had very (**2**)............. success at first and in 1902, nine years (**3**)............. it had moved to its present site, the owners decided (**4**)............. change its name. Someone suggested Manchester Central, but the fans were not keen (**5**)............. this name, saying that it sounded more like a railway station (**6**)............. a football club. A better suggestion – Manchester United – was proposed and readily accepted. Six years later the club won the national championship.

But it was not until Matt Busby (**7**)............. over as manager in 1945, (**8**)............. , that the club started to become special. Busby recruited a team of talented young players who helped turn Manchester United (**9**)............. the greatest English team of the 1950s. Then, in 1958, just as they (**10**)............. beginning to do well in the European Cup, a number (**11**)............. the players died in a tragic air accident. It was a major setback for the club.

However, Busby's 1950s team was followed (**12**)............. another great side, which finally succeeded (**13**)............. winning the European Cup in 1968. After Busby retired, the club had quite (**14**)............. few problems, although more recently it has (**15**)............. on to achieve even greater success.

Part 4: error correction

Read the text below and look carefully at each line. Some of the lines are correct, and some have a word which should not be there.

If a line is correct, put a tick (✓) by the number. If a line has a word which should **not** be there, write the word in the space. There are two examples at the beginning (**0** and **00**).

MY STRUGGLE WITH CIGARETTES

Usually I am the quite a strong person, but I have to admit	**0**	the
I started smoking at the incredibly young age of twelve, and	**00**	✓
then found myself unable to stop. I did knew I had a problem,	**1**	
but I didn't want to admit it. One day, our head teacher insisted	**2**	
on by registering me as an 'addict', and said that for half a	**3**	
term I was allowed for to smoke in the car park in the lunch	**4**	
break! I was absolutely amazed. I was also given many advice	**5**	
and support, and my doctor prescribed any nicotine patches.	**6**	
The head teacher believed that by getting us to admit we were	**7**	
been smoking he was helping us get back our self control.	**8**	
His experiment immediately stopped me to smoking secretly	**9**	
in the school toilets and prevented many of other pupils from	**10**	
inhaling my smoke. I tried to give up smoking completely.	**11**	
I found it difficult so for a few days, but I'm pleased to say	**12**	
that after a week, I was no more longer interested in smoking.	**13**	
Indeed, despite the plenty great many opportunities I have had,	**14**	
I have never smoked a cigarette again in whole my life.	**15**	

Part 5: word formation

Read the text below. Use the word given in capitals at the end of each line to form a word that fits the space in the same line. There is an example at the beginning (**0**).

CHASING TORNADOES

Tornadoes are the **(0)** amazing spinning storms which are common in the **AMAZE**
midwest of the USA. Although they can often be **(1)**.............. short-lived, lasting **FAIR**
only 1–2 hours, tornadoes can spin at up to 400 kph, and can **(2)**............ destroy **EASY**
whole areas, even throwing **(3)**............ farm animals on to the tops of trees. **TERRIFY**
People who are **(4)**............ enough to live in their path, often feel threatened by **FORTUNE**
tornadoes, and yet, **(5)**............ , some travel companies in the USA organise trips **REMARK**
for tourists who **(6)**............ go in search of them. Some enthusiasts travel **ACTIVE**
thousands of kilometres in the hope of seeing a violent but **(7)**............ storm! **EXCITE**
Apart from the great rush of adrenaline they get as they **(8)**............ anticipate **NERVOUS**
the **(9)**............ of the tornado, these people are also motivated by the thought **ARRIVE**
that they may go home with some **(10)**............ , and possibly valuable, photographs. **IMPRESS**

Discovery

Overview

- **Reading:** multiple matching: questions (Paper 1 Part 4)
- **Language development 1:** future forms
- **Writing:** formal transactional letter (Paper 2 Part 1)
- **Listening:** multiple-choice questions (Paper 4 Part 4)
- **Speaking:** collaborative task and discussion (Paper 5 Parts 3 and 4)
- **Use of English 1:** error correction (Paper 3 Part 4)
- **Language development 2:** reflexives; structures with question words
- **Use of English 2:** word formation (Paper 3 Part 5)
- **Language development 3:** forming nouns; phrasal verbs with *come*

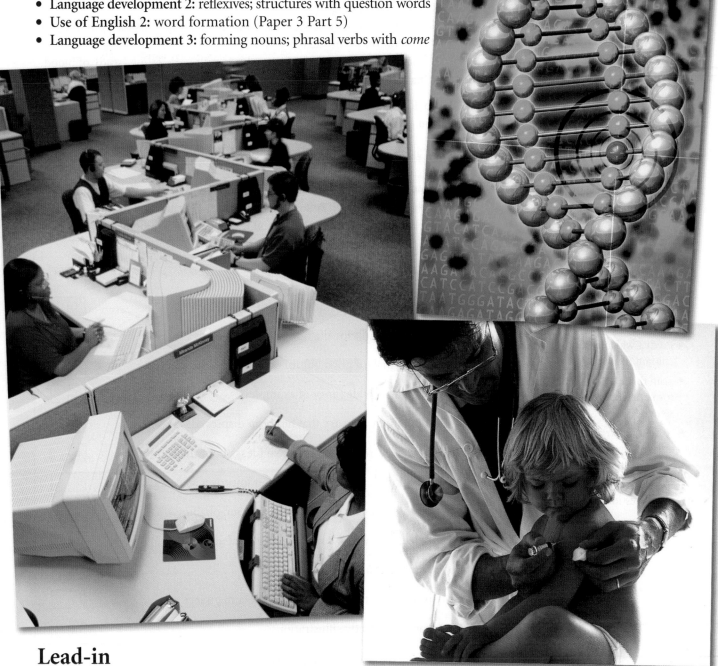

Lead-in

- Look at the photos. What benefits have these inventions and discoveries brought?
- How would our lives be different without them?
- When is 'progress' not necessarily a good thing?

Human science

Reading (Paper 1 Part 4)

Before you read

1 a Match the fields of science in the list below to the definitions 1–6.

psychology   genetics   astronomy
forensic science   linguistics   archaeology

1 the study of the stars and planets
2 the study of ancient societies by examining what remains of their buildings, graves, etc.
3 the study of how the mind works
4 the study of language
5 the study of the characteristics that living things pass on from one generation to the next
6 methods used for finding out who is guilty of a crime (study of blood, hair, fingerprints, etc.)

b Look at the title of the article opposite and the subheadings A–D. What are you going to read? What field of science do you think each book is about?

Skimming

2 Skim each text and check your answers to Exercise 1b.

Multiple matching:

questions ▶ page 188

Task strategy

- Read the lead-in line very carefully. (**Which review states ...**)
- Read the questions and mark the key words.
- Predict which sections of the text contain the answers.
- Scan the relevant section, looking for parallel phrases and parts of sentences.
- Read that part carefully to check it answers the question.
- If you can't find the answer, leave it for the moment and go on to the next question.

3 a For Questions 1–12 choose from the book titles (A–D). There is an example at the beginning (0). Follow the task strategy. For the first four questions, the key words in the questions and text have been highlighted for you.

Which review states that the book:	
follows on from the author's earlier book?	0 C
includes a number of funny stories?	1
is not difficult for the non-scientist to read?	2
would make a good gift for someone?	3
contains a wide range of examples?	4
talks about a theory that has been disproved?	5
puts forward the author's own ideas about the subject?	6
mentions a part of the body that improves as you get older?	7
discusses research carried out on young babies?	8
reflects the writer's wider educational aims?	9
covers important topical issues?	10
is intended to go with a filmed documentary?	11
has very effective illustrations?	12

b Compare and justify your answers.
1 Why is **A not** the answer to question **0** although it refers to *earlier books*?
2 Which key words did you mark in the questions?
3 What related phrases or parts of sentences did you find in the text?

Four Popular Science Books

Oliver Mansell reviews four books, all of which tell us more about ourselves.

A In the Blood *by Steve Jones*

This is the book for anyone who wants to keep up-to-date with the latest influential theories. Did you know, for 5 example, that whoever our parents may be, we are all united by DNA, 'the basic stuff of life', which contains our genes? And did you know 10 that most of the population of the world may have descended from fewer than 100 people?

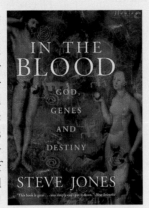

New and surprising discoveries like this are being made almost every week, which is why genetics is now 15 at the forefront of twenty-first-century science. Before they'd heard of genes, people believed that family traits were carried in the blood. Today we know that they were wrong. Issues like these are among those discussed in this thrilling new book by Professor Jones. 20 As with his earlier books on other subjects, you will find it hard to put down, even if you don't have a scientific background.

B The Human Face *by Brian Bates with John Cleese*

This fascinating book collects together the findings 25 of various scientific studies, old and new, concerning the human face. One of these has shown that 30 minutes after birth, when our eyes can 30 hardly focus, we gaze at faces rather than anything else. And it seems that we continue to be fascinated

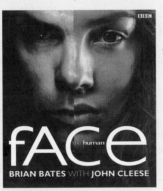

with them all through life. There have been a number of 35 psychological tests designed to investigate beauty, but their conclusions only prove what the Ancient Greeks always knew – a beautiful face is one with regular features.

So, maybe this is not the book to buy if you want to be surprised with new facts, but it does provide some 40 fascinating insights into how faces have developed over the years, and whether one can judge a person by their appearance alone. Although rather serious in places, the book is packed with eye-catching photos, making it an ideal birthday present even for the most reluctant student 45 of science.

C Brain Story *by Susan Greenfield*

As Director of the Royal Institution of Science, Susan Greenfield's main objective is to encourage the 50 greater public understanding of scientific ideas. In this book, she introduces us to the inside of our heads and shows the kind of 55 enthusiasm about the brain that other writers reserve for fine art or football. The idea

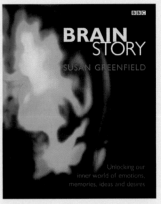

of 'intelligence' worries her, however, because this suggests that a person's 'brain power' is pre-determined. She agrees 60 with those who insist that the brain, which is capable of amazing things, is constantly developing, and gets better and better with age, providing you look after it. Although this book develops the ideas introduced in her previous one, *The Private Life of the Brain*, it clearly has television 65 audiences in mind (a tie-in series has just begun on BBC1) and as a consequence it is rather shorter on detail, focusing instead on one or two interesting examples.

D The Language Instinct *by Steven Pinker*

Where does our feeling for language come from? How do 70 we learn to speak it so effortlessly? Why is it so hard for adults to learn a foreign language? Cleverly structured, with many amusing anecdotes, 75 linguist Stephen Pinker's book examines why we use language and where this ability comes from. His personal belief is that language is as instinctive 80 to us as flying is to geese, and

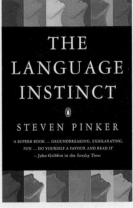

that we use it to great effect in order to communicate. He illustrates his theory with examples of language taken from various sources, including children's conversations, pop culture and politicians' speeches. A 85 clever user of language himself, Pinker has packed his book full of original thoughts. Because of this, it does not make for light reading, but it will nonetheless appeal both to specialists and anyone who is interested in language and human beings in the 90 widest sense.

Discussion

4 Discuss these questions.

1 Based on the reviews, which of these books would you most and least like to read? Why? What else would you like to know about the subject?

2 Do you ever read popular science books or watch science programmes on TV? Why/Why not?

Language development 1

Future forms

1 a Read the extracts. Guess who is talking to who, and what the situation is.

EXAMPLE: 1 A child talking to a parent, in a car. The child is feeling travel-sick.

1
I don't feel well. I think I'm going to be sick.

4
I know what she's like. If you tell her, she'll tell everyone.

2
I can't, I'm afraid! I'm taking my driving test tomorrow.

5
Hurry up! It starts at eight.

3
Did I tell you it doesn't work? I'm going to take it back to the shop.

6
That bag looks heavy. I'll carry it for you.

b Mark the verb forms in Exercise 1a that express the future.

c Match the meanings in the list a–f to each extract above. Then complete the table below.

a planned, decided earlier (intention)

b unplanned, decided now (e.g. an offer, a promise)

c planned, a definite arrangement (e.g. in a diary)

d prediction: we notice something in the present that will make something happen

e planned, fixed event (e.g. a public timetable)

f prediction: we expect something to happen (it is our opinion or we have experience of it)

Form	Meaning	Example
A Present continuous	....	....
B Present simple	....	....
C *Going to* + infinitive	....	1 ....
(two meanings)	....	2 ....
D *Will/Shall* + infinitive	....	1 ....
(two meanings)	....	2 ....

▶ Grammar reference pages 199–200

Time Clauses

Use the present simple in time clauses with a future meaning.

Which example below is **not** correct?

1 I'll give her the message **as soon as** she **arrives**.

2 **When** everyone **is** on the coach, it will leave.

3 Are you going to have a drink **before** the show **will start**?

4 **After** we **move** offices, we'll start on the new project.

2 Mark the most likely verb form in each pair.

1 He adapts quickly; I'm sure he *will be / is going to be* fine in his new job.

2 Sorry, I can't. I'*ll go and visit / 'm going to visit* Tom in hospital tonight.

3 We'll call you as soon as we'*ll get / get* there.

4 It says here that the play *starts / is going to start* at seven.

5 You look tired. You rest, and I'*ll cook / 'm going to cook* dinner tonight.

6 I'd love to come tomorrow but I *have lunch / 'm having lunch* with my brother.

7 Have you heard the news? Tara'*ll have / 's going to have* a baby.

8 Just before you *go / will go*, can you check this for me?

3 a Read the quotation below and mark examples of the future continuous and the future perfect.

❝I am confident that in 50 years' time we will have established a permanent base on Mars and that later this century people will be having holidays in space.❞
Martin Rees, astronomer.

The Fifth Element, dir. Luc Besson

b **Which verb form in the box below refers to an action:**
- which will be complete by a point in the future?
- which will still be in progress at a point in the future?

A Future continuous: *will/won't be + -ing*
  People **will be having** holidays in space.
B Future perfect: *will/won't have + past participle*
  We **will have established** a permanent base …

4 **Complete these predictions for the year 2100. Put the verbs in brackets in the future continuous or the future perfect.**

1 We .... (*find*) life on other planets before then.

2 We .... (*travel*) around in aerial vehicles, like flying saucers.

3 Long before then, scientists .... (*discover*) how to make fresh food last for years.

4 Many people .... (*live*) in space, which will help with the overpopulation problem.

5 The Internet .... (*take over*) most teachers' jobs and .... (*provide*) most of our entertainment.

6 Scientists and engineers .... (*make*) parts of the body routinely. When we're sick, we .... (*go*) to mechanics, not doctors!

5 a **Read the statements and decide which are:**
- very certain
- fairly certain
- not very certain at all

1 *I am confident that* in fifty years' time we will have established a permanent base on Mars.
2 *We may have* found life on other planets, *but I doubt it.*
3 *I think it's quite likely that* scientists will be making blood.
4 *There could be* holidays in space.
5 *We should be* travelling in aerial vehicles.

b **Use the expressions to comment on the predictions in Exercise 4.**

c **What other things do you think will be possible in a hundred years' time? Think about these questions.**
1 What will we be eating?
2 What progress will have been made in medicine and technology?
3 What changes will have taken place in education and entertainment?

6 a **Complete these sentences with information about yourself. Think about your arrangements, plans, hopes and dreams.**
1 At the weekend … .
2 In the next few days … .
3 For my next holiday … .
4 On my birthday … .
5 In the future I hope … .
6 By this time next year … .
7 Within the next ten years … .

b **Discuss your arrangements, plans, hopes and dreams from Exercise 6a with other students.**

7 **Correct the mistakes in this piece of student's writing.**

After I will finish the last year of university, I am definitely going to have a long holiday. I expect I am going with my friend, Luis, to a place where we will be doing lots of sport and relaxing in the sun to recover from all our hard work.

But before that there is a lot of work. My exams will start on the 15 June and they are lasting two weeks. The results will not have been here before the end of August, so I am having a long time to wait. For the next month I will study for two hours every evening and I am not going out during the week.

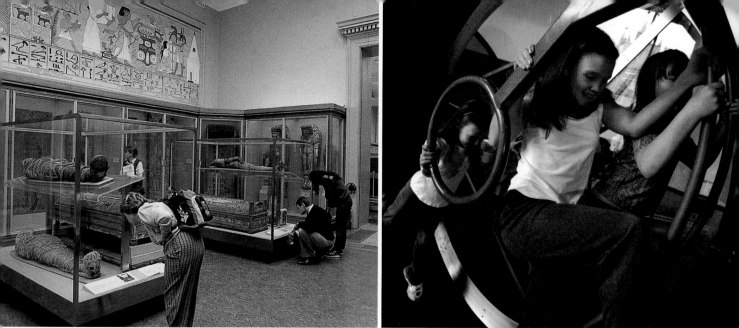

The British Museum: the oldest museum in the world   *Explore-At-Bristol: a true 21st-century science museum*

Writing   Transactional letter (Paper 2 Part 1)

Lead-in   1 **Discuss these questions.**

1 What are the most popular museums in your country? Have you been to them? Which would you recommend?

2 If you had to organise a visit by your college to a museum, what things would you have to consider?

Understand the task   2 **Read the task below and answer the questions.**

1 WHO are you writing to?

2 WHY are you writing?

3 WHAT information will you include?

4 HOW will you write? In what style? (Remember who you are writing to.)

You are the secretary of your college Science Club. You have seen this advertisement and are interested in organising a group visit. You have written some questions to ask the museum. Read the advertisement and the questions carefully. Then write a letter to the groups organiser of the museum explaining what you would like to do and asking for the information you need.

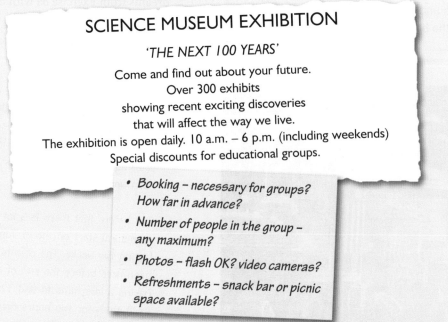

SCIENCE MUSEUM EXHIBITION

'THE NEXT 100 YEARS'

Come and find out about your future.
Over 300 exhibits
showing recent exciting discoveries
that will affect the way we live.
The exhibition is open daily. 10 a.m. – 6 p.m. (including weekends)
Special discounts for educational groups.

- Booking – necessary for groups? How far in advance?
- Number of people in the group – any maximum?
- Photos – flash OK? video cameras?
- Refreshments – snack bar or picnic space available?

Write a **letter** of between **120** and **180** words to the museum in an appropriate style. Do not write any postal addresses.

Plan your letter

3 a Number these key points in a logical order for the letter.
- asking about eating
- asking about booking
- conclusion
- saying why you're writing
- introducing myself
- asking about video cameras
- asking about numbers
- asking about photos

b Write the key points from the list above in this paragraph plan.

Paragraph 1: introducing myself **Paragraph 3:** ....

.... **Paragraph 4:** ....

Paragraph 2: ....

.... **Paragraph 5:** ....

Language and content

4 a Complete the expressions in the table for the letter.

Requesting	*I would be grateful …*
Asking for information/ permission	*Could you …?* *Would it be possible … ?* *I would also like … .*
Introducing a request	*We will (probably) be arriving … so … .* *Since we will (probably) be coming for the whole day … .* *When we arrive, can we …/will we able to …?* *Our group is quite large so … .*

b Complete these opening and closing sentences.
Opening: *I am the … . I saw your … and I was wondering if I could ask … .*
Closing: *I look forward to … .*

c Which phrase from the list below will you use to close the letter?
Goodbye   Yours faithfully   Cheers!   All the best

Write your letter

5 Now write the letter, using the ideas and some of the language above. Avoid copying whole phrases from the question. Do not write any postal addresses. Write your answer in 120–180 words.

Check and improve your letter

▶ Writing reference page 206

6 When you edit your letter, what things will you check? Refer to the checklist in the Writing reference.

LANGUAGE SPOT: polite questions

Look at the examples of polite questions.

Where's the café? ➡	Do you think I wonder if I would be very grateful if	you could tell me	where the café is(?)
Is the café open? ➡	Could you (please)	tell me let me know	whether the café is open?

Make each question more polite using a phrase above, including the word in brackets.

1 Where can we leave our bags? (*think*)
2 Is there a toilet on this floor? (*could*)
3 How much will we have to pay? (*grateful*)
4 When does the museum close? (*wonder*)
5 Where's the cloakroom? (*tell*)
6 What time does the museum close? (*grateful*)
7 Can we pay by credit card in the shop? (*tell*)
8 Who's the person in charge? (*wonder*)

10 Invention

Listening (Paper 4 Part 4)

Before you listen

Task strategy

Before you listen, read the instructions and the question stems. Mark key words in the questions and think about what you will hear. Don't be distracted by the options at this stage.

1 a Look at the cartoon. How does it relate to the title of the unit?

   b Look at the listening task below. Read the questions but not the answers A–C.
   1 Do you know anything about the inventor Trevor Baylis?
   2 Discuss possible answers which you might hear.

Multiple-choice questions

▶ page 190

Task strategy

- Listen for the answer to each question. The questions follow the order of the text.
- Choose the option which is closest. The words in the options will not be the same as the words you hear.
- During the second listening, check the other options are not possible.

2 a 🔲 You will hear part of a radio programme about inventors. For questions 1–7, choose the best answer A, B or C. Follow the task strategy.

1 What led Trevor Baylis to become an inventor?
   A It was something he'd enjoyed studying.
   B It grew out of his childhood hobby.
   C It was what his parents did.

2 What influenced Trevor's choice of first job?
   A the salary that was offered
   B the opportunities for further study
   C the amount of free time he would have

3 How does Trevor get ideas for new inventions?
   A people come to him with problems
   B from his own knowledge of engineering
   C by realising that there is a need for something

4 Trevor's idea for the wind-up radio came as a result of
   A remembering a dream he had once had.
   B examining a piece of outdated technology.
   C realising that there was a simple solution to a problem.

5 What criticism does Tanya have of young inventors?
   A They arc financially motivated.
   B They work for large companies.
   C They lack the necessary imagination.

6 According to Tanya, what is the hardest part of being an inventor?
   A accepting that an idea is no good
   B persuading others of the value of an idea
   C keeping your ideas a secret from other inventors

7 What gives Trevor Baylis greatest satisfaction?
   A large numbers of people benefiting from his inventions
   B the pride he gets from having had an original idea
   C the idea that his work may help people in need

   b Compare and justify your answers. Listen to the recording again if necessary. Discuss this question.
   Were the questions mainly about facts or about feelings and opinions?

Discussion

3 Which <u>single</u> invention do you think has benefited people most?

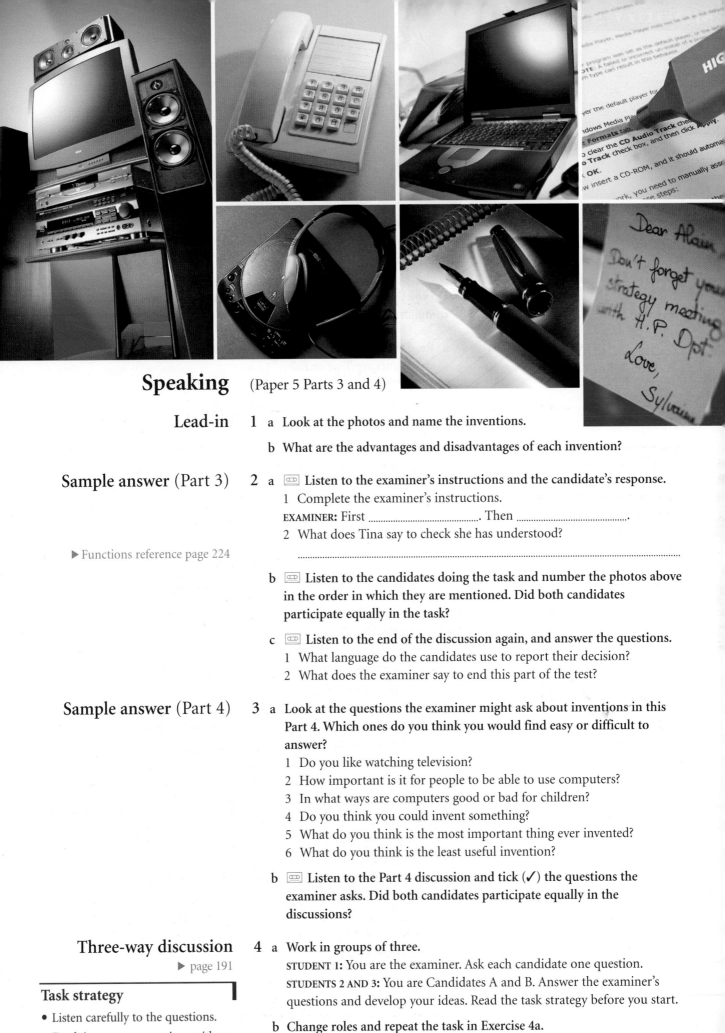

Speaking (Paper 5 Parts 3 and 4)

Lead-in

1 a Look at the photos and name the inventions.

b What are the advantages and disadvantages of each invention?

Sample answer (Part 3)

2 a ▣ Listen to the examiner's instructions and the candidate's response.
   1 Complete the examiner's instructions.
   EXAMINER: First .... Then ....
   2 What does Tina say to check she has understood?

   ....

▶ Functions reference page 224

b ▣ Listen to the candidates doing the task and number the photos above in the order in which they are mentioned. Did both candidates participate equally in the task?

c ▣ Listen to the end of the discussion again, and answer the questions.
   1 What language do the candidates use to report their decision?
   2 What does the examiner say to end this part of the test?

Sample answer (Part 4)

3 a Look at the questions the examiner might ask about inventions in this Part 4. Which ones do you think you would find easy or difficult to answer?
   1 Do you like watching television?
   2 How important is it for people to be able to use computers?
   3 In what ways are computers good or bad for children?
   4 Do you think you could invent something?
   5 What do you think is the most important thing ever invented?
   6 What do you think is the least useful invention?

b ▣ Listen to the Part 4 discussion and tick (✓) the questions the examiner asks. Did both candidates participate equally in the discussions?

Three-way discussion

▶ page 191

4 a Work in groups of three.
   STUDENT 1: You are the examiner. Ask each candidate one question.
   STUDENTS 2 AND 3: You are Candidates A and B. Answer the examiner's questions and develop your ideas. Read the task strategy before you start.

b Change roles and repeat the task in Exercise 4a.

5 Did you follow the advice given in the task strategy?

Task strategy

- Listen carefully to the questions.
- Don't just answer questions with *yes* or *no*. Give your opinions, justify them and develop your ideas.

75

Use of English 1 (Paper 3 Part 4)

Lead-in

1 Do you think modern technology makes our lives simpler or more complicated?

Error correction

➤ Task strategy Unit 8 page 60

2 a Read the title and text below quickly and decide whether the following statements are *True* or *False*.
   1 Tom has always happily used modern technology.
   2 He lost all the college computer records.
   3 Luckily, it never destroyed his confidence.

Tip

Incorrect words only occur **once** in a line. If you see a word twice in one line it is correct. For example, in line 15 the word *him* occurs twice so it must be correct.

b Do the task. Follow the task strategy and use the Help clues if necessary.

Read the text below and look carefully at each line. Some of the lines are correct, and some have a word which should not be there. If a line is correct, put a tick (✓) by the number. If a line has a word which should not be there, write the word in the space. There are two examples at the beginning (**0** and **00**).

HELP

➤ Line 3
   Is an idea repeated here?
➤ Line 4
   A grammatical rule about possessives is being broken.
➤ Line 8
   What is the object of the verbs *press* and *pressed*?

COMPUTER BLUNDERS

Tom's not usually the kind of person who has a fear of modern	**0** ✓
technology. He doesn't get nervous when is trying to operate	**00** is
a own video recorder and he enjoys using the Internet – he even	**1**
does most of his shopping on it. When he sits in front of a screen,	**2**
he is himself like an explorer, as though the whole world	**3**
is at the his fingertips. Last year, he was working on his own	**4**
in college and managed to get by into the important program	**5**
that ran the whole system. He realised that he had been made	**6**
a mistake and tried to get out of the system. Unfortunately,	**7**
he went to press *Enter* but he pressed it *Delete*. Everything	**8**
disappeared from his own screen and every other one screen	**9**
around him. He was furious with himself and he didn't know	**10**
what for to do. Luckily, the college had copies of everything and	**11**
was able to recover most of it. They never found out why it	**12**
had happened, and for weeks he never used him a computer,	**13**
either in college or at home. In fact, the sight of a keyboard	**14**
filled him with complete terror and made him to go cold.	**15**

c Which questions test:
   • reflexives?
   • question word structures?

d Find a correct example of a reflexive and a question word structure in the text.

Discussion

3 Have you ever had a problem with modern technology?

Language development 2

Reflexives

A Reflexive pronouns
- when the subject and object of a transitive verb are the same:
  He **hurt himself** when he fell off the chair.
  (Compare: He hurt his sister when he bumped into her.)
- = without the help of others:
  I repaired the television **myself**.
- with enjoy when there is no direct object:
  They **enjoyed themselves** at the party.
- with by to mean alone.
  She went to the cinema **by herself**.

B Own
- = without the help of others:
  I repaired the television **on my own**.
- = alone:
  She went to the cinema **on her own**.
- = belonging to no other person:
  My (very) **own** room.
  I saw it with **my own** eyes.

C Each other/One another
- = each of two or more does something to the other:
  They talked to **each other/one another**. They talked to ~~themselves~~.

(LOOK) **Find correct examples of this language in the Use of English text opposite.**

1 a Tick (✓) the correct sentences. Correct the incorrect ones.
   1 I used to work myself abroad.
   2 My printer turns itself off.
   3 Can you help myself?
   4 Robots can't talk to each one another.
   5 This was her very own invention.
   6 Have you enjoyed you?
   7 He found himself in trouble.
   8 Relax yourself!
   9 I built the model my own.
   10 Clare and Rob met themselves last year.

  b Complete the text opposite with reflexives where possible (see the box above), and pronouns (e.g. me, them).

2 Discuss these questions.
   1 What things do you prefer to do yourself?
   2 Do you like being on your own?
   3 Do you and your best friend ever argue with each other?

ROBOTS

Robots are not new. As long ago as 400 BC, the philosopher and mathematician Archytus built a wooden bird that could fly on **(1)**............. And in the seventeenth century, Johann Muller created both an iron fly and an artificial eagle that could take to the air by **(2)**.............. These days of course robots are everywhere, but I sometimes ask **(3)**............. whether they are a good thing. There are even robot dogs that we can have as pets, but I can't imagine buying one **(4)**.............. For a start, I can't believe we'd ever manage to communicate with **(5)**............., unlike real animals. I suppose there is some point in having a robot helping **(6)**............. in our daily lives – like doing the household chores that some people can't do **(7)**............., or doing a mechanical job in a factory – but I wouldn't want a robot carrying out a delicate operation on **(8)**............. in hospital, would you? I'd rather the surgeons did it **(9)**............!

Structures with question words

A Question word + to-infinitive: He didn't know **what to do**.
B Question word + clause:
  They never found out **why it had happened**.
  Do you know **how to programme** the video?

3 a Complete the second sentence so that it has a similar meaning to the first sentence, using the word given.
   1 Mike can't use a camcorder. **how**
     Mike doesn't .... camcorder.
   2 When you've done the things I want you to do, you can go out. **what**
     You can go out when .... want you to do.
   3 We don't know the right places to find the information. **where**
     We aren't sure .... information.
   4 I'm not sure which person I should believe. **who**
     I don't .... believe.

  b Complete these sentences about yourself.
   1 Next year I have no idea what ... .
   2 I can't explain why ... .
   3 I wish I could decide where ... .
   4 It would be useful if I knew how to ... .

Use of English 2 (Paper 3 Part 5)

Lead-in 1 **Match the people to their discoveries.**

1 Sir Isaac Newton   a penicillin
2 Alexander Fleming   b a comet
3 Alan Hale and Tom Bopp   c water displacement principle
4 Archimedes   d gravity

Word formation (A)

▶ page 190

▶ Task strategy Unit 4 page 32

2 a **Read the title and text below quickly and complete this summary.**

Sir Alexander Fleming discovered .... by accident when he found that
.... was killing the .... he was growing. He didn't think it was a
very .... discovery.

b **Do the task. Follow the task strategy and use the Help clues if necessary.**

Read the text below. Use the word given in capitals at the end of each line
to form a word that fits in the space in the same line. There is an example
at the beginning (**0**).

HELP

➤ Question 1
Did he expect it or not?
➤ Question 2
Is the suffix *-ness* or *-ity*?
➤ Question 4
Is this an adjective or adverb?

THE DISCOVERY OF PENICILLIN (1928)

One of the most (**0**) amazing advances ever made in medicine	**AMAZE**
began with an (**1**)............. event. Sir Alexander Fleming had been	**EXPECT**
looking into the (**2**)............. of finding a better way of killing germs	**POSSIBLE**
when he came upon something (**3**)............. in his laboratory. Some	**PUZZLE**
mould that had (**4**)............. landed on one of the dishes appeared to	**ACCIDENT**
be killing the bacteria he was growing. At first he was (**5**)............. about	**EXCITE**
his (**6**)............. and grew more of the mould, giving it the name of	**DISCOVER**
penicillin. However, in his view it was only really (**7**)............. as an	**EFFECT**
antiseptic against skin (**8**)............. and soon lost interest. It wasn't until	**INFECT**
ten years later that two other (**9**)............. managed to isolate the	**SCIENCE**
substance that killed the bacteria, and (**10**)............. began to save	**SUCCESS**
people's lives with it.	

c **Answer these questions about the task.**

1 How many nouns did you have to make?
2 Which answers were adverbs?
3 Which words required a prefix?

Word formation (B)

3 **Read the title and text below quickly and find out why the comet was
named after two people. Then do the task.**

Read the text below. Use the word given in capitals at the end of each line
to form a word that fits in the space in the same line. There is an example
at the beginning (**0**).

THE HALE-BOPP COMET (1995)

Since the (**0**) beginning of history, people have seen comets	**BEGIN**
travelling through the night sky. Amateur (**1**)............. are always so	**ASTRONOMY**
fascinated by comets that they get hours of (**2**)............. following	**PLEASE**
them and trying to make new (**3**)............. How did it come about,	**DISCOVER**
though, that a recently-discovered comet has a (**4**)............. of two	**COMBINE**
names, Hale and Bopp? On July 23, a (**5**)............. star-watcher,	**PROFESSION**
Alan Hale, was at home in New Mexico when he saw an (**6**).............	**USUAL**
bright dot in the sky. Coincidentally, Tom Bopp, a (**7**)............. in a	**SUPERVISE**
big (**8**)............. company, 400 miles away in Arizona – and a keen	**CONSTRUCT**
(**9**)............. of the night sky – saw the dot at exactly the same	**OBSERVE**
time through a friend's home-made (**10**)............. As a result,	**EQUIP**
it was decided to name the comet after both men.	

HELP

➤ Question 3
Singular or plural?
➤ Question 6
Positive or negative?
➤ Questions 7/9
Is the suffix *-ion, -er* or *-or*?

Language development 3

Forming nouns

1 a Look at the examples in the table of nouns formed from verbs.

-ment	-ure	-ance	-ence
achievement	failure	assistance	presence
	departure	appearance	existence
		performance	correspondence
(t/s)ion	-y	-er	-or
decision	delivery	explorer	sailor
organisation	recovery	employer	

b Copy and complete the table with nouns from the Use of English texts opposite.

2 a Do the quiz below. Guess the answers if you don't know.

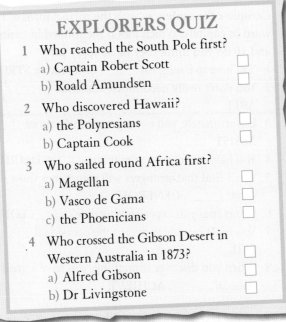

EXPLORERS QUIZ

1 Who reached the South Pole first?
 a) Captain Robert Scott ☐
 b) Roald Amundsen ☐

2 Who discovered Hawaii?
 a) the Polynesians ☐
 b) Captain Cook ☐

3 Who sailed round Africa first?
 a) Magellan ☐
 b) Vasco de Gama ☐
 c) the Phoenicians ☐

4 Who crossed the Gibson Desert in Western Australia in 1873?
 a) Alfred Gibson ☐
 b) Dr Livingstone ☐

b Read the information below and check your answers. Complete the sentences with nouns formed from the verbs in brackets.

1 Norwegian Roald Amundsen reached the South Pole in 1911, with the .... (*assist*) of a determined team and through brilliant .... (*organise*).

2 The Polynesians discovered Hawaii In 400 AD, nine hundred years before the Europeans knew of its .... (*exist*). Making such a journey by canoe was a remarkable .... (*achieve*).

3 The Phoenicians were the first .... (*sail*) to travel round Africa. They completed their journey in the seventh century BC, without the technical .... (*equip*) which is available today.

4 The Gibson Desert is named after the .... (*explore*) Alfred Gibson, who died after his .... (*fail*) to reach a camp in search of help.

3 a Copy and complete the table below with nouns formed from the adjectives in the list.

able long kind generous dark strong
sad equal ill real popular

-ness	-th	-ity
loneliness	truth	activity

b Add one noun from the Use of English texts opposite.

4 Complete the sentences with nouns formed from the words in brackets.

1 The .... (*popular*) of travelogues has increased recently.

2 The best travelogues have always been .... (*describe*) of cultures which are new to the writer.

3 The *Hai-Lu*, a Chinese traveller's account of the west, was written in the eighteenth century by the writer Hsieh Ch'ing Kao, who had the .... (*able*) to write vividly about Europe from a Chinese point of view. Its .... (*important*) has recently been recognised.

4 In the fourteenth century, Moroccan writer Ibn Buttuta spent 29 years travelling and making .... (*observe*) about Africa, Asia and Europe. We can only imagine the .... (*lonely*) he must have felt at times.

Phrasal verbs with *come*

5 a Match this phrasal verb from the Use of English text to the correct definition:
How did it *come about* that ...?
a visit   b calculate   c happen

b Match the phrasal verbs to the definitions.

1 come across	a visit (somebody) at home
2 come off	b find by chance
3 come up	c receive (praise or criticism)
4 come round	d succeed
5 come up against	e get uncovered
6 come up with	f get mentioned
7 come out	g encounter (something difficult)
8 come in for	h suggest

6 Complete the sentences with phrasal verbs from Exercise 5b. Use each verb once only.

1 The team has .... a number of problems so far.

2 Did anything important .... at the meeting?

3 Tania .... last night but you weren't in.

4 I'm sure the truth will .... one day.

5 We .... some old school photos the other day.

6 The plans have .... a lot of criticism.

7 Jackson's attempt to break the record didn't ....

8 Has anybody .... any new ideas?

Module 5: Review

1 Put the verbs in brackets in the correct future form. Use the present continuous, present simple, *going to* or *will/shall.*

1

A: Have you decided to go to university?

B: Yes, I have. I .... (*study*) astronomy.

A: Have you decided which university?

B: I don't know yet. Maybe I .... (*go*) to Hull. I've got friends there.

2

A: I .... (*not/think/I/find*) the building without a map.

B: When you .... (*get*) to the college, you .... (*see*) it on the right.

3

A: Oh, you're busy. I .... (*come*) back tomorrow.

B: No, wait. I .... (*not/be*) long. I .... (*be*) with you as soon as I .... (*can*).

4

A: They say the weather .... (*be*) good tomorrow. Are you free for a game of tennis?

B: Yes, I .... (*not/work*) tomorrow. .... (*I/book*) a court?

2 a Make questions about the future, using the verbs in the list. Use the future simple, future perfect or future continuous. If there is more than one possible future form, give reasons for your choice.

work live have retire go study move buy

Do you think you:

1 .... abroad on holiday next year?

2 .... in a foreign country in five years' time?

3 .... English ten years from now?

4 .... house by 2020?

5 .... a big family?

6 .... two cars by the time you are 30?

7 .... from home 25 years from now?

8 .... from work by the time you are 60?

b Answer the questions in Exercise 2a about yourself.

3 Correct the mistakes in the text. There may be more than one possibility.

Andy is a brilliant inventor. When he first got **(1)** *own* workshop, he had an assistant called Rob. But they never really talked to **(2)** *themselves.* Rob annoyed Andy because he never told **(3)** *himself* what he was doing, and he did things **(4)** *on own* without checking with Andy first. Andy soon realised it would be better to work **(5)** *by his own* and do everything **(6)** *on himself.* His best ideas come when he is completely **(7)** *himself.* His latest idea is a TV which switches **(8)** *it* off when no one is watching it!

4 Complete the sentences with the correct form of the word in capitals. Which job(s) mentioned in Units 9 and 10 do you think they most apply to?

1 You have to have great .... of character. **STRONG**

2 You don't really need much academic .... **ABLE**

3 Unfortunately, you never get much financial .... **ASSIST**

4 You have to be good at making .... **DECIDE**

5 You'll find that strangers will sometimes show you great .... **GENEROUS**

6 Sometimes you experience terrible .... **LONELY**

7 You must be able to accept the occasional .... **FAIL**

8 When you discover something, you have a great sense of .... **ACHIEVE**

5 Read the text and decide which answer A, B, C or D best fits each space.

At times we thought our Arctic expedition would never come **(1)**............ . During our preparations, we came **(2)**............ a lot of technical problems, and we also had problems raising the money we needed. Our university finally came **(3)**............ the money, but many people said there were more important things to spend the money on, so we came **(4)**............ a lot of criticism. Eventually we set off as planned, and everything went well until we were nearly at our destination, and we came **(5)**............ another group of explorers!

1 **A** out	**B** round	**C** off	**D** across
2 **A** up with	**B** in for	**C** round	**D** up against
3 **A** up with	**B** in for	**C** up against	**D** off
4 **A** up with	**B** in for	**C** up against	**D** off
5 **A** off	**B** across	**C** up against	**D** up

MODULE 6
The arts

Overview

- **Reading:** multiple-choice questions (Paper 1 Part 2)
- **Language development 1:** relative clauses; reduced relative clauses
- **Writing:** article (Paper 2 Part 2)
- **Speaking:** individual long turn (Paper 5 Part 2)
- **Listening:** extracts (multiple-choice questions) (Paper 4 Part 1)
- **Use of English 1:** structural cloze (Paper 3 Part 2)
- **Language development 2:** adjectives and nouns + preposition; *be used to/get used to + -ing*
- **Use of English 2:** word formation (Paper 3 Part 5)
- **Language development 3:** word formation: music; word formation: prefixes; verbs and nouns

Lead-in

- Which of the following are especially important to you and why?
  music   books   cinema   dancing   theatre
- Do governments have a responsibility to support and develop the arts, or should this be left to private enterprise?

11 A dream come true

Reading (Paper 1 Part 2)

Before you read

1 a Look at the photo. What qualities do you think a ballet dancer needs to be successful?
EXAMPLE: *They need to be very fit to be able to jump like the dancer in the photo.*

b Look at the title of the article opposite and the introduction. What do they tell you about this dancer's ambitions?

Skimming

▶ Reading strategy Unit 3 page 22

2 Skim the text to find out the main events in Alina's career.
1 How did she start dancing?   3 How does her career affect her private life?
2 Where did she train?

Multiple-choice questions

▶ page 188

Task strategy

• Read the questions and mark key words. Don't look at the options yet.
• Find and mark the parts of the text that contain the information you need.
• Read the options. The correct option will match the meaning of the text but use different words.

3 a For questions 1–7 choose the answer A, B, C or D which you think fits best according to the text. Follow the task strategy. Question 1 has been done for you. The highlighted words show how the answer was found.

b Compare and justify your answers.
1 Which part of the text answered each question?
2 Which parallel words or phrases helped you to identify the correct answer A, B, C or D?

4 Discuss these questions.
Alina says '*I don't have enough time for close friendships.*' For the sake of your career, would you:
• sacrifice friendships?
• give up your free time?
• commit a crime?
• leave your country?
• tell a lie?

Vocabulary: idiomatic expressions

5 Find idiomatic expressions and phrasal verbs in the text that mean:
1 cry (v.) (para. 1)
2 gradually become understood (para. 1)
3 get in someone's way (para. 2)
4 be successful (para. 3)
5 someone who is important or who has influence over a small area (para. 4)
6 everyone knows the rest of the story you are telling (para. 5)

A dream come true

Jeffrey Taylor meets Romanian Alina Cojocaru, the Royal Ballet's youngest ever principal dancer.

There aren't many people who have risen to the top of their profession by the age of 19, but Romanian ballerina Alina Cojocaru is one. When she danced the leading role in the ballet *Giselle* for the first time, her performance was so breathtaking that people in the audience were in tears. As soon as the final curtain fell, the director of the Royal Ballet Company rushed backstage and told Alina that she was promoted to the role of principal dancer. She was still feeling emotional after her performance and the news took time to sink in. As she recalls, 'I just stared at him and said "Sorry?" Then I understood. I couldn't speak. It was a dream come true'.

As a child, Alina had no idea what ballet was. 'I was a very lively little girl,' she says. 'I was always jumping around the flat, breaking chairs and getting under my mother's feet. A family friend thought ballet would quieten me down.' Only two months after she started dancing lessons, Alina got an audition with the famous Kiev Ballet Academy. She was successful and only two weeks later, at just nine years old, she set off on the 27-hour train journey from her home city of Bucharest to Kiev to join the Ballet Academy.

From the beginning, Alina always **stood out** from her classmates. 'I had to show the others how the steps should be done and I always got top marks. It made me feel very lonely,' she remembers. Although everyone was kind to her, she was never happy in Kiev. 'It was dark and cold in our hostel, we had to sleep in our clothes at night. I was very homesick and used to cry myself to sleep.' Her parents had said that if she didn't like it there, she could go home. But after seeing her first ever ballet performance, she became determined to stay there and become a dancer. By the time she was 16, this determination had paid off. She won a scholarship to train with the Royal Ballet School in London.

After her training in London, Alina decided to go back to Kiev, not because she preferred the Kiev Ballet, but because there was more chance of dancing leading roles there. A year later, however, having successfully performed many such roles, she phoned the Royal Ballet and asked if she could join the company in London. 'I felt like a very little fish in a very big pond when I first came back to London,' she says, 'but I didn't want to be a big fish in a little pond either. I felt I needed to be stretched.'

Joining the Royal Ballet was a brave but ultimately successful career move and it wasn't long before Alina was given her big opportunity. A principal dancer became ill and Alina was asked to replace her, with only five days to learn the role. It was hard work, but it was worth it. Her triumphant first night as *Giselle* followed. The audience adored her and the reviews were excellent. The rest, as they say, is history.

Her meteoric rise to stardom doesn't appear to have changed Alina. After that first night as *Giselle*, she still travelled home by train to a tiny rented flat and cooked supper for her father. Exhausted by her work, she spends her free time sleeping and reading, and admits: 'I don't have enough time for close friendships. But I don't mind being on my own. I'm fine as I am.'

---

1 How did Alina feel when she was made a principal dancer?
   A She was unable to control her emotions.
   (B) She was unable to say what she felt about it.
   C She was unsure whether she really deserved it.
   D She was unprepared for the audience's reaction.

2 Why did Alina first start learning ballet?
   A She wanted to find out more about it.
   B She was offered lessons by a friend.
   C She was given a place at an academy.
   D She was in need of physical exercise.

3 The phrasal verb *stood out* (line 36) tells us that Alina
   A was more able than her classmates.
   B was well liked by the class.
   C was a useful member of the class.
   D was impatient of her classmates.

4 Why did Alina stay with the Kiev Ballet?
   A She'd made a promise to her parents.
   B She knew she wouldn't be there long.
   C She saw it as the way to achieve her ambitions.
   D She hoped to get a place at a ballet school in London.

5 Why did Alina decide to go back to London as a dancer?
   A She was in need of new challenges.
   B She realised how much she liked the place.
   C She had regretted turning down a previous offer.
   D She was dissatisfied with the roles she was getting.

6 How did Alina come to dance her first principal role with the Royal Ballet Company?
   A It was the result of a lucky break.
   B It was a role that she already knew.
   C She had gained the necessary experience.
   D She was becoming popular with ballet fans.

7 From the last paragraph, we understand that Alina
   A does not find it easy being a star.
   B is content with her current lifestyle.
   C is looking forward to her next move.
   D wishes she had time for other interests.

A

B

C

D

E

F

Language development 1

Relative clauses

1 a Look at the photos from famous films that starred child actors. Match the photos to the film titles.
   1 E.T. the Extra-Terrestrial   4 Oliver!
   2 Harry Potter and the   5 Billy Elliot
     Philosopher's Stone   6 Home Alone
   3 The Wizard of Oz

   b Discuss these questions.
   1 Which of the films are based on books?
   2 Have you seen any of the films?
   3 What are they about?

2 a Read about Rupert Grint, who gained a role in the film *Harry Potter and the Philosopher's Stone*. Answer these questions.
   1 Why was Rupert Grint so keen to play the part?
   2 What did he do to try and get an audition?

The boy who plays Harry's best friend Ron Weasley says he used to 'live the Harry Potter books' and knew all of them. For 12-year-old *Rupert Grint, who looks like Ron*, being chosen was like *a dream that had come true. Rupert, whose family all have red hair like the Weasleys*, felt he was destined to be Ron. When the auditions were advertised he wrote off. But he got no reply to *the letter he sent*, so his mum helped him to make *a video, which he says was terrible*. He also wrote *a rap song in which he explained* why he wanted the role so much.

   b Complete the information in the box with examples from the text.

Relative clauses

A Defining relative clauses add essential information.
  Examples:
  1 ....
  2 ....
  3 ....
  Use *who* or *that* for people, and *which* or *that* for objects.

B Non-defining relative clauses add extra, non-essential information, and are separated by commas.
  Examples:
  1 ....
  2 ....
  3 ....
  Use *who* for people, and *which* for objects.
  Whose is the possessive relative pronoun.

C The relative pronoun can be omitted when the clause defines the object of the clause.
  Example: ....

▶ Grammar reference pages 196–197

---

3 Complete the sentences with a pronoun from the list below and add commas if necessary. Show where two different pronouns could be used, and where the pronoun could be omitted.

that   who   whose   where   which

1 *Billy Elliot* is set in an English mining town .... there is high unemployment and poverty. It tells the true story of a boy .... wants to become a ballet dancer, but .... father wants him to become a boxer.

2 *Oliver!* .... is a musical based on Charles Dickens' novel *Oliver Twist* is set in London .... there was a lot of poverty in the nineteenth century.

3 The alien E.T. .... most famous line was *'Phone home'* was later used in an advertising campaign for a telephone company. Drew Barrymore .... co-starred as Gertie in *E.T. the Extra-Terrestrial* is now an established Hollywood actress.

4 Judy Garland .... daughter Liza Minnelli is also an actress starred as Dorothy in *The Wizard of Oz*. It is basically the story of a girl .... has a vivid dream.

5 *Home Alone* in .... parents leave their young child at home on his own touches on a theme .... is not uncommon in real life today.

6 In the book *Harry Potter and the Philosopher's Stone*, Harry does not want to return to his cruel uncle and aunt .... motivates him to succeed in the tasks .... the school sets him. But this is not so obvious in the film version, for .... it has been criticised.

4 Join these pairs of sentences with relative clauses. Add commas to the non-defining relative clauses.

1 I saw a poster. It was advertising a new dance show.

2 I phoned the box office. It was in London.

3 There was an answering machine. It was telling me to call another number.

4 I spoke to a man on the other number. He told me there were only expensive seats left.

5 I booked two tickets. They cost 60 Euros each.

6 I paid by credit card. This is a very convenient way to pay.

7 On the day, we went to the theatre. It overlooks Leicester Square in London.

8 We couldn't get into the theatre. It had been closed because of technical problems.

9 I went home with my friend. She was very disappointed.

10 Next day I phoned the theatre. They were very helpful and offered replacement tickets.

5 Expand the sentences about *Bugsy Malone* by adding the extra information in brackets.

1 The 1976 film *Bugsy Malone* is a musical satire of 1930s gangster movies.
(all the actors in it are children)

2 Director and writer Alan Parker had the idea for *Bugsy Malone* when he was watching *The Godfather*.
(it was only the second film he wrote)

3 14-year-old Scott Baio was acting in his first film.
(he played the leading role of Bugsy Malone)

4 Co-star Jodie Foster had already appeared in seven films. *(she was 13 when the film was made)*

5 The cast of more than 40 children didn't actually sing in the film themselves.
(their acting and dancing made the film a success)

Reduced relative clauses

Some relative clauses can be 'reduced' to participle clauses.

A A present participle clause (*-ing*) can replace:
- a relative clause in the present or past continuous.
*The woman **singing** that song is a famous actress. (The woman **who is singing** …)*
*The car **going** round the corner was the new BMW. (The car **that was going** …)*
- a relative clause describing a permanent state.
*The people **living** in that house work in the theatre. (The people **who live** …)*
*The flat **belonging** to my brother was the nicest. (The flat **which belonged** …)*

B A past participle clause can replace a passive relative clause.
- *All TVs **sold** in this shop have a one-year guarantee. (All TVs **which are sold** …)*
*The video **released** last week has sold a million. (The video **which was released** …)*

6 Look at the information in the box above. Join the pairs of sentences 1, 3, 5 and 7 in Exercise 4. This time use reduced relative clauses.

7 Look at Exercise 4 again. Make notes about a time when you went to see a play or film. Write pairs of sentences. Then talk about it, using relative clauses and reduced relatives to link your sentences.

Writing   Article (Paper 2 Part 2)

Lead-in   1 Discuss these questions.

    1 How do you decide what films to see, or books to read?

    2 Do you read reviews of films or books? Do you follow their advice?

Understand the task   2 Read the task below and answer the questions.

    1 What is the PURPOSE of the article?

      (e.g. to inform, to persuade, to entertain, to teach)

    2 How many PARTS are there to the question?

    3 Which of these are you being asked for in each part:

      • an opinion • an anecdote • facts • to describe a situation?

    4 What STYLE will you use? Neutral, lively, informal?

You have just seen this advertisement:

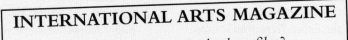

INTERNATIONAL ARTS MAGAZINE

What is your favourite book or film?
Why do you like it?

We are looking for short articles answering these questions,
and we will publish some of them next month.

Write your **article** for the International Arts Magazine in **120–180** words in an appropriate style.

Plan your article   3 a Complete the paragraph plan below with the topics in the list.

    • brief description of the story • what you don't like • conclusion

    • title • attention-grabbing introduction • what you like

    • recommendation

    Paragraph 1: ....

    ....

    Paragraph 2: ....

    Paragraph 3: ....

    Paragraph 4: ....

    Paragraph 5: ....

    ....

    b Which is the most eye-catching title to get the reader's attention?

    A My favourite book

    B The best read of my life

    C An interesting read

Language and content   4 a Choose the best opening paragraph.

A My favourite film is *Titanic*. It's very good.

B A great story about a great ship! For me, *Titanic* is the best film ever made. I was on the edge of my seat from start to finish.

    b Choose the best closing paragraph.

A A wonderful love story, high drama, superb special effects. This film has got everything – you really must see it.

B I think you will like *Titanic*. I do.

c Complete some of the sentences in the table for your favourite book or film.

Catching the reader's attention (para. 1)	*Have you seen/read …?* *I have to tell you about my favourite book/film … .* *It's the best … .* *It's a book/film called … written/directed by … .*
Describing the story (para. 2)	*It's set in … (place) in … (time).* *It's about … who … .*
Saying what you like (para. 3)	*I think the story/characters/descriptions/special effects are … .*
Saying what you don't like (para. 4)	*I must admit some of the acting isn't so good … .* *The story is a bit slow in places … .* *It gets a bit confusing when … .*
Conclusion/ Recommendation (para. 5)	*Although … it is still a great film/book.* *You really must/should see/read it.* *If you like (romance/drama/comedy) you'll love this … .*

Write your article

5 Now write your own article, using the ideas and some of the language above. Write your answer in 120–180 words.

Check and improve your article

6 Edit your article using this list. Check your:
- plan (Have you covered everything?)
- style (Is it lively and interesting?)
- language (Is it varied and interesting?)
- use of relative clauses.

▶ Writing reference page 206

Fame, the Movie

LANGUAGE SPOT: avoiding repetition

a **What do the words in italics refer to?**
Fame – the musical
Good musicals make sure *their* audience feel good when *they* leave the theatre. In *this* musical the acting and singing are wonderful. The actors hit *their* notes with gusto and give *the show* all *they*'ve got. The youngest *ones* are the best. *You* won't know *their* names but *they*'re as good as any professional. However, *these* are the plus points. The plot is less than satisfactory. *It*'s very thin and *this* is the reason *we* don't really care about the characters or what happens to *them*.

b **Change the words in brackets to avoid repetition.**
1 I like *Phantom of the Opera* and *Les Miserables*. (*Phantom of the Opera* and *Les Miserables*) are both musicals.
2 *Phantom of the Opera* is on at the Adelphi. (The Adelphi) is a lovely theatre. We've been (to the Adelphi).
3 I'd love to see *Grease* but I can't afford (to see *Grease*).
4 Can you get me tickets for Friday? I've got a day off (on Friday).
5 These seats are quite near the stage, but the (seats) over there are nearer.

Speaking (Paper 5 Part 2)

Lead-in 1 Look at the two photos, which show two different kinds of art. Which do you prefer?

Sample answer 2 a 🎧 Listen to the examiner and complete the instructions.

EXAMINER: *I'd like you to compare and contrast these photographs, and say which ....*
... .

b 🎧 Listen to Alice doing the task and answer the questions.
1 Does she give enough time to both parts of the task?
2 Does she make full use of the minute?

c 🎧 Listen to the first part again, and tick (✓) the expressions she uses to speculate about the photos.

The statue could be/might be … .	It must have/must have had … .
It can't be … .	I get the impression that … .

▶ Functions reference page 224

d 🎧 Listen to the second part and complete her personal opinions.
ALICE: *Well, I like .... but if ...., I think I .... because ....*

Short response 3 a 🎧 Listen and complete the examiner's question for Robert.
EXAMINER: *Robert, are you ....?*

b 🎧 Listen to Robert's answer and complete what he says.
ROBERT: *I'm .... art. I prefer ....*

Individual long turn

▶ Task strategy Unit 6 page 45

4 a Work in pairs. Do Task 1 (on this page). Then turn to page 219 and follow the instructions for Task 2.
Task 1
Look at the photographs on pages 88 and 89.
STUDENT A: Compare and contrast the photographs, and say which type of art you think is more interesting.
STUDENT B: Listen to Student A without interrupting. Stop him/her after one minute, and say briefly whether you are interested in art.

Task strategy

Student B, remember: Just give a brief response to the question, maximum 20 seconds.

b Did you follow the strategy on page 45?

c What language did you use to compare and contrast, speculate and give personal opinions?

Listening (Paper 4 Part 1)

Before you listen

1 Look at the listening task in Exercise 2. The extracts are not related. What kind of information does each question 1–6 ask for? Mark key words.

Extracts (multiple choice)

▶ page 190

▶ page 190

Task strategy

- Focus on the speaker's main idea – you don't need to understand every word.
- Choose one of the options after listening the first time.
- Check your answer during the second listening. Make sure the other options are wrong.
- Guess the answer if necessary.

---

2 a 🔊 You will hear people talking in six different situations. For questions 1–6, choose the best answer A, B or C.

1 You overhear a woman talking on her mobile phone. What is she doing when she speaks?
 A thanking a friend who's done something for her
 B asking a friend for information about an event
 C inviting a friend to an event she's organising

2 You hear part of an arts programme on the radio. What is the speaker talking about?
 A a film
 B a stage play
 C a novel

3 You hear an extract from a radio play. Where is this scene taking place?
 A in a restaurant
 B in a hotel reception
 C in a motorway café

4 You overhear two teenagers discussing a film they have just seen. How does the boy feel about it?
 A uninterested by the storyline
 B disappointed by the acting
 C unimpressed by the photography

5 You overhear two people talking. Who are they talking about?
 A a close friend
 B a colleague
 C a relation

6 You overhear a man talking about an art exhibition. What does he criticise?
 A the way it is laid out
 B the information available to visitors
 C the quality of the works of art on show

b Compare and discuss your answers. Listen to the recording again if necessary. What words and phrases give the answer?
 EXAMPLE: 1B – *So do they give the exact dates?*

Use of English 1 (Paper 3 Part 2)

Lead-in

1 Discuss these questions.
1 Which of these paintings do you prefer and why?
2 Do you like going to art galleries?

Structural cloze

▸ Task strategy Unit 4 page 30

2 a Read the title and text quickly. Are these statements *True* or *False*?
1 The Tate Modern is a great success.
2 The building is not very interesting.
3 The art is arranged in order of date.

b Do the task. Follow the task strategy and use the Help clues if necessary.

Read the text below and think of a word which best fits each space. Use only **one** word in each space. There is an example at the beginning (**0**).

Tate Modern

The Tate Modern, a gallery (**0**) of modern art in London, opened (**1**)............ doors in May 2000. In its first year, it attracted more (**2**)............ 5.25 million visitors, but some people were surprised (**3**)............ its success. A lot of people in the UK are not interested (**4**)............ modern art, and even get angry (**5**)............ the large sums of money which are spent (**6**)............ it. The museum's success has been to bring (**7**)............ a new audience for art. Half the visitors are under 35 years of age, and the gallery (**8**)............ helped to make modern art 'cool'.

How is this possible? Firstly, many visitors talk to each other (**9**)............ the building itself, (**10**)............ than the art on display. The building (**11**)............ converted from a power station, and the architects (**12**)............ designed the Tate Modern decided to keep many of the building's industrial features. Secondly, the gallery organises its collection into themed areas, such as 'Still life, Real Life and Objects', (**13**)............ of arranging the works in the order they were produced, (**14**)............ is the approach people have got used (**15**)............ over the years.

HELP
➤ **Question 3**
This is a use of the passive.
➤ **Question 5**
Which two prepositions can combine with *angry* in this sentence? Which one fits better here?
➤ **Question 7**
Which phrasal verb can mean *attract*?
➤ **Questions 10/13**
These phrases have a similar meaning, but different prepositions!

c Which questions test:
• adjectives + prepositions?
• verbs + prepositions?
• verb forms?

d Which did you find the most difficult, and why?

3 Make a note of the word + preposition combinations you want to remember. You can record them by main word (A), by preposition (B), or by example sentence (C):

Language development 2

Adjectives and nouns + preposition

A Adjective + preposition
Walter's **interested in** modern classical music.
It's **unusual for** him to be late.

(LOOK) **at the Use of English text opposite and find examples of adjectives with a preposition.**

B Noun + preposition
Congratulations on an excellent performance!
What's the **relationship between** the two women in the play?

C Some adjectives and nouns go with different prepositions:
He's **good at** singing. (= he is skilful)
Relaxation is **good for** you. (= it benefits you)
That's very **good of** you. (= you are kind and thoughtful)
My sister's **good with** children. (= she deals with them well)

1 a **Mark the correct preposition in each sentence.**
   1 What was the result for / on / of the art competition?
   2 Audiences often feel sorry for / by / with the bad guy!
   3 Chris didn't have any success for / in / on getting tickets.
   4 There's no comparison of / with / between Mozart and Madonna.
   5 I'm tired of / in / on watching television every night.
   6 Moira always gets involved on / in / of discussions about art.
   7 I have difficulty for / in / by understanding opera.
   8 The musician's excited by / for / about making his first CD.
   9 Ellie was annoyed with / on / in her husband for forgetting the tickets.
   10 Alan's got no hope from / to / of ever selling a painting!

   b **Complete the article with the correct prepositions. There may be more than one possibility.**

Vermeer

The seventeenth-century Dutch painter Johannes Vermeer is famous (1)............. his very realistic paintings. Many experts have tried to work out how he was so good (2)............. painting accurate details. In his day, it was usual (3)............. painters to draw the picture first, but Vermeer seemed capable (4)............. painting without doing this. Even the Victorians, who were responsible (5)............. Vermeer's present great reputation, were puzzled (6)............. why his paintings were so similar (7)............. photographs.
  Philip Steadman of University College, London has no doubt (8)............. the reason. He claims Vermeer used an early form of camera, called a camera obscura, as a means (9)............. creating accurate images. Steadman was suspicious (10)............. a mysterious black box in one painting, saying that it is exactly where Vermeer's camera would have been. But Steadman says even if he is right (11)............. Vermeer's method, we shouldn't lose respect (12)............. the artist's talent.

2 **Answer these questions about yourself.**
   1 What are you shocked by/keen on/bad at?
   2 Who are you impressed by/scared of/worried about?

be used to/get used to + -ing

(LOOK) **at this example from the Use of English text opposite:**

... the approach people have **got used to** over the years.

I'm used to eating spicy food. (= accustomed to it)
I'm not used to eating spicy food. (= it's new and strange for me)
I can't/couldn't **get used to driving** on the left. (= become accustomed to, it was difficult)
I left home last year. I had to **get used to living** alone.

Compare:
I **used to listen to** a lot of pop music when I was younger but I don't now.

3 **Complete the sentences. Mark the correct form of *used* and use the correct form of the verb in brackets.**
   1 He used / is used / get used to (live) .... in Hollywood but he moved to Cannes in July.
   2 It took him a long time to used / be used / get used to (live) .... in France.
   3 Katie got tired quickly. She didn't used / wasn't used / didn't get used to (film) .... so early.
   4 If you want to be an artist, you'll have to used / be used / get used to (hear) .... criticism of your work.
   5 Newspapers weren't used / didn't use / couldn't get used to (print) .... such awful stories.
   6 These days we aren't used / don't used / can't get used to (watch) .... films in black and white.
   7 When he became famous, he had to be used / get used / used to people (stare) .... at him in the street.
   8 I'm exhausted. I don't used / didn't use / 'm not used to (go) .... round art galleries.

4 **What things do you have to *get used to* when you:**
   ● get married?
   ● start work?
   ● go on a diet?
   ● go travelling?
   ● change college?

Use of English 2 (Paper 3 Part 5)

Lead-in

1 Who is your favourite pop or rock singer now? Who did you use to like five years ago?

Word formation (A)

2 a What advice would you give someone doing the word formation task below? Check your answer with the task strategy on page 32 if necessary.

▶ Task strategy Unit 4 page 32

b Do the task. Follow the task strategy and use the Help clues if necessary.

Read the text below. Use the word given in capitals at the end of each line to form a word that fits in the space in the same line. There is an example at the beginning (**0**).

HELP
➤ Question 4
  Is a prefix or suffix needed?
➤ Question 5
  What suffix do you need?
➤ Question 8
  Do you a need a prefix, a suffix or both?

STEVIE WONDER

Stevie Wonder is a highly (**0**) inventive American musician. **INVENT**
Blind from birth, he quickly developed (**1**)............ skills beyond **ART**
his age. By the age of nine he was not only a good (**2**)............, he **SING**
had mastered an (**3**)............ range of instruments, including the **IMPRESS**
piano, organ, harmonica and drums. His (**4**)............ talent was **ORDINARY**
soon discovered, and he was offered his first (**5**)............ **RECORD**
contract at the age of 11. His early records sold (**6**)............ **EXTREME**
well and, despite a couple of (**7**)............ years, in 1965 he **DISAPPOINT**
began a run of hit records that continued (**8**)............ until 1971. **INTERRUPT**
From then on he was given total artistic (**9**)............, and his **FREE**
music started to get more unusual and more (**10**)............ **POLITICS**

c Which were the hardest answers, and why?

Word formation (B)

3 Do the task.

Read the text below. Use the word given in capitals at the end of each line to form a word that fits the space in the same line. There is an example at the beginning (**0**).

MUSICAL GENIUS

Scientists now agree that the best (**0**) musicians are born, not **MUSIC**
made. An (**1**)............ recent study of twins has shown that our genes **AMBITION**
account for 80 per cent of our (**2**)............ to recognise musical notes **ABLE**
exactly, which is the key to musical (**3**)............ Most of us on **GREAT**
the other hand are quite (**4**)............ of telling one note from **CAPABLE**
another and have a limited potential for (**5**)............ This **DEVELOP**
discovery probably accounts for the (**6**)............ large number of **CURIOUS**
musical families, like the (**7**)............ talented family of pop stars, **CREDIBLE**
the Jacksons. However, we should be careful not to (**8**)............ the **ESTIMATE**
(**9**)............ of training and hard work. Some people may have **IMPORTANT**
an (**10**)............ in-born talent but they still have to develop it. **ASTONISH**

HELP
Three of the words require a prefix.
You have to make **four** nouns.

Discussion

4 Discuss these questions.
  1 Do you have musical ability? Do you practise?
  2 What would you like to be able to do in music?

Language development 3

Word formation

1 a **What do we call a person who:**
1 plays the piano? 4 composes music?
2 plays the drums? 5 conducts an orchestra?
3 plays the trumpet?

b **Complete this article with the correct form of the nouns in brackets.**

Every year, festivals of world music take place in more than 12 countries. This year's three-day festival in Reading, UK, had 60 bands from across the globe. First on stage was a group of ten **(1)**.............. (*dance*), five **(2)**.............. (*music*) and three **(3)**.............. (*sing*) from Cuba, who immediately created a carnival of song and dance. Other **(4)**.............. (*perform*) included the Soweto String Quartet: three **(5)**.............. (*violin*) and a **(6)**.............. (*cello*), who play a wonderful mix of classical music, contemporary jazz and **(7)**.............. (*tradition*) African music. I particularly enjoyed Makana, an acoustic **(8)**.............. (*guitar*) from Hawaii, and Faisal Taher, a **(9)**.............. (*sing*) whose vocals in the Village tent gave things a Middle Eastern tone. A live **(10)**.............. (*perform*) by Zimbabwe's best-selling artist Oliver Mtukudzi was also memorable.

2 a **Find two adjectives with negative prefixes in the Use of English texts opposite and write them in the correct place in the table.**

un-	in-	dis-
unpleasant	inconvenient	dissatisfied

im-	il-	
impossible	illegal	

b **Choose the correct negative prefix for each of the adjectives in the list. Copy and complete the table.**
polite   loyal   experienced   tidy   patient
honest   fair   literate   practical   fit
secure   satisfactory   logical

3 a **Choose an adjective from Exercise 2 to describe:**
1 a child who never puts his things away.
2 a man who can't cook or change a tyre on a car.
3 a good student who feels her homework is not good enough.
4 homework which is not good enough.
5 someone who can't read or write.
6 a graduate who has just started in her first job.
7 a man who is exhausted after running for a bus.

b **Answer these questions.**
1 Are you ever impatient, impolite or unfair?
2 What's the most illogical or impractical thing you've done?
3 Is your room untidy?

Verbs and nouns

Look at these verb + noun combinations with *say, tell, speak* and *talk.*
- *say*
  anything/something (to someone)
  a few words
  yes/no
  a prayer
  hello
  your name

- *tell*
  someone
  the time
  the truth/a lie
  a joke/a story/a secret
  someone's fortune

- *speak*
  a language
  your mind

- *talk*
  sense/nonsense/rubbish
  business/sport/politics

4 a **Read the information in the box above and correct the mistakes in these sentences.**
1 The teacher spoke us a horror story.
2 I can't stand it when artists say politics.
3 We all talked a prayer together.
4 Excuse me, could you say me the time?
5 My brother talks three languages.
6 Tell hello to Rosie for me.
7 Mike said the police what he had seen.
8 Don't trust him. He's always speaking lies.

b **Now complete this letter with the correct form of *say, tell, speak* or *talk.***

Why don't we go to Spain together – for a holiday perhaps – I **(1)**.............. a little Spanish and it would be fun. Please **(2)**.............. yes, but don't **(3)**.............. anything to Jason – he'll be very jealous.
I like Jason but sometimes he **(4)**.............. a lot of rubbish. Last week he **(5)**.............. me that he had seen the musical *Les Misérables* in Paris but I knew he was **(6)**.............. a lie – he's never been to France. I didn't **(7)**.............. anything to him at the time because I was in a hurry but when I get the chance I'll **(8)**.............. my mind and **(9)**.............. him exactly what I think about him and his lies.
OK, I've got to go now. Hope you can come!

5 **Make sentences about yourself, using the prompts and *say, tell, speak* or *talk.***
1 I/languages   3 I/politics   5 I/no
2 I/lies   4 I/jokes

Exam practice 3

Paper 1: Reading

Part 3: gapped text (sentences)

You are going to read a newspaper article about exploring the oceans. Seven sentences have been removed from the article. Choose the most suitable sentence from the list **A–H** for each part (**1–6**) of the article. There is one extra sentence which you do not need to use. There is an example at the beginning (**0**).

Filming the mysteries of the deep

More people have travelled into space than have dared venture into the deep ocean. The oceans cover 70 per cent of our planet. However, 60 per cent of their area is more than 1,000 metres below the surface, a depth at which very little has been explored. Below 200 metres there is a strange and gloomy world where very little life survives. At 1,000 metres there is permanent darkness, where the only light is created by the animals that live there. **0** **H** We know almost nothing about it.

Alistair Fothergill has just been down there to make *The Blue Planet*. This natural history documentary cost more, and took longer to make, than any other television series before it. **1** What is more, at least ten of these strange, wonderful and sometimes horrific groups of creatures were completely new to science.

Among the fish filmed for the first time was the Deep Sea Angler, which illuminates itself by bacteria in its body, and the Fangtooth, which has teeth so large that it can never close its mouth. Their most exciting discovery, however, was one which had never been heard of before, which they called the Hairy Angler fish. **2** And with its huge mouth, full of sharp teeth, it is therefore able to kill passing fish – even those far larger than itself – and put them into its expandable stomach. In the deep ocean, where there is very little food, it's important to eat whatever is available.

While Fothergill went to a depth of 'only 1,000 metres' to film these creatures, some specially trained members of his team descended a further 3,000 to visit the so-called 'black smokers' in the middle of the ocean. **3**

Until about 20 years ago, when these areas were found, all life on our planet was thought to be dependent on the sun's energy. The discovery of the smokers disproved that theory. 'We now realise that even right down at the very bottom of the deep ocean there are extraordinary pockets of life.' explains Fothergill. 'The energy comes from bacteria, that feed on salt from a rock. **4** The most amazing of these creatures are the tube worms, which are about two metres long, as thick as your arm, with bright red feathers. They have no stomach or mouth, but are completely packed full of bacteria.'

5 'But we'll be back,' he insists. 'The deepest point in the ocean, at more than 12,000 metres, is the Marianas Trench in the Pacific. There is still so much to discover down there in the depths of the sea. The giant squid, for instance, is the size of a London bus, and has never been seen alive.' What he would find even more thrilling, however, would be to discover the secrets of an even larger ocean creature.

6 He explains that scientists are studying a big population which goes up and down the coast of California at an incredible speed of over 30 kilometres an hour, and then disappears under the surface for long periods at a time. However, American biologists have finally succeeded in attaching satellite tags to a few individuals. 'We're now getting some exciting information back to suggest that they're heading for a place off Costa Rica,' says Fothergill. 'That's where I want to go looking for them.'

A The features from which it gets its name are actually sensors that can detect the slightest vibration made by other marine life nearby.

B These are openings created when water flows through cracks in the sea bed, hits very hot volcanic rock and comes shooting out again.

C Fothergill's most passionate ambition is to discover where the blue whale goes to have its young.

D These tiny life forms, in turn, provide food for a whole range of 'new' animals.

E Excited by these discoveries, Fothergill would have sent a camera down even further, but this proved impossible.

F For a long time scientists thought they must be a completely different species of fish.

G And in filming natural history, he made real history too, because his team found 50 species that had never been filmed before.

H This vast black world is a desert, a bottomless hole.

Paper 3: Use of English

Part 1: lexical cloze

Read the text below and decide which answer **A**, **B**, **C** or **D** best fits each space. There is an example at the beginning (**0**).

BELIEVE THE EYES

How do you know when someone is lying? Scientists studying the human face with sensitive cameras may have discovered the answer, almost by **(0)** ...A.... . When someone in the laboratory dropped a book, **(1)**............ a loud noise, the camera they were using to study someone's face showed an unexpected **(2)**............ . The sudden fear had caused the **(3)**............ of the person's face around the eyes to change. This led the researchers to **(4)**............ the idea that if a super-sensitive camera could spot fear, it would be quite **(5)**............ of showing when people were **(6)**............ a lie.

The researchers then **(7)**............ up an experiment to test out their theory. Some volunteers were told a secret which they were forbidden to **(8)**............ with another set of volunteers, who were told to **(9)**............ what it was. The results were **(10)**............ , with the camera correctly identifying which of the volunteers was lying.

Some people believe that these tests could lead to the **(11)**............ of a camera which would **(12)**............ airport security staff who, at the moment, have to **(13)**............ on their own judgement when asking passengers about the contents of their luggage. However, although the camera could be more **(14)**............ than traditional ways of discovering whether people are lying, most scientists believe that more **(15)**............ tests are needed before it goes into widespread use.

0	A	accident	B	surprise	C	fortune	D	shock
1	A	getting	B	making	C	having	D	doing
2	A	remark	B	relation	C	reply	D	reaction
3	A	example	B	description	C	appearance	D	variety
4	A	get away with	B	stand up to	C	look forward to	D	come up with
5	A	capable	B	clever	C	skilful	D	talented
6	A	saying	B	speaking	C	telling	D	talking
7	A	set	B	put	C	held	D	gave
8	A	argue	B	share	C	inform	D	spill
9	A	find out	B	catch up	C	ask after	D	call for
10	A	famous	B	amazed	C	wondering	D	impressive
11	A	innovation	B	growth	C	development	D	increase
12	A	appeal	B	assist	C	attract	D	accept
13	A	support	B	lean	C	rely	D	rest
14	A	accurate	B	correct	C	right	D	honest
15	A	persuading	B	convincing	C	proving	D	agreeing

Part 3: key word transformation

Complete the second sentence so that it has a similar meaning to the first sentence, using the word given. **Do not change the word given.** You must use between **two** and **five** words, including the word given. Write **only** the missing words.

EXAMPLE:

0 You must do exactly what the manager tells you.

carry

You must <u>carry out the manager's</u> instructions exactly.

1 John will have finished his work in a short while.

long

It won't .... finished his work.

2 What's the name of the man who had his nose broken in a fight?

whose

What's the name of the man .... in a fight?

3 I find it very difficult to believe anything he says.

have

I .... anything he says.

4 For several years, I felt strange driving on the left.

used

It took me several years .... on the left.

5 Excuse me, could you please tell me the time?

wonder

Excuse me, ... tell me the time.

6 I think it was a very stupid thing for him to do.

what

I think that .... very stupid.

7 He took the money – I saw him myself.

own

I saw him take the money .... eyes.

8 I don't think we'll finish this crossword.

hope

I don't think there's .... finishing this crossword.

9 Kate is the name of the woman who is brushing her hair.

called

The woman who is .... Kate.

10 The band will already have started to play before the Queen comes in.

be

The band .... when the Queen comes in.

Part 5: word formation

Read the text below. Use the word given in capitals at the end of each line to form a word that fits the space in the same line. There is an example at the beginning (**0**).

POEMS BY MOBILE PHONE

Mobile phones may be very (**0**) <u>useful</u> gadgets, but many people find the **USE**
noise which they make rather (**1**)............. , especially when they ring at **ANNOY**
awkward moments. Others complain about receiving (**2**)............. text messages **NECESSARY**
which often require great (**3**)............. on the part of the reader because **PATIENT**
they are written so (**4**)............. . With this in mind, a new mobile-phone **BAD**
service is being introduced which aims to bring (**5**)............. , as well as a **PLEASE**
moment of pause and (**6**)............. , into the stressful lives of businesspeople. **REFLECT**
The service will send people a short daily poem. Some will be (**7**)............. , **AMUSE**
others more serious, but all will be (**8**)............. understood. Although the **EASY**
service, set up by the experienced poet, Fredrik Lloyd, sounds rather (**9**)............. , **AMBITION**
it has already attracted subscribers from a wide (**10**)............. of businesses. **VARY**

MODULE 7
What's in fashion?

Overview

- **Reading:** multiple matching: headings (Paper 1 Part 1)
- **Language development 1:** permission and necessity: present and past; advice and recommendation
- **Writing:** transactional letter (Paper 2 Part 1)
- **Listening:** multiple matching (Paper 4 Part 3)
- **Speaking:** collaborative task, discussion (Paper 5 Parts 3 and 4)
- **Language development 2:** speculation and deduction
- **Use of English 1:** key word transformation (Paper 3 Part 3)
- **Use of English 2:** lexical cloze (Paper 3 Part 1)
- **Language development 3:** prepositional phrases; verbs with similar meanings

Lead-in

- Look at the photos. How have fashions changed over the last 25 years in your country in these areas?
  a food and how we eat it   b clothes and dress codes
- 'There's never a new fashion but it's old.' (Geoffrey Chaucer 1342–1400)
  What does this quotation mean? Do you agree with it?

Fast food

Reading   (Paper 1 Part 1)

Before you read

1 Look at the title of the article opposite. Discuss these questions.
1 What is *fast food*? What are *fast-food giants*? Can you name any?
2 Do you know **where**, **when** and **why** fast food started?
3 Why have fast-food restaurants been so successful?
4 Will the fast-food industry continue to grow? Why/Why not?

Skimming

2 Skim the text to check your answers to Exercise 1. Don't worry if there are words you don't understand. You only need to understand the main points.

Multiple matching: headings ▶ page 188

3 Choose the most suitable heading from the list A–H for each part (1–6) of the article. There is one extra heading which you do not need to use. There is an example at the beginning (0).

a Look at the example (0 – H). Which words in the heading match the key phrases in the text? Mark them.

b Do the task. Follow the task strategy. Key phrases in sections 1 and 2 of the text have been highlighted for you.

Task strategy

- Read the paragraph headings and mark key words.
- For each heading, look for the paragraph that contains the same ideas.
- Read the paragraph carefully and mark key phrases.
- Check that the heading matches the key phrases in the text.
- Cross the headings off as you use them.

A Simplicity is the key to success
B Identifying a need for further changes
C Achieving the same standard worldwide
D A model for other companies to follow
E Responding to the changing demands of the customer
F A challenge to the basic idea of fast food
G Gradual acceptance of the benefits
H A surprising amount of evidence

c Compare and justify your answers.

Discussion

4 Discuss these questions.
1 Fast food is often called *junk food*. Why? Do you think it's a fair description?
2 How different is your diet from that of your parents and grandparents? Do you think it's better or worse?

Vocabulary: classifying

5 The text mentions the following categories. Can you think of more examples to add to each category in the table?

staff	crockery	cutlery	ways of preparing food
waitress	dish	knife	grill

How fast-food giants changed the world

0 — H

When future archaeologists start digging up the remains of modern western civilisation, they will be
5 astonished at how many hamburger and pizza boxes they come across. For over the last 50 years, the passion for what has become known
10 as 'fast food' has created both a social revolution and an enormous amount of wealth.

1

The story of fast food began in the USA in the 1930s and
15 1940s, a result of the country's love affair with that other great innovation of the twentieth century, the automobile. Indeed, in southern California, people were becoming so attached to their cars that they were happy to spend all evening in them. Realising that this was bad for trade,
20 restaurants began to employ waitresses known as 'car hops'. Their job was to carry trays of food out to those customers who preferred eating in their vehicles in the car park to sitting round a table in the traditional manner.

2

Brothers Richard and Maurice McDonald ran one of these
25 successful 'drive-in' restaurants in a town near Los Angeles. The business was not without its problems, however: staff were always leaving for higher-paid jobs, and the teenagers who were their main customers were constantly breaking or stealing the crockery and cutlery. So
30 the McDonalds decided to look again at the basic idea of the take-away restaurant to see if they could find a way round these drawbacks.

3

In 1948 they came up with the solution – a completely new method of providing customers with food. They
35 decided to streamline the process by keeping it as straightforward and uncomplicated as possible. For example, they got rid of two-thirds of the items on the menu, including anything that had to be eaten with a knife, fork or spoon. Meanwhile, the kitchen became like a
40 factory with machines doing most of the cooking and each unskilled employee performing just one routine task according to strict rules and regulations.

4

What the McDonald brothers had understood
45 was the importance of uniformity. The success of any fast-food chain depends on the reliability of its product. Consumers can
50 order a 'Big Mac' at any McDonald's on the planet and know exactly what they will get. In order to achieve this guaranteed level of
55 quality, the food must be heavily processed and the whole system of food preparation must be tightly controlled. McDonald's has a handbook for employees which contains precise
60 instructions on how everything is to be cooked, from how thick the French fries should be to how far apart burgers should be placed on the grill.

5

The fast-food industry now employs millions of people worldwide. McDonald's alone now trains more new
65 workers every year than the US army. It is the largest owner of retail property in the world and its corporate symbol, the golden arches, is recognised everywhere. Inspired by the success of the McDonald brothers, dozens of lookalike fast-food chains have spread out across the
70 world from the USA. And the influence of the McDonald approach can be seen throughout the service economy. There are now chains of coffee bars, shops and all manner of other businesses which benefit from bring organised according to the same principles.

6

75 Although fast food does have its good points – it's convenient, cheap and tasty – there are some people who question its long-term appeal. The leading US chains are no longer growing so quickly, and some people have linked this slowdown with a new attitude towards food in the
80 western world. As people increasingly turn to the healthier lifestyle associated with fresh produce, local food and old-fashioned methods of food preparation, it will be interesting to see whether the fast-food industry has perhaps had its day.

Language development 1

Permission and necessity: present

1 a Look at these comments made in a restaurant. Which ones are more likely to be made by a waiter, and which ones by a customer?

> 1 We're not allowed to smoke, are we?

> 2 You don't have to give them a tip.

> 3 I'm afraid you can't sit there – it's reserved.

> 4 You're allowed to smoke in this area.

> 5 Excuse me, sir, children over 12 mustn't use the play area.

> 6 Steve, you're not supposed to use your mobile phone here. Turn it off.

> 7 I'm sorry, but you have to wear a tie to eat here.

> 8 I must try one of the desserts – they look delicious.

> 9 You can choose any table on this side, madam.

> 10 I think we are supposed to leave a tip.

b Write the words in italics 1–10 in the correct place in the table below.

Function	Example
A Giving permission	1 ....
	2 ....
B Prohibiting	1 ....
	2 ....
	3 ....
	4 ....
C Expressing obligation	
• the speaker feels it's necessary	1 ....
• the rules or situation make it necessary	2 ....
	3 ....
D Expressing lack of necessity	....

▶ Grammar reference pages 200–201

2 a Complete the sentences with the correct form of the words in brackets. You may need to make the verb negative.
1 They're very busy at the weekend, so we (*must/book*) .... a table.
2 It's a formal dinner. You .... (*can/wear*) jeans.
3 Lorna's a club member. Of course she (*allow/come*) .... in!
4 I think we (*suppose/wait*) .... for a waiter to show us to our table.
5 You (*have to/have*) .... a starter if you don't want one.
6 You (*must/bring*) .... your own food or drink to this restaurant!
7 Children under 16 (*allow/drink*) .... alcohol; they're too young.
8 You (*can/pay*) .... by cash, cheque or credit card.

b What rules are there in a café or restaurant that you know?

Permission and necessity: past

3 **a** Read the extract from a letter about a new restaurant and answer the questions.
1 Was it necessary to wear a suit?
2 What was the worst thing about the restaurant?

We went to that new restaurant yesterday. It's very big, so we *didn't have to* book a table. John wore a suit because he thought it would be very formal, but in fact it wasn't, so he *needn't have* dressed so smartly. Of course, the children *couldn't* play in the restaurant but they *were allowed to* use the play area outside. The meal was very expensive though – we *had to* pay by credit card because we didn't have enough money with us. And worst of all, I *wasn't allowed to* smoke!

b Complete the table with examples from the letter.

Meaning	Example
It was permitted.	....
It was prohibited.	1 ....
	2 ....
It was necessary.	....
It wasn't necessary.	....
It was done but it wasn't necessary.	....

▶ Grammar reference pages 200–201

4 **a** Mark the correct forms in each pair.

When I was a student I worked as a waiter during the holidays. The best thing was that I **(1)** *needn't have paid / didn't have to pay* for my meals, as they were all free. We **(2)** *were allowed to / had to* eat as much as we wanted during breaks, but the work was tiring because we **(3)** *could / had to* work long hours. And although customers **(4)** *had to / could* give us tips, we **(5)** *couldn't have kept / couldn't keep* the money – we **(6)** *had to / were allowed to* share it with the other staff. I was nervous when I started because they said that sometimes I would **(7)** *need to have cooked / have to cook* the food, but I **(8)** *couldn't worry / needn't have worried* because I **(9)** *was allowed to / didn't have to* cook at all while I worked there.

b What rules about food and eating did your family have when you were a child?

Advice and recommendation

Find and correct the mistakes in these sentences.
1 You ought complain about that soup – it's cold.
2 You shouldn't having a dessert if you're full up.
3 If you don't like pasta, you'd better to have a pizza.
4 You must have try that new restaurant in Castle Street.

▶ Grammar reference page 201

5 Replace the words in italics in the letter below with words from the list in the correct form.

can	must	have to	had better

Dear Melanie,

Thanks for agreeing to look after our house while we're away. Just a few things to remember:

Be careful with the front door lock. *It's necessary to* **(1)**........................... pull it up before turning it. But *it's very important not to* **(2)**........................... force the key or it'll break!

Please feed the cat twice a day. You *are allowed to* **(3)**........................... give him anything from the bottom shelf.

It's not necessary for you to **(4)**........................... pay us to use the phone, and the kids *are permitted to* **(5)**........................... use the PlayStation. *We strongly recommend you* **(6)**........................... try the local restaurant. *It's a good idea to* **(7)**........................... book though.

Have fun,

Louise

6 Complete these sentences about yourself.
1 This year I really must ... but I mustn't ... .
2 At college / work we have to ... but we don't have to ... .
3 When I was younger I could ... but I wasn't allowed to ... . I had to ... but I didn't have to ... .

Writing Transactional letter (Paper 2 Part 1)

Lead-in 1 Discuss these questions.

1 Have you been to a meal or a party on a river-cruise boat?
2 Would you like to? Why/Why not?

Understand the task 2 Read the task below. What four things must you decide before you start writing? Look back at Unit 5, page 42, Exercise 2, if you need help.

You work for a language school in the UK. A group of students is coming next month and you have organised a lunch cruise for them on a river near the school. You have sent the programme to their group leader, who has written back to you with some questions. Read the questions and the notes you have made. Then write a letter to her, giving all the necessary information.

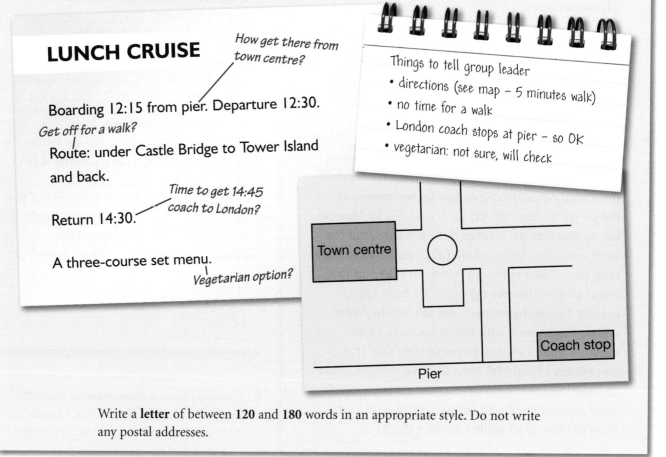

LUNCH CRUISE *How get there from town centre?*

Boarding 12:15 from pier. Departure 12:30.
Get off for a walk?
Route: under Castle Bridge to Tower Island and back.

Time to get 14:45 coach to London?

Return 14:30.

A three-course set menu.
Vegetarian option?

Things to tell group leader
• directions (see map – 5 minutes walk)
• no time for a walk
• London coach stops at pier – so OK
• vegetarian: not sure, will check

Town centre

Coach stop

Pier

Write a **letter** of between **120** and **180** words in an appropriate style. Do not write any postal addresses.

Plan your letter 3 a Make a list of key points to include in the letter.

b How many paragraphs will you have? What will you include in each?

Language and content

4 a How could you continue these sentences for the opening paragraph?

Thank you very much for … .

Here are the … .

b Which of these expressions for giving directions would be appropriate in this letter?

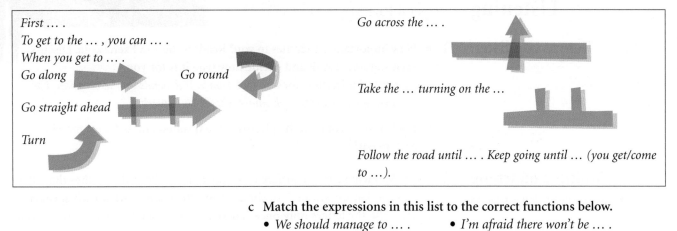

First … .
To get to the … , you can … .
When you get to … .
Go along
Go round
Go straight ahead
Turn

Go across the … .
Take the … turning on the …
Follow the road until … . Keep going until … (you get/come to …).

c Match the expressions in this list to the correct functions below.

- *We should manage to … .*
- *You asked about … .*
- *We might be able to … .*
- *I'm afraid there won't be … .*
- *You wanted to know whether … .*
- *Unfortunately, I don't think … .*

Referring to questions	*As for (X) itself … .*
Talking about possibilities	*You'll be able to … .*
Apologising	*I'm very sorry but … .*

d Complete some of the expressions in the table to use in your letter.

e How will you close the letter?

Write your letter

5 Now write your letter, using the ideas and some of the language above. Avoid copying whole phrases from the question.

Check and improve your letter

6 Edit your work.

▶ Writing reference pages 207–208

LANGUAGE SPOT: giving directions

a Mark the correct preposition in each sentence.

1 There's a bus *in / on / over* the corner.

2 Get off *on / between / at* the cinema. I'll be waiting for you outside.

3 The car park is right next *to / at / by* my house.

4 Go *past / on / at* the supermarket.

5 You'll see the café *at / on / in* the right at the end of the road.

6 Drive *on / across / at* the bridge.

7 Turn sharp right *in / on / at* the crossroads.

8 Follow the road *across / past / over* the police station at the bottom of the hill.

b Mark the more informal alternative in each pair.

1 I've never *visited / been to* your house before. Could you *give me directions / tell me the way*?

2 *Where do we go / Which direction do we take* once we get to the top of the hill?

3 *You should / I think you ought to* be able to *find the route without any difficulty / find the way OK*.

4 *There's no need / It isn't necessary* to get a taxi but *it is possible that you will / you might* have to wait *a short time / a bit* for a bus.

5 When you *get there / arrive at your destination* you *will notice / 'll see* my house on the other side of the road.

14 How do I look?

Listening (Paper 4 Part 3)

Before you listen

1 a How important are clothes to you? Read the task in Exercise 2a. Discuss each statement A–F and decide how true it is for you.
   EXAMPLE: *I sometimes dress to look smart. It depends on the occasion. For example, I have to look smart when I go to work.*

   b Look at the people in the photos. Which statement A–F best matches each person?

Multiple matching

▶ Task strategy Unit 8 page 58

2 a ☐ You will hear five different people talking about the clothes they like to wear. For questions 1–5, choose from the list A–F what each speaker says. Use the letters only once. There is one extra letter which you do not need to use.

   A I dress to look smart.

   B I buy good quality clothes.

   C I don't care what I wear.

   D I choose clothes that are easy to look after.

   E I wear fashionable clothes.

   F I like to be comfortable.

   Speaker 1 ☐ 1
   Speaker 2 ☐ 2
   Speaker 3 ☐ 3
   Speaker 4 ☐ 4
   Speaker 5 ☐ 5

   b Compare and justify your answers. Listen to the recording again if necessary.
      1 What phrases helped you choose your answer?
         EXAMPLE: 1A – *I tend to wear fairly elegant clothes ... at work ... businesslike ... I don't feel right in casual clothes ...*
      2 Did you need to change any answers the second time you listened?

Discussion

3 Discuss these questions.
   1 Speaker 5 says she is not a *fashion victim*. What does she mean? Why do people become fashion victims?
   2 In your opinion are dress codes a good or a bad thing? Are dress codes becoming more relaxed in your country?

Vocabulary: adjectives

4 a The table shows the usual order of adjectives describing clothes. Complete the table with the words in the list.
      linen   baggy   checked   high-heeled   scruffy   tight   fitted
      cotton   patterned   old-fashioned   navy   viscose   flowery   Scottish

opinion	size/shape	colour	pattern	origin	material
elegant	straight	khaki	striped	French	silk

   b Use some of the words to help you describe what the people in the photos are wearing. Add more words to the table.

   c Look around your classroom. What styles and colours seem to be most popular in your group?

Speaking (Paper 5 Parts 3 and 4)

Lead-in 1 Look at the clothes in the photos. Say which of the clothes you like best and why.

Collaborative task 2 a Work in groups of three.

▸ Task strategy Unit 8 page 59

STUDENT 1: You are the examiner. Turn to page 219 and read the instructions.
STUDENTS 2 AND 3: You are Candidates A and B. Look at the photos on this page. Follow the examiner's instructions.

b Look at the task strategy on page 59. Did you follow each piece of advice?

Discussion 3 Look at the six Part 4 questions below. Which questions ask you to:

a give an opinion?   d make a comparison?
b give personal information?   e describe an experience?
c make a prediction?   f talk about likes or dislikes?

1 Do you enjoy shopping for clothes?
2 Have you ever bought clothes which you didn't like later, or never wore?
3 Do you think we can decide what a person is like by the clothes they wear?
4 How much do you think the media decides what clothes we buy?
5 Do you notice a big difference in the way different generations dress?
6 Do you think clothes will generally be more or less casual in ten years' time?

Sample answer (Part 4) 4 a 🔊 Listen to Julia and Paul answering Question 3 above. Do you agree with what they said?

b Who gave a better answer? In what way was it better?

c Which of these expressions did Paul use to begin his answer? Why did he use it? What is wrong with the other two expressions?
1 *I really haven't a clue. Can I have a different question?*
2 *To be honest, I haven't thought much about it but ... .*
3 *I don't know.*

d Julia added her opinion to what Paul said. Was she agreeing or disagreeing? Which of these expressions did she use? Tick (✓) them. Which of the others could she use?

Apart from that	*Not only that ... .*
And there's another thing	*Actually ... .*

Three-way discussion 5 a Work in groups of three. Take turns to be the examiner and ask two questions each from Exercise 3.

▸ Task strategy Unit 9 page 75

b When you have finished, discuss these questions.
1 Did you give your partner an opportunity to respond to what you said?
2 Did you develop all your answers fully?

Language development 2

Speculation and deduction

Use	Present: modal + verb	Past: modal + *have* + past participle
A *must* Certainty (we are sure it's true)	*The light's on. Ken **must be** at home.*	*Helen's late. She **must have missed** the train.* *He **must have been going** to work. That's* *why he was in a hurry.*
B *can't/couldn't* Certainty (we are sure it's **not** true)	*Jamie **can't/couldn't be** in the library.* *It's closed.*	*It **can't/couldn't have rained/been raining**.* *The roads are dry.*
C *may/might/could* Possibility (we are less sure)	*Sally **may/might/could be** at home. I don't* *know.* *They **may/might/could be watching** us.* *Who knows?*	*She **may/might/could have left** already. I'll* *check.* *The train may have been delayed.*

Present speculation and deduction

1 a Look at the first two columns (Use and Present) in
   the table above and correct the mistakes in the
   sentences below.
   1 Marlie's in her pyjamas. She can be going to bed.
   2 It mustn't be his jacket – it's too small.
   3 That might be Kate. I recognise that voice.
   4 I think that's John's case, so he couldn't be here.
   5 She's decided not to buy those shoes. She could
     have enough money.
   6 Mike must work in a clothes shop – he knows
     nothing about fashion!

   b Look at these bags and make guesses about each
   owner.
   1 *It … a woman. She … rich because … . She …*
     because … .
   2 *It … someone on holiday or … because … .*
   3 *It … either a man or a woman … . I think they …*
     because … .

Speculation/deduction in the past

2 Look at the third column (Past) in the table. Complete
   the conversations with modals of deduction in the
   past and the verbs in the list in the correct form.

   steal   be   have   go   leave   cost   buy

   1 A Have you seen my make-up box in the bedroom?
     B No, you .... it there. I've just tidied up
       and I didn't see it.
   2 A What happened to Sarah's necklace?
     B Nobody knows, but it ....
   3 A Those shoes are so elegant! They ....
       you a lot of money.
     B Not really – I got them in a sale.
   4 A Why is Mark looking so suntanned?
     B He .... to the beach yesterday or else
       he .... a sunlamp!
   5 A I saw Frank at the gym this morning.
     B Oh. So his illness .... very serious!
   6 A Jane's nose looks completely different.
     B She .... plastic surgery!

3 Complete these sentences about yourself and the
   class, and speculate using modals.
   EXAMPLE: *The road outside sounds noisy. There must be*
             a lot of people going home from work.
   1 The teacher looks … . He/She … .
   2 The classroom feels … . It … .
   3 The student next to me seems … . He/She … .

Use of English 1 (Paper 3 Part 3)

Lead-in 1 a Look at the three completed transformations below. In what way has the candidate not followed good exam strategy in each one?

> 1 I'm sure Sue was pleased when she saw the coat you bought her. **been**
> Sue ...*must be pleased*... when she saw the coat you bought her.
> 2 I'd love to go to the cinema tonight, but I've got to do the ironing. **wish**
> I *wish I could go with you to* the cinema tonight, but I've got to do the ironing.
> 3 Although it was raining, I went out without an umbrella. **spite**
> I went out without an umbrella ~~in~~ *despite the fact that* it was raining.

b Check your answers by looking back at the task strategy on page 17.

Key word transformation

▶ Task strategy Unit 2 page 17

2 a Now do the task below. Follow the task strategy and use the Help clues if necessary.

Complete the second sentence so that it has a similar meaning to the first sentence, using the word given. **Do not change the word given**. You must use between **two** and **five** words, including the word given. Write **only** the missing words.

1 There's someone at the door, but it's too early for Kate.
be
There's someone at the door, but .... because it's too early.

2 I'm sure Tom's tired because he's yawning a lot.
must
Tom .... because he's yawning a lot.

3 I'm hungry because the last time I ate was five hours ago.
not
I'm hungry because I .... five hours.

4 He's so relaxed, I'm sure he's just got back from holiday.
been
He's so relaxed, he .... holiday.

5 I'm not fit enough to go in for a marathon.
too
I'm .... go in for a marathon.

6 It was possible that he was having a shower, so he couldn't hear the bell.
may
He .... shower, so he couldn't hear the bell.

7 You can borrow my computer, but you must look after it.
as
You can borrow my computer .... look after it.

8 I'm sure she hasn't left because her coat's still here.
have
She .... because her coat's still here.

9 I think he probably didn't hear me because of the traffic.
could
I don't think .... me because of the traffic.

10 'Have you finished the novel, Lucy?' Tony asked.
she
Tony asked .... the novel.

HELP
➤ Question 1:
You need to use a modal.
➤ Question 3:
Be careful. You need to change the tense.
➤ Question 6:
You need to add a preposition.
➤ Question 7:
An expression which means *provided that*.
➤ Question 9:
Positive or negative verb?

b Answer the questions about the task.
1 Which questions test modals of speculation and deduction?
2 Which modals are in the present and which are in the past?
3 What do the other questions test?

Use of English 2 (Paper 3 Part 1)

Lead-in

1 Discuss these questions.
  1 Do you recognise the designer labels below?
  2 How easy is it to buy counterfeit designerwear?

Lexical cloze

▶ Task strategy Unit 2 page 18

2 a Read the title and text quickly and answer the questions. (Ignore the spaces.)
  1 What do British children think of designerwear?
  2 Why do they have little choice in what they wear?

b Do the task. Follow the task strategy and use the Help clues if necessary.

Read the text below and decide which answer **A**, **B**, **C** or **D** best fits each space. There is an example at the beginning (**0**).

  0 A hope   B trust   C imagine   D believe

LACOSTE
DEVIENS CE QUE TU ES

DESIGNER LABELS

In Britain these days, it seems even very young children (0) **A** to wear a Calvin Klein watch or Nike trainers. Fashion experts (1)............ that brand names have become so important that their followers (2)............ to be able to buy the company's products no matter what. In an (3)............ to get people to buy, these companies' symbols are (4)............ so extensively that they have become more important than the products themselves.

In a (5)............ survey of British teenagers, only one out of 60 would (6)............ that they did not own any designer clothes of the (7)............ fashion. The survey also (8)............ that a staggering 60 per cent are willing to spend the same (9)............ of money on one designer item as on two non-designer items which might do harm to their image. Some people (10)............ that on the (11)............ designer labels offer a guarantee of quality, but 35 per cent said they would rather buy counterfeit designerwear than a non-label (12)............ of clothing.

The survey suggests that we have less (13)............ choice in what we buy than we might think. The media make the decisions about what is (14)............ fashion, and so a whole generation is trying to (15)............ smart by wearing identically labelled trainers, jeans, shirts and sweatshirts.

HELP

➤ Question 4
Not all of these nouns can be combined with *in a(n)*, and only one makes sense in context.

➤ Question 8
This is a verb that often combines with *survey*.

➤ Question 10
In this context, the verb means *state*.

	A	B	C	D
1	demand	request	claim	wish
2	require	suppose	assume	expect
3	labour	effort	work	affair
4	played	used	exercised	acted
5	recent	just	late	present
6	allow	permit	consent	admit
7	final	closing	latest	concluding
8	announced	revealed	exhibited	displayed
9	amount	number	total	cost
10	quarrel	discuss	debate	argue
11	sum	main	whole	general
12	object	item	thing	matter
13	real	authentic	factual	pure
14	on	at	by	in
15	see	watch	look	show

c Which questions test preposition + noun combinations?

Discussion

3 Discuss these questions.
  1 When you buy something, do you compare quality and price or look at the label?
  2 Do you mind paying a lot of money for items with famous labels even though they were cheap to make?

Language development 3

Prepositional phrases

> (LOOK) at these examples of prepositional phrases from the Use of English text opposite.
>
> *Some people argue that **on the whole** designer labels offer a guarantee of quality.*
> *The media make the decisions about what is **in fashion**.*

1 a Mark the correct phrase in each pair.

Before I went to Milan last year for Fashion Week, I hadn't realised that you are expected to look good **(1)** *at all times / at the moment* there. So, when I got off the plane wearing jeans and trainers, people stared at me as if they were **(2)** *in danger of / in favour of* contracting some dreadful disease.

Things went **(3)** *from bad to worse / from time to time*. When I arrived at my hotel, **(4)** *at least / at first* the receptionist assumed I had walked in **(5)** *by the way / by mistake*, and **(6)** *to my surprise / to my advantage* asked the porter to give me directions. After some embarrassment, and **(7)** *in a bad mood / in a loud voice*, I hurried to my room and changed.

(8) *From time to time / From then on* I never went out without dark glasses and my best clothes. But this was, **(9)** *to a certain extent / to the point*, not really me.

b Which noun in each group does not combine with the preposition? Cross it out.
1 **on:** sight   purpose   the beginning
2 **for:** fun   conclusion   a change   nothing
3 **in:** uniform   the end   luck   time to time   conclusion   fashion
4 **out of:** date   fashion   sight   purpose   breath

c Replace the words in italics with a phrase from Exercise 1b.
1 Ellen didn't turn up, so *finally* I decided to go in by myself.
2 My clothes were no longer *a popular style*.
3 The doorman said my pass was *no longer valid*.
4 I'm sorry, I didn't do it *deliberately*.
5 Please be honest with me *in contrast with your usual behaviour*.
6 You're *fortunate* today – I've found your wallet.

Verbs with similar meanings

2 Look at these examples from the Use of English text opposite and mark the correct verb in each pair.

1 ... *very young children* **hope / expect** *to wear a Calvin Klein watch* ...
2 ... *their followers* **hope / expect** *to be able to buy the company's products* ...
3 ... *60 per cent are willing to* **buy / spend** *the same amount of money* ...
4 ... *which might* **make / do** *harm to their image.*
5 ... *they would rather* **buy / spend** *counterfeit designerwear* ...

3 a Complete the phrases with *make* or *do*.

1	your hair	7	a difference
2	friends	8	a job
3	a suggestion	9	an excuse
4	a course	10	something for a living
5	the washing-up	11	a profit
6	a phone call	12	a good impression

b Complete the text below with these phrases.

it would be comfortable   feel so good
a lot of money on it   to show my friends
in cash   trying it on   an Armani suit

I've just bought **(1)**.................................... . I spent
(2).................................... , and paid
(3).................................... not by credit card. I was
looking forward to **(4)**.................................... in the
shop and I hoped **(5)**.................................... , but I
wasn't expecting it to **(6)**.................................... .
And of course it looks great – I can't wait
(7).................................... !

4 Mark the correct word in each pair.
1 That fashion company's profits didn't *raise / rise* at all last year.
2 It all started when Johnson *became / grew* the Director.
3 It soon emerged that he *earned / won* $20 million a year.
4 Their reputation was badly *damaged / injured* by the scandal.
5 He was forced to *retire / resign* and look for another post.
6 But the company's wounds have still not *cured / healed*.

5 Complete the text with an appropriate verb in the correct form.

After I **(1)**............. from work at 60, I
decided to **(2)**............. some money on a day
at Royal Ascot, the most popular horse
race meeting in the UK. I didn't **(3)**.............
to get a ticket for the Royal Enclosure, but
I **(4)**............. the decision that I would
(5)............. my best to look good. So I
(6)............. a dress from a London store and
paid a designer to **(7)**............. me a hat. On
the day, my hat **(8)**............. such a great
impression that I was invited to the Royal
Enclosure and met the Queen!

6 Discuss this question.
What do you like spending money on?

Module 7: Review

1 Complete the text with the words in the list.
linen scruffy elegant patterned cutlery
baggy old-fashioned grill

When we reopened our restaurant we had to get a new oven with a more modern **(1)**............. , and we had to get new **(2)**............. because we'd thrown out our old knives, forks and spoons. We also changed the staff's **(3)**............. old uniforms because they'd got rather dirty and were looking rather **(4)**............. , so they needed to be more up-to-date. We couldn't decide whether to have loose-fitting, **(5)**............. clothes or to go for a smarter, more **(6)**............. style. In the end we decided on something smart but casual; for the men a plain **(7)**............. shirt, and in contrast a **(8)**............. blouse for the women.

2 Replace the incorrect words in italics in these texts with an appropriate form of *must, have to, needn't, can* or *be supposed/allowed to*.

I work in a bank – I'm glad we **(1)** *have to* wear a uniform because I don't like them. But there are some rules about dress. Men **(2)** *can't to* wear a jacket and tie so that they look smart, but they **(3)** *must* take off their jacket in summer so they are comfortable. Women **(4)** *must to* wear trousers or a skirt – they can choose – but it **(5)** *is allowed to* be smart. And we **(6)** *don't have to* wear very bright colours like red and yellow; only black, blue and white.

I was a police officer for 30 years. When I started I bought some strong shoes for all the walking, but I **(7)** *can't* have done that because they give you shoes with the uniform! I **(8)** *must to* wear a uniform at all times – I **(9)** *didn't have to* appear in public without it. I **(10)** *couldn't* take off my coat and jacket in summer, but my head still got hot because I **(11)** *was allowed to* wear my helmet all the time. I liked having a uniform though, because I **(12)** *wasn't allowed to* think about what clothes to wear to work every day!

3 Complete this conversation with modals *can, may, might, could, must* and the correct form of the verb in brackets. There may be more than one possibility.

JILL: Our new designer jeans aren't in the warehouse. Have you any idea where they **(1)**.......................... *(be)*?

ALAN: No, but they **(2)**.......................... *(be)* in the shop. Shall I ring and find out?

SUE: No, they **(3)**.......................... *(be)* there. The shop's closed for the weekend. Someone **(4)**.......................... *(steal)* the jeans from the warehouse during the night. That's the only possible explanation.

ALAN: But how **(5)**.......................... the thieves .... *(get in)*? They **(6)**.......................... *(break in)* through the window, because there's an alarm.

SUE: They **(7)**.......................... *(have)* a key or we **(8)**.......................... *(leave)* a door unlocked by mistake, or perhaps someone **(9)**.......................... *(hide)* in the warehouse when we left last night.

JILL: I'm sure there **(10)**.......................... *(be)* some other explanation.

JOHN: Good morning everyone! Guess what? I sold our new jeans collection to a private buyer last night ... Why are you looking at me like that?

4 Complete the text with the correct prepositions.

(1)............. first, I liked being a waiter, although **(2)**............. time **(3)**............. time it got a bit boring. **(4)**............. the end, though, I felt I was working **(5)**............. nothing, so I decided it was time **(6)**............. a change. I borrowed some money, and opened a Mexican food stall **(7)**............. the end of the High Street, **(8)**............. the corner, next **(9)**............. the bank. I was **(10)**............. luck and, **(11)**............. my surprise, the stall was very successful right **(12)**............. the beginning. **(13)**............. the moment I have 20 stalls in different towns but I would like to have **(14)**............. least 100. My friends say I'm **(15)**............. danger of becoming boring because I work all the time, but **(16)**............. the whole they're very supportive.

5 a Mark the correct word in each pair. Then match the questions in A to the answers in B.

A
1 What job would you like to *do / make*?
2 Would you *make / do* the washing-up in a big hotel?
3 How would you *spend / buy* any money you earned?
4 How often would you like the company to *raise / rise* your salary?
5 Have you any ambitions to *become / grow* a manager?

B
a Every year, or I'd *resign / retire* and get another job.
b I'd buy a lot of clothes. I like to *make / do* a good impression.
c Of course, because it *makes / does* a big difference to your salary!
d No, because I don't *expect / hope* they would pay me very much.
e One where I can *earn / win* plenty of money.

b Answer the questions in A about yourself. Give reasons.

MODULE 8
The important things in life

Overview

- **Reading:** gapped text: paragraphs (Paper 1 Part 3)
- **Language development 1:** reported speech and questions
- **Writing:** discursive composition (Paper 2 Part 2)
- **Listening:** sentence completion (Paper 4 Part 2)
- **Speaking:** interview (Paper 5 Part 1)
- **Use of English 1:** error correction (Paper 3 Part 4)
- **Language development 2:** ways of expressing ability
- **Language development 3:** phrasal verbs with *get*
- **Use of English 2:** key word transformations (Paper 3 Part 3)

Lead-in

- Look at the photos. Which important things in life do they illustrate? Which are the most important for you? Do you think you devote the right amount of time to each?
- 'The man who goes alone can start today; but he who travels with another must wait until that other is ready.' (Henry David Thoreau 1817–1862) What do you think the quotation means? Which is better: to go alone or to wait for the other?

Reading (Paper 1 Part 3)

Before you read

1 a Where or how do people usually meet their future husband/wife in your country? For example:
- in a bar/nightclub
- at work
- through a dating agency
- on public transport
- through friends
- through their parents

b Read the title and subheading of the article opposite and look at the photo.
1 Where did this couple first meet? How do you think it happened?
2 What does the title mean?

Skimming

2 Skim the text and compare your ideas in Exercise 1b. (Ignore the gaps at this stage.)

Gapped text: paragraphs

▶ page 188

Task strategy
- Read the base text and example paragraph carefully.
- Reread the paragraph before and after each gap and think about what information is missing.
- Read the paragraph options and decide which one fits in terms of topic and language links.
- Read the text again with your answers, to check it makes sense.

HELP
➤ **Gap 1**
  Which paragraph in the box explains who *the man sitting opposite* was?
➤ **Gap 2**
  Which paragraph in the box refers to the sleeping businessman?
➤ **Gap 3**
  Look at paragraph 9 (after gap 3). Which paragraph in the box explains who is speaking?
➤ **Gap 4**
  Where is Dennis in paragraph 11 (after gap 4)? Which paragraph in the box fills in the story?

3 Seven paragraphs have been removed from the article. Choose from the paragraphs A–H the one which fits each gap (1–6). There is one extra paragraph which you do not need to use. There is an example at the beginning (0).

a Look at the highlighted words in the example paragraph H. What ideas in paragraphs 1 and 3 of the base text do they link to?

b Do the task. Follow the task strategy and use the Help clues if necessary.

c Compare and justify your answers.

Discussion

4 Discuss these questions.
1 What is your reaction to the way Wendy and Dennis met? Do you think this is a true story?
2 Do you believe that everyone has one 'soul mate' who is just right for them?
3 Which of these things do you think is most important in a successful relationship?
  appearance   shared interests   age   education   sense of humour

Vocabulary

5 a What preposition is used with these verbs? How do they translate into your language?
- go out .... someone
- get on .... someone
- fall in love .... someone

b The text contains a lot of vivid words and phrases. Find the ones that mean:
1 extremely full (para. 3)
2 fall asleep (para. 3)
3 stand up (para. 7)
4 confused and nervous (para. 11)
5 write in a hurry (para. 11)
6 go somewhere very quickly (para. 13)

Meant to be

Five minutes later, and Wendy would never have met Dennis on the tube.

Wendy Hatton, 39, and her husband Dennis, 32, live in London. She works in publishing and he is a scientist.

(1) On 18 October, Dennis and Wendy celebrated their second wedding anniversary – three years to the day after they first met on a crowded underground train in London. But it was only a chance in a million that they got to know each other at all.

0	H

(3) She remembers: 'The tube was packed. There was only one seat free – next to a businessman in a smart suit who had dropped off to sleep. As I pulled out my book, I caught the eye of the man sitting opposite, who gave me a little nod. I smiled briefly and got on with my reading, but I could feel myself blushing.'

1	

(5) Meanwhile, the businessman's head was slowly moving towards Wendy's shoulder as he fell into a deeper sleep. Suddenly, to her horror, it was resting on her arm. Wendy felt very embarrassed, but didn't know what to do.

2	

(7) As Wendy reached her stop and got to her feet, Dennis pushed a note into her hand. To this day, he doesn't know what made him do something so totally out of character, but he felt he couldn't just let her disappear into the night.

3	

(9) 'I'm sorry,' he said. 'I honestly don't make a habit of meeting women on trains, but would you come for a coffee with me?' As Wendy explains: 'I know it seems ridiculous, but it never occurred to me to refuse.' There was, however, nowhere open serving coffee at that time of night, so they ended up going back to Wendy's flat. As she recalls: 'He was so non-threatening that I felt instantly comfortable with him.'

4	

(11) Five minutes later, Dennis rang. 'I was worried that I might never see you again,' he said and started to explain. He'd been as flustered as Wendy was when he'd scribbled down his mobile number on that scrap of paper in the train. On his way home in a taxi, however, the horrible truth had suddenly hit him. He hadn't given her the right number – he could never remember his own number and without thinking, he'd written a more familiar one: that of his ex-girlfriend.

5	

(13) 'It seemed too soon to think about anything like that,' said Wendy. 'But later that night, he had a bad fall – he slipped on some wet stairs and managed to knock himself out. At the hospital, they found my number on a slip of paper in his wallet and called me. I dashed straight round. It was when I saw him lying there on that hospital trolley that it really hit me – I had fallen in love with him.'

6	

(15) They got married the following year. Wendy is still stunned by her good fortune.

A 'So I really had met my Mister Right on an underground train. Fate must have been on my side that first night, because there's no way we'd have met at any other time.'

B Wendy's heart was pounding as she stepped onto the platform, clutching the scrap of paper. Then she felt a tap on her shoulder. It was Dennis, who had run after her.

C Seeing this, Dennis suddenly felt irritated. He gave the man's briefcase a kick to wake him up, and Wendy smiled her appreciation.

D They sat and talked for hours, both realising that they'd met someone special. When Dennis left, he asked Wendy to call him.

E Fortunately, Wendy saw the funny side of this and they started going out regularly. They got on incredibly well. Two weeks later, realising they were made for each other, Dennis proposed.

F This came as a shock to Wendy. She looked him straight in the eye and told him it was out of the question.

G Although Dennis had noticed Wendy as she got on and found her attractive, he was trying hard not to stare. 'Late night trains are horrible enough without strange men staring at you,' he says.

H It was late and Wendy had intended to get a taxi home that night. But seeing the long queue, she changed her mind and got the tube instead; a decision that was to change her life.

Language development 1

Reporting exact words

1 a Iris and George married 50 years ago. In what ways do you think customs before marriage were different then?

b Read what Iris says and answer the questions.
1 Why didn't Iris accept George's proposal immediately?
2 What does she think is the secret of a happy marriage?

> 'George was taking me home from the cinema and he suddenly asked me if I would marry him. I didn't say anything. He asked what the matter was. I replied that we'd only met the previous summer and said that we'd only known each other for a year. He said he loved me. I told him to ask my father, and of course my father said "Yes"! Somebody once asked me what the secret of a happy marriage is. I replied that nothing's changed — the husband still has to be the "king of the castle"!'

c Complete the table with the exact words each person used.

Present simple	Past simple
1 'I .... ?'	He said he loved me.
Present perfect	**Past perfect**
2 'We .... each other for a year.'	I said that we'd only known each other for a year.
Past simple	**Past perfect**
3 'We only .... summer.'	I replied that we'd only met the previous summer.
Imperative	***tell* + object + *to* + infinitive**
4 '............................ my father.'	I told him to ask my father.
***Yes/No* question**	
5 '............................ marry me?'	He asked me if I would marry him.
***Wh-* question**	
6 'What .... the matter?'	He asked what the matter was.
No tense change	
7 'What .... the secret of a happy marriage?'	Somebody asked me what the secret of a happy marriage is.
8 'Nothing ....'	I replied that nothing's changed.

d Why is there no tense change in examples 7 and 8?

▶ Grammar reference pages 203–204

e What do these words and expressions usually change to in reported speech?

today   tomorrow   yesterday   last week
next month   this   here   come   bring

2 Read the conversation, then complete the text below.

TIM: Hi Sarah, it's Tim. What are you doing tonight?

SARAH: You're nosy! Anyway, I'm studying.

TIM: That's boring – come out for a meal instead.

SARAH: Well, I've nearly finished, I suppose. Which restaurant do you have in mind?

TIM: That new Indian one. I went there last week - it's great.

SARAH: OK, then. Can you pick me up?

TIM: Sure. I'll be there at seven.

SARAH: Great. I must be back early though.

Tim took me out last night – he called and asked me
(1)............................ doing, so I said that
(2)............................ studying. He said (3)............................
boring, and told me (4)............................ for a meal
instead. I replied that (5)............................ finished and
asked him which restaurant he (6)............................ in
mind. He told me that he (7)............................ the new
Indian restaurant the previous week, and that
(8)............................ great. I asked him (9)............................
up, and he said he (10)............................ there at seven. I
said I (11)............................ back early.

3 a Tell each other about a person, place or pet that is important to you. As you listen, ask each other questions and make notes.

b Report your conversations to the rest of the group.

Reporting verbs

4 a Complete the 'report' of Sarah and Tim's conversation with these verbs.

accused   agreed   explained
persuaded   suggested

1 Sarah .... Tim of being nosy.
2 Tim .... Sarah to go out for a meal.
3 She .... to go out for a meal.
4 Tim .... going to the new Indian restaurant.
5 He .... that he'd been there before.

b Write the verbs in Exercise 4a in the correct place in the table.

verb + *to*	
verb + object + *to*	
verb + *-ing*	
verb (+ object) + prep + *-ing*	
verb (+ object) + *that* + clause	

c Now write these verbs in the correct place in the table.

admit   advise   apologise   decide
deny   insist   offer   refuse   remind
recommend   warn

d Which verbs in Exercises 4b and c could go into more than one place in the table?

▶ Grammar reference page 204

5 Report what the people say, using a reporting verb from Exercise 4.

1 'You shouldn't get married yet,' Jane's father told her.
Jane's father ....
2 'I started the argument,' Nadia said.
Nadia ....
3 'I don't care what you say, I'm cooking dinner tonight,' Paul said.
Paul ....
4 'Don't go out with Mike, he's not nice,' Adela told her sister.
Adela ....
5 'I'm sorry if I hurt your feelings,' Nick told his girlfriend.
Nick ....
6 'Why don't we stay in this weekend?' Mark said.
Mark ....
7 'I'll carry that bag for you,' Marta said to her mother.
Marta ....
8 'I'm not listening!' Carol said.
Carol ....

6 Complete these sentences about yourself.

1 Once I had to apologise … .
2 … asked me if … .
3 … persuaded me … .
4 I've decided … .

7 Make sentences from these words.

1 Sometimes people / suggest / marriage / old-fashioned idea.
2 Parents often / persuade / children / get married.
3 Some people / insist / get married / while / still teenagers.
4 One couple / admit / get married / for financial reasons.
5 Some couples / refuse / have / religious wedding.
6 A few women / decide / not / change their surname.

Writing Discursive composition (Paper 2 Part 2)

Lead-in   1   Discuss these questions.
1   Would you prefer to live alone or with
    someone else? Why?
2   What are the advantages and disadvantages
    of each? Make notes.

Understand the task   2   Read the task below and answer the questions.
1   WHO is going to read the composition and what is its PURPOSE?
2   Will you just give your OPINION, or will you give both sides of the
    argument (FOR and AGAINST)?
3   What STYLE will you use?
4   What do you think makes a GOOD composition?

> After a class discussion on different kinds of relationships, your teacher has asked
> you to write a composition, giving your opinions on the following statement.
> *Living alone is more enjoyable than living with someone else.*
>
> Write your **composition** in **120–180** words in an appropriate style.

Plan your composition   3   a   Look at your notes from Exercise 1 and decide on the two most
           important advantages and disadvantages.

           b   This is a possible paragraph plan for the composition. Which of your
               points would you include in each paragraph?

               Paragraph 1:   Introduction
                               A general statement/rhetorical question
                               Qualifying the argument

               Paragraph 2:   Advantages
                               Introduction
                               Advantage 1   →   Reason   →   Specific example
                               Advantage 2   →   Reason   →   Specific example

               Paragraph 3:   Disadvantages
                               Introduction
                               Disadvantage 1   →   Reason   →   Specific example
                               Disadvantage 2   →   Reason   →   Specific example

               Paragraph 4:   Conclusion
                               Summing up/Balancing the argument
                               Your overall point of view

Language and content   4   a   Choose the best statement for the composition from each pair below.

A   1   On balance, despite the various advantages,
        it would be difficult to live alone.
    2   Fine, yes there are good things about it, but
        overall, no, not really.

C   1   I like being with my mates, don't you?
    2   Most people would find it lonely and
        miss the friendship.

B   1   I agree with this statement.
    2   Nowadays more people are deciding to live
        by themselves.

D   1   There is nobody to tell us what to do.
    2   We make the decisions – no one else.

       b   Match the statements (A–D) to the paragraphs in Exercise 3.

c Complete some of the expressions below with your own ideas for the composition.

Introducing the topic	First of all I'd like to say that … . The first point I'd like to make is … . I'd like to begin by … . Many people think that … . Some people say/claim … . Why do some people believe … ? However, if that is the case, then why … ?
Advantages	In the first place … . The main advantage is that you are free to … . There is no one else to … . Then there is … . What's more … . Another advantage is that … .
Disadvantages	On the other hand … . Secondly, … . Another disadvantage is … . Last but not least, … .
Summarising	In conclusion (I believe that) … . To sum up, there are arguments … . However, in my view … .

Write your composition

5 Now write your composition, using the ideas and some of the language above. Write your answer in 120–180 words.

Check and improve your composition

6 Which of the statements are true about your composition?
- I have answered the question.
- The sentences and organisation are clear and logical.
- Arguments are followed by reasons and examples.
- Both sides of the argument are given equal treatment.
- It is clear what I think by the end.
- The style is consistent and neutral.
- I have checked: length, grammar, spelling, punctuation and linking expressions.

▶ Writing reference page 213

LANGUAGE SPOT: linking expressions

Mark the correct phrase in each pair.

1 Flatmates often don't get on very well at first. *In addition / In fact*, they can have a lot of arguments.
2 Flats in my city are very expensive for one person. *In addition / In other words*, I like sharing.
3 Most people share household tasks. *For instance / That is to say*, they take it in turns to wash up.
4 I haven't got room for a flatmate. *Moreover / For example*, I like living on my own.
5 I think that house would be too expensive. *Similarly / Besides*, it's a long way from the centre.
6 He's a nice guy to live with. *Nevertheless / What's more*, he needs to help out more.
7 The flat's on the fifth floor, and there's no lift. *Because of this / Even so*, we decided to rent it.
8 It's not very big. *Even so / On the other hand*, it's right in the centre.

16 Hobbies

Kate Moss

Julia Roberts

Listening (Paper 4 Part 2)

Before you listen

1 a You will hear an interview about the hobbies of famous celebrities. Can you match the stars in the photos with their hobbies (A–E)? There is one extra hobby.

   b Check your answers on page 219. Are you surprised? Why do you think they have these hobbies?

Sentence completion

▶ page 190

2 a ▭ You will hear a radio interview with Robin, a psychologist who has studied people's free-time interests and hobbies. For questions 1–10, complete the sentences. Follow the task strategy.

Mick Jagger was pleased to be seen as a ⬚ [1] on young people.

Robin says most people think that ⬚ [2] is a boring hobby.

Robin explains that certain types of hobby may not match a celebrity's ⬚ [3].

In the past, the only free-time interest regarded as suitable by rock stars was ⬚ [4].

Robin found out about Jarvis Cocker's hobby when he asked about a ⬚ [5] his band had made.

Robin mentions ⬚ *and* [6] as things which rock stars tend to collect.

On film sets, Robin found that actors were particularly keen on ⬚ [7].

For young people, the sport called ⬚ [8] is a popular free-time activity at the moment.

Various forms of ⬚ [9] are getting more popular with people of all ages.

Robin finds ⬚ [10] the best activity when he wants to relax.

   b Compare and discuss your answers.

   1 Did you predict the missing information correctly? Were you able to work out whether you needed to listen for the name of an activity, an object or another type of word?

   2 How are the sentences in the task different from the recording?

Vocabulary: idiomatic expressions

3 Ask and answer these questions.

   1 Is there any free-time activity you are really *keen on*?

   2 What is the *fastest-growing* free-time activity in your country? Why is it *all the rage*?

   3 What do you do to *pass the time* if you have to *hang about* waiting for someone or something?

   4 What really helps you to *wind down* after a hard day?

Task strategy

• Read the sentences and decide what kind of information is missing.

• Listen and complete the sentences with a word, number or short phrase from the recording. Write no more than three words. Only use words from the recording.

• Check your answers during the second listening. Don't leave any blanks.

• Check your spelling and grammar.

Rod Stewart

Jarvis Cocker

Speaking (Paper 5 Part 1)

Lead-in

1 In this part of the exam you may be asked questions about:
- your home town
- your family
- your job or your studies
- your spare-time activities
- your future plans.

a Write two possible questions for each topic above. Make notes about your answers to the questions.

EXAMPLE: Home town: Do you live in ....? Yes – here all life.

b Practise asking each other the questions.

Sample answer

2 a 📼 Listen to Anna and Giorgio's Part 1 Interview and answer the questions.
1 What topics did they each talk about?
2 Do you think they made a good first impression?

b 📼 Listen again. Which two words didn't they know? How did they explain them?

Interview ▶ page 191

Task strategy

- Try to be calm and make a good first impression.
- Give full answers, but don't speak for too long.
- If you don't know a word, express it in a different way.
- Listen when your partner speaks.

3 a Work in groups of three. Take turns to be the examiner (asking the questions), the assessor (listening and assessing the candidate) and the candidate.

EXAMINER: Ask some of your questions from Exercise 1a. Don't repeat questions already asked.

ASSESSOR: Make notes on the candidate's performance.

CANDIDATE: Answer the questions. Try to follow the task strategy.

b Discuss the task.
1 How well did you each do?
2 Did you give full answers?
3 Were any answers too short or too long?
4 Did you have to think of different ways of saying things?
5 What would you do differently next time?

Use of English 1 (Paper 3 Part 4)

Lead-in

1 **Discuss these questions.**

1 What are the similarities and differences between these activities?
painting   reading   model making   doing puzzles
2 Which of them have you done?
3 What do you like/dislike about them?

Error correction

▶ Task strategy Unit 8 page 60

2 **Do the task. Follow the task strategy and use the Help clues if necessary.**

Read the text below and look carefully at each line. Some of the lines are correct, and some have a word which should not be there. If a line is correct, put a tick (✓) by the number. If a line has a word which should **not** be there, write the word in the space. There are two examples at the beginning (**0** and **00**).

ORIGAMI

Origami is the Japanese art of paper folding. You may not think	0	✓
this sounds very interesting, but when you will see some of the	00	will
amazing models that can to be made from one sheet of paper, you	1	
start to appreciate of it. First, you must learn the basic techniques.	2	
Then, as soon as you know how many to copy other people's	3	
designs, you can decide on a model of your own, such as a	4	
new dragon. But remember, you are not allowed to use no scissors.	5	
Some people say that origami it began in China, soon after	6	
paper was being invented by a Chinese court official. Origami	7	
then spread from China to Korea and Japan. Others claim that	8	
folding paper is such a natural thing for to do that it began	9	
independently in many countries. No one really knows its origin,	10	
but, what is a certain is that, over time, the Japanese, who are	11	
often said to be gifted with their hands, can were able to turn it	12	
into a decorative art. Today, origami is widely practised, and	13	
there are lots tens of thousands of known folds, attracting the	14	
interest of mathematicians and artists around the world.	15	

HELP

➤ **Line 1**
What grammatical rule about modals is being broken here?

➤ **Line 5**
How many negative forms are needed?

➤ **Line 11**
What kind of word is *certain*, a noun, adjective or adverb?

Discussion

3 **Discuss these questions.**

1 Have you ever tried origami? Would you like to?
2 Is it popular in your country?
3 Do you like making things?

Language development 2

Ways of expressing ability

A Present: *can*
   Can is more common than *be able to* in the present:
   Can you play tennis? No, I can't.

Note: *can* also expresses future ability, if we are deciding now about the future:
   I can play tennis tomorrow if you want.

B Past: *could/was able to*
- Use *could* for general past ability:
  Could you play chess when you were a child?
- Use *was able to*, not *could*, for ability in a specific situation:
  I was finally able to finish my model plane last weekend.
- Use *wasn't able to* or *couldn't* for both general and specific ability:
  I couldn't/wasn't able to beat Tom at squash yesterday.

C Future/Perfect tenses/Infinitive form: *be able to*
   Can has no infinitive or past participle, so we use *be able to*:
   I will be able to play more tennis in the summer.
   Has he ever been able to finish a marathon?
   I might be able to go hiking next weekend.

D Other ways of expressing ability
   *I **know how to** play chess.* (I have learned the skill)
   *I **succeeded in** beating my sister last week.* (suggests some difficulty)
   *I **managed to** beat my brother as well.* (suggests a lot of difficulty)

(**LOOK**) **at the Use of English text opposite and find examples of A–D .**

1 a **Mark the correct form in each pair. Sometimes both options may be correct.**
   1 I *can / manage to* play the piano quite well.
   2 Last week I *was able to / could* get away for a few days.
   3 I *could / have been able to* ride a bike from a very early age.
   4 When I was at school, I *couldn't / wasn't able to* draw very well.
   5 In the last month I *have managed to / knew how to* get some outdoor exercise every weekend.
   6 Once the exams are over, I *will be able to / can* spend more time on my favourite hobby.
   7 I *could / managed to* beat my father at chess eventually, but it wasn't easy.
   8 I was very pleased when I finally *managed to find / succeeded in finding* a salsa class.

   b **Which of the sentences in Exercise 1a are true for you and your partner?**

2 **Complete the sentences with the correct forms of the words in brackets.**
   1 If Paul doesn't get some help, he .... that model. (*able/finish*)
   2 How do you .... so slim? (*manage/stay*)
   3 After five years Nico has .... his driving test. (*succeed/pass*)
   4 I'm afraid I .... to the party on Saturday night. (*can/come*)
   5 After making three big mistakes, Tara realised she .... the match. (*could/win*)
   6 We .... (*know/play*) chess. Can you teach us?
   7 Sergio .... (*able/stay*) ahead at the end, so he lost the race.
   8 I .... (*could/swim*) until I was twelve, but then I learned very quickly.

3 **Complete the sentences with the verb in brackets and *can, could, be able to, succeed* or *manage* in the correct form. There may be more than one possibility.**

I've been making models all my life. When I was nine I had my first Meccano set – you know, those metal pieces which you (1).......................... (*use*) to make machines – and everyone was amazed that I (2).......................... (*put together*) cars that moved.

   Later I (3).......................... (*build*) a larger car which (4).......................... (*reach*) quite high speeds. I also built a radio-controlled machine that looked like a plane, but unfortunately it (5).......................... (*not/fly*).

   Now I make radio-controlled robot machines that battle with other machines. Last year I (6).......................... (*get*) 'Victor', my warrior robot, onto the TV programme *Robot Wars* and we actually (7).......................... (*win*) every battle. I hope I (8).......................... (*carry on*) making machines for many years to come.

Language development 3

Phrasal verbs with *get*

1 a Discuss these questions.
  1 What is the average working week in your country?
  2 Do you think it is too long, too short or about right?

b Read the article and find out what happened in France in 2000.

FRENCH SHORTER WEEK IS A WINNER

Are long working hours **getting** you **down**? Then look at what the French Government did in 2000. They insisted that employers and workers **got together** and negotiated a reduction in the working week to an average of 35 hours a week over a year.

The rest of Europe thought they would never **get away with** it. The Government had to work hard to persuade many employers that it would benefit their company. But they succeeded in **getting** their message **across**.

At first, many employees worked long hours one week and took time off the next. Some employers **got round** the problem by giving workers an average of 15 extra days' holiday a year.

But in general, the experiment **got off to a good start**. In Paris, the traffic decreased on Wednesday afternoons as working mothers **got off** work earlier to spend time with their children. On Fridays, the city emptied as workers took the opportunity to **get away** for a long weekend.

When people **got back to** their workplace, they **got down to** work with renewed energy, according to their employers. The shorter working week has helped reduce unemployment, and enabled everyone to live a better life.

c Look at the verbs and expressions with *get* in bold and decide if these statements are *True* or *False*, according to the text.
  1 Long working hours make some people unhappy. ☐T
  2 Employers and workers in France went on holiday together. ☐F
  3 Europe didn't believe the French Government would succeed in introducing a shorter working week. ☐
  4 The Government was unable to convince employers that a shorter working week was a good idea. ☐
  5 Some employers gave workers longer holidays to avoid a problem. ☐
  6 The experiment was not very successful at first. ☐
  7 Working mothers left work earlier on Wednesday afternoons. ☐
  8 Workers stayed at home for long weekends. ☐
  9 When people returned to work, they did their jobs more energetically. ☐

d What do you think are the disadvantages of a shorter working week?

2 Choose the correct paraphrase A or B for each sentence below.
  1 I get on very well with my sister.
    A My sister and I have a good relationship.
    B My sister and I often go out together.
  2 It's difficult to get by in New York on less than $300 a week.
    A You need at least $300 a week to live in New York.
    B You need at least $300 a week to travel around New York.
  3 It takes ages to get through to the complaints department.
    A Travelling to the complaints department takes a long time.
    B Contacting the complaints department takes a long time.
  4 She always gets round her dad so that he gives her a lift.
    A Her dad gives her a lift because she contacts him.
    B Her dad gives her a lift because she persuades him.
  5 It took me a long time to get over the problem.
    A I didn't recover from the problem for a long time.
    B I didn't tell people about the problem for a long time.
  6 What have the children been getting up to?
    A What have the children been buying?
    B What have the children been doing?

3 a Complete the questions with a phrasal verb from Exercises 1 and 2.
  1 How often do you .... with friends from your previous school/job?
  2 When did you last .... for a long weekend? Did it .... a good start?
  3 What kind of things .... you .... ? What do you do to cheer yourself up again?
  4 Have you ever done anything wrong and .... it?
  5 How well do you .... with your parents?
  6 How much money do you need to .... ?
  7 Do you ever try to .... people so that they do what you want?
  8 What time will you .... lessons today?

b Ask a partner the questions.

Use of English 2   (Paper 3 Part 3)

Lead-in   1   Look at the three completed transformations below. What vocabulary is tested in each one?
a   prepositions following a noun, verb or adjective
b   fixed phrases (e.g. *on purpose, apart from, as a result of/owing to*)
c   phrasal verbs

> 1   I am here as a representative of the Government.
> **behalf**
> I am here .... on behalf of .... the Government.
> 2   They employ extra staff at the weekends.
> **on**
> Extra staff .... are taken on .... at the weekends.
> 3   Prices have gone up sharply again.
> **increase**
> There has been .. a sharp increase in .. prices.

Key word transformation

▶ Task strategy Unit 2 page 17

2   a   Look at the task below. What language is being tested in each question?

b   Now do the task. Follow the task strategy and use the Help clues if necessary.

Complete the second sentence so that it has a similar meaning to the first sentence, using the word given. **Do not change the word given.** You must use between **two** and **five** words, including the word given. Write **only** the missing words.

1   Phil knows how to cheat successfully at cards.
away
Phil knows how to .... at cards.

2   I'll take my CD player because we might want to listen to music.
case
I'll take my CD player .... listen to music.

3   It's time you started some serious work at college.
down
It's time you .... serious work at college.

4   There probably won't be any more customers today.
unlikely
It .... be any more customers today.

5   They had to cancel the outdoor exhibition because of the bad weather.
called
The outdoor exhibition .... because of the bad weather.

6   His kids never take any notice of what he says.
pay
His kids never .... he says.

7   I failed to persuade Tom to take up stamp collecting.
succeed
I .... Tom to take up stamp collecting.

8   Nicola's only punishment was a small fine. **off**
Nicola .... a small fine.

9   We found it difficult to write the story. **trouble**
We .... the story.

10   Don't worry! I'll make him tell the truth.
out
Don't worry! I'll .... him.

HELP
▶ Question 1
You need to use a phrasal verb.
▶ Question 5
You need a phrasal verb and the passive!
▶ Question 7
What preposition follows *succeed*?

c   Compare and discuss your answers.

Exam practice 4

Paper 1: Reading

Part 2: multiple choice You are going to read a magazine article about the author Dick Francis. For Questions 1–7, choose the correct answer **A**, **B**, **C** or **D**.

STRAIGHT FROM THE HORSE'S MOUTH

Dick Francis, the novelist, has written over 40 thrillers based on the world of horse racing.

Dick Francis has written his last book. Actually, he's said that four times before, but every time he decides to stop writing, he meets someone interesting or something unusual happens to him, and he gets the idea for a story which he feels he really must write. This must delight his publishers, for whom he has been turning out best-selling novels at the rate of one a year for the last 40 years. But now, at the age of 80, he may actually mean it about not writing any more. Until something else fires his imagination, of course!

It is hard to see what else Francis could aim for apart from a pleasant retirement. Since 1991, he has lived in the Cayman Islands with his wife, Mary. Both have medical conditions which get worse in the cold, damp weather of their native Britain, so for five months a year Francis works at his desk overlooking the sea. He writes by hand, only transferring his novel to the computer once it is complete. The other seven months, he takes holidays and does research for his books.

Francis' first career was in horse racing, where he trained as a jockey. He rode 74 winning horses and became national champion before being persuaded to take early retirement after suffering a number of terrible injuries. It was at this point that he wrote his first book – his autobiography. But another 16 years, during which he worked as a racing writer for a national newspaper, passed before he attempted another. His first novel was published in 1962 to great acclaim, after which he never looked back.

Although his novels, mostly thrillers based on the world of horse racing, are unfairly looked down on by some educated readers of literature, all sorts of people around the world buy and enjoy them in their millions. Francis provides thrilling stories in which criminals drink champagne while the hero battles against all odds to bring them to justice. Good always wins, although you never know how it will happen until the last couple of pages.

However, Francis' achievements were once called into question recently when a rather critical biography suggested that his books were partly the work of his highly intelligent wife, Mary. Francis denies this, but it is undoubtedly true that once he has **come up with** the idea for a book, researching *line 39* the locations and details of a new story is something they do together as a team. To help him in **this**, Mary *line 41* has, amongst other things, qualified as a pilot and learned photography.

So why does he find it so difficult to give up writing? Up to a point, it's helped to make up for having to give up his first career. The loss of his old life left a huge hole which has never, despite the fame and the great wealth, quite been filled. 'I started writing stories about it, which helped to compensate,' he concludes. But one doesn't feel that he's been so dissatisfied with the result. 40 years of compensation, after all, is not so bad.

1 What do we learn about Dick Francis in the first paragraph?
   A He denies that his writing career is over.
   B Not all of his books have been equally successful.
   C His books are partly based on his own experiences.
   D His publishers have asked him to write another book.

2 Why does Dick Francis choose to live in the Cayman Islands?
   A It's a good place to do his research.
   B Most of his novels are based there.
   C His wife comes from that area.
   D The climate is good for his health.

3 Why did Dick Francis give up horse racing?
   A He was offered a job working for a newspaper.
   B He was advised to do so for medical reasons.
   C He wanted to concentrate on writing a book.
   D He had reached the retirement age for jockeys.

4 What do we learn about Dick Francis' novels in the fourth paragraph?
   A They have won literary prizes.
   B They do not all have happy endings.
   C They appeal to a wide range of people.
   D They deal with all sorts of different subjects.

5 What does *come up with* (line 39) mean?
   A He's suggested something.
   B He's agreed to something.
   C He's invented something.
   D He's accepted something.

6 What does the word *this* in line 41 refer to?
   A doing the research
   B qualifying as a pilot
   C being a photographer
   D having a good idea

7 What impression of Dick Francis' life do we get from the last paragraph?
   A He is happier now than he's ever been.
   B He wishes that he had started writing earlier.
   C Horse racing was the thing he always loved best.
   D He has no regrets about changing career.

Paper 3: Use of English

Part 2: structural cloze

Read the text below and think of a word which best fits each space. Use only **one** word in each space. There is an example at the beginning (**0**).

FISH AND CHIPS

If you ask any British person (**0**)....to.... name the country's national dish, you (**1**)............ probably receive the answer: 'fish and chips'. But that person might be surprised to learn that the chips, or fried potatoes, (**2**)............ probably invented by the French, and that the whole dish only dates back (**3**)............ around 1860. This was (**4**)............ the first shop selling fish and chips together opened in London.

Over the years, the dish has occasionally gone (**5**)............ of fashion, as people tried other types of take-away food (**6**)............ a change – but each time, a new generation (**7**)............ come along and rediscovered it. Now there must (**8**)............ well over 8,000 shops in the UK, eight for (**9**)............ one McDonald's restaurant, and a British-style shop has just opened in New York.

Apart (**10**)............ a few fish-and-chip shops in European holiday resorts, the dish is rarely served abroad. But the owners of the new shop in Manhattan will be offering the 'real thing' from (**11**)............ beginning. They have (**12**)............ running a traditional British tea-shop in New York for several years and so already know (**13**)............ to recreate a 'British experience' for the Americans. But New Yorkers had (**14**)............ be prepared for a shock. As well as covering the food in salt and vinegar, the shop even wraps (**15**)............ in old newspapers – British style!

Part 3: key word transformation

Complete the second sentence so that it has a similar meaning to the first sentence, using the word given. **Do not change the word given.** You must use between **two** and **five** words, including the word given. Write **only** the missing words.

EXAMPLE:

0 You must do exactly what the manager tells you.

   carry

   You must <u>carry out the manager's</u> instructions exactly.

1 Amy went to the doctor's, although she didn't really need to.

   gone

   Amy really .... the doctor's.

2 'Stop running, Lucy!' said her father.

   told

   Lucy's .... running.

3 This season our football team started well.

   got

   Our football team .... start this season.

4 I bet Harry was very upset not to have got a place at university.

   been

   Harry didn't get a place at university so he .... upset.

5 Holly doesn't look well. I don't think she should go to work.

   better

   Holly .... work because she doesn't look well.

6 'I didn't hit your car deliberately!' Emily said to the man.

   denied

   Emily .... car deliberately.

7 The man dived into the river and so was able to escape.

   managed

   The man .... into the river.

8 It's not true that Luke was staying in London last night – I had dinner with him at home.

   can't

   I had dinner with Luke at home last night, so he .... in London.

9 'Don't touch that plate, it's hot!' Alexis said to Tom.

   to

   Alexis warned .... hot plate.

10 It's not a good idea for teachers to use bad language in front of their classes.

   ought

   Teachers .... bad language in front of their classes.

Part 4: error correction

Read the text opposite and look carefully at each line. Some of the lines are correct, and some have a word which should not be there. If a line is correct, put a tick (✔) by the number. If a line has a word which should **not** be there, write the word in the space. There are two examples at the beginning (**0** and **00**).

THE DAY I MET AN OLD FRIEND

I like going bird-watching in the countryside and, after my	0	✔
girlfriend and I split up, a friend of mine suggested me that	00	me
I should and get together with a few other people with the	1	
same hobby and make some new friends. He persuaded at me	2	
to spend a weekend with a group of bird-watchers from his local	3	
club, in what must have be the remotest part of the country.	4	
He said I would easily be able for to find the hotel – it was	5	
the first hand turning on the left after I reached a forest. I was	6	
supposed to be get to the hotel by six o'clock on Friday night,	7	
and he told to me to carry binoculars, so the others could	8	
recognise me on a sight. Anyway, after a good journey, I got	9	
there well before six. When I drove into the car park I saw	10	
another car. I was in the luck! Someone else in the group must	11	
have got there early too much, and I could make at least one friend	12	
before the others arrived. Imagine my surprise when I went inside	13	
and saw a woman what I recognised, with a pair of binoculars,	14	
who looking at me. My ex-girlfriend had had the same idea!	15	

MODULE 9
The consumer society

Overview

- **Reading:** multiple matching: questions (Paper 1 Part 4)
- **Language development 1:** conditionals
- **Writing:** transactional letter (Paper 2 Part 1)
- **Speaking:** individual long turn (Paper 5 Part 2)
- **Listening:** extracts (multiple choice) (Paper 4 Part 1)
- **Use of English 1:** structural cloze (Paper 3 Part 2)
- **Language development 2:** number and concord
- **Use of English 2:** word formation (Paper 3 Part 5)
- **Language development 3:** money and banks; forming verbs

Lead-in

- What are the benefits and drawbacks of the consumer society?
- 'The people who do all the work don't get their fair share of the profits.'
  How far do you agree with this?

Reading (Paper 1 Part 4)

Before you read

1 a Imagine you want to set up your own business. Which of the following do you consider to be the most important factors for success?
- having your own money to start up with
- funding from an organisation
- having parents in the same business
- specific skills
- help from friends
- energy and determination
- talent and creativity
- supplying a real need

b Look at the title and subheading of the article opposite and the photos. Can you guess what kind of business each young person started?

Skimming and scanning

2 Skim and scan the text to check your guesses in Exercise 1b.

Multiple matching: questions

▶ Task strategy Unit 9 page 68

3 a You are going to read an article about five young people who have each made a lot of money by setting up a business. For Questions 1–15 choose from the people (A–E). The people may be chosen more than once. When more than one answer is required, these may be given in any order. There is an example at the beginning (0).

HELP

➤ **Question 1**
If something is *hard* you can say it's *a struggle*.

➤ **Questions 3/4**
You are not careful with money if you *splash it around*.

➤ **Question 5**
A sum of money given by an organisation is *a grant*.

➤ **Questions 6/7**
Look for different ways of referring to *money*.

➤ **Question 9**
If you ignore someone, you *take no notice of them*.

➤ **Question 15**
Another word for *prize* is *award*.

Which young person:		
is carrying on a family tradition?	**0**	**C**
found one part of the work hard at the beginning?	1	
says that he/she prefers to be his/her own boss?	2	
is careful with money?	3	4
got financial help from an organisation?	5	
says he/she does the work mostly for the money?	6	7
feels that further education would be a waste of time?	8	
ignored advice that he/she was given?	9	
says he/she finds the work itself the main motivation?	10	
has turned an initial disappointment to his/her advantage?	11	12
says he/she enjoys the creative side of the business most?	13	
is willing to give up aspects of his/her social life for the business?	14	
has received a prize in recognition of what he/she has achieved?	15	

b Compare and justify your answers.

Discussion

4 Work in groups.
The Government runs an award scheme for promising small businesses. Annual awards are given in each of these categories:
- Best service to the local community
- Most innovative
- Most helpful to young people

You are members of the judging panel. Decide which of the businesses described in the article you will offer an Annual award to. Prepare to explain your choice.

How to get rich young

*We asked five young people who have already made their fortunes in business
to tell us the secret of their success.*

A Justin Etzin (24)

It all began when Justin, then aged 16, tried to get into a nightclub and was turned away for being too young. 'After that, I kept on at them until they let me organise an under-20s party,' he recalls. 'They were expecting about 50 teenagers to turn up, but I'd found them 2000!' Justin continued organising parties during his school holidays and had made enough money by the age of 18 to buy himself a speedboat. Today, at 24, he has other business interests and a fortune of £2 million. But Justin's not just in it for the financial rewards. 'What gets me excited is coming up with new ideas,' he insists, 'and at the end of the day, I'd rather be healthy than wealthy.'

B Lee Allen (20)

Lee set up a sports-coaching business when he was just 18. 'Everyone warned me that it was a tough world and I wasn't experienced enough to take the disappointments that lay ahead. But I felt confident in what I was doing, so I took no notice of them. My idea was to coach children with special needs and because nobody else was doing that, I got a grant and an office from Mencap, a charity which helps the mentally disabled. At first, the administrative side was a real struggle, but I managed it somehow.

Last year, the company I set up won an award for being the most innovative new business in the country. That means more to me than any money I've made out of it.'

C Charlotte Crossley (18)

Charlotte first started up in business when she was 12 years old, making and selling things called 'friendship bracelets.' She paid friends to make them, using her materials and designs. Since then, she's expanded into make-up and hair accessories and was able to buy herself a brand new car last year. 'My father and grandfather were both successful businessmen, so making money seemed natural to me. I am studying for A levels, but I have decided not to go to university because I don't feel it has anything more to offer me. Work excites me more. I can work all day every day without a break and never get bored. I lead a hectic life – socialising, schoolwork and working. But why not? I feel like I can have it all.'

D Thomas Jones (16)

Tom started playing with computers when he was five. By the time he was 12, he'd set up his own web page on the Internet and was selling advertising space. He now runs a profitable business from his bedroom at home, offering a complete Internet and technical support service. 'I have always been fascinated by computers. I'm proud of what I've achieved. But what really keeps me going is the thought of all the cash I'm making. I think it's worth giving up a few nights out in case there aren't the same opportunities later. Our projected turnover for next year is £160,000, so the business is a huge investment.' Apart from buying himself a few treats, Tom mainly reinvests his money. 'But I still intend to go to university, no matter how much I make, because in any business you need to keep up with new developments.'

E Louise Bagshawe (25)

Things haven't always gone well for Louise. After she'd written her first book at the age of 23, a publisher took one look at it and advised her to tear it up and start again. 'I was so upset by their reaction,' said Louise. 'that I bought a pile of very successful novels and read them from cover to cover to remind myself of my business aim. This was to write 'popular' books that would earn me a fortune by working for myself, rather than earning peanuts working for someone else.' The rewritten novel became the first of four 'blockbusters' which have made Louise a millionaire. However, she does not splash her money around. 'I'm saving up for a rainy day. Who knows what will happen in the future.'

**Vocabulary:
prepositions and particles**

5 Fill in the missing prepositions or particles and complete the sentences about yourself.

1 My friends keep .... at me to … .

2 I'm very good at coming .... with ideas for … .

3 I take no notice .... people who … .

4 I would find it hard to give .... … .

5 I think it's important to keep .... with … .

Language development 1

Conditionals

1 a Would you go on a TV quiz show to try to win money?

b Read the conversation about a quiz show and answer the questions.

1 How do you win a million pounds on the show?

2 Why didn't the man win a million pounds?

A
That new quiz show is on TV – what do they have to do to win?

B
If they answer fifteen questions correctly, they win a million pounds. It's a bit more complicated than that but *if you watch it now, you'll soon learn the rules.* Last week a man got the last question wrong and lost everything. *If he had got it right, he would have won a million.* It looks easy when you're watching it on TV, but I'm sure *if I went on the show, I wouldn't win a million!*

c Complete the Example column in the table with the clauses in italics from the conversation.

Explanation	Example	Form
Always true. (*if = when*)		
Possible and likely.		
Unlikely or imaginary.		
Unreal in the past.		

d Now complete the Form column in the table with these forms:

- *If* + past + *would*
- *If* + past perfect + *would have*
- *If* + present + present
- *If* + present + future

2 a Make questions with *if* about the present or future using the ideas below. Choose conditionals depending on how likely you think the situation is.
1 you / win a lot of money / what / you / spend it on?
2 a classmate / ask / lend / small amount of money / what / you / do?
3 a classmate / ask / lend / large amount of money / what / you / do?
4 what / you / do / you / need change for the phone?
5 you / find a lot of money / what / you / do?
6 what / you / do / lose / wallet or purse?
7 what / you say / you / receive / a present you / not / like?
8 what / you / buy / you / go / shopping at the weekend?

b Ask each other the questions.

3 Write a sentence with *if* about each sentence in the story below.
1 James forgot to set his alarm, so he overslept.
   If James had remembered to set his alarm, ...
2 Because he was late for work, he got the sack.
3 He couldn't find another job, so he started his own business.
4 The business was a great success because it was such a good idea.
5 James worked very hard and became a millionaire.
6 So, he became very rich because he didn't set his alarm!

▶ Grammar reference page 202

'Mixed' conditionals

4 a Complete the quotes below with *last week* and *now*.

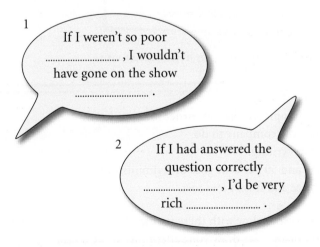

1 If I weren't so poor .... , I wouldn't have gone on the show ....

2 If I had answered the question correctly .... , I'd be very rich ....

b Match the examples above to these explanations.
A If I had done something different in the past, the present would be different.
B If the present were different, I would have done something different in the past.

5 Mark the correct form in each pair.
1 If I *earned / had earned* more money in my present job, I *wouldn't have gone / wouldn't go* for a job interview last week.
2 Sheila *would be able / would have been able* to go out now if she *hadn't spent / didn't spend* so much on clothes yesterday.
3 If the company *had invested / invested* more when they started, their profits *would be / would have been* bigger now.
4 If I *were / had been* the President, I *would reduce / would have reduced* taxes as soon as I was elected.
5 She *would be / would have been* at home now if she *didn't miss / hadn't missed* her train.
6 Paul *couldn't have bought / couldn't buy* that new car last week if he *weren't / hadn't been* so well-off.

Conjunctions

6 Mark the correct conjunction in each pair.
1 The company will be a success *even if / provided that* we all work hard.
2 *If / Unless* we get more customers, we will have to close.
3 *As long as / Even if* we get more customers, we may have to close.
4 We can move to bigger offices *as long as / unless* they're not too expensive.

▶ Grammar reference pages 201–202

7 Complete the sentences with *if, unless, even if, provided that, as long as* and put the verbs in brackets into a suitable tense.
1 .... you .... (*hurry up*) we .... (*miss*) the bargains in the sale!
2 We buy our office equipment from PenCo, who .... (*give*) us a discount .... we .... (*spend*) more than £100.
3 I'm really grateful. .... you .... (*not/lend*) me the money I .... (*have*) big problems now.
4 I .... (*come*) with you .... you .... (*pay*). What time does it start?
5 .... we .... (*not/run*) a business we .... (*have*) more free time, but we enjoy what we do.
6 .... Peter .... (*ask*) me to invest in his company, I .... (*not/be*) able to. I didn't have enough money at that time.
7 .... you .... (*not/work*) so many hours you .... (*not/feel*) so tired all the time. You really should try it.
8 .... this .... (*be*) my company, I .... (*not/spend*) so much on new computers last year.

Writing   Transactional letter (Paper 2 Part 1)

Lead-in   1   Discuss these questions.

1   Have you ever wanted to complain about something? Did you actually complain?
2   Why might you complain to:
a shopping website? an airline? a hotel?

Understand the task   2   Read and analyse the task. (See Unit 5, page 42, Exercise 2.)

You have just played a new game and you were very disappointed. Read this advertisement carefully and the notes you have made. Then write a letter to the Director of the company complaining about the advertisement, saying that future advertisements should not be so misleading.

TRY YOUR LUCK

The new game that gives everyone the chance to win.

No! £5 a game!

• Big cash prizes — *only one!*

• Very low cost

no, it isn't! — • Easy to play

but 50% goes on 'administration'!

• All money goes to charity

Claims within three months through your local store.

Write a **letter** of between **120** and **180** words in an appropriate style. Do not write any postal addresses.

Plan your letter   3   Put these paragraph topics in the best order for your letter.

A   What you expect the company to do.
B   Saying why you're writing.
C   Not easy to play and 50 per cent goes on 'administration'.
D   Only one big prize and it isn't low cost.

Language and content   4   a   Complete the phrases below with these verbs.

object   complain   draw your attention   express
I am writing to:

1   .... about your advertisement.
2   .... to your advertisement.
3   .... my dissatisfaction.
4   .... to some incorrect statements.

b Match the inappropriate phrases in A with the more appropriate ones in B.

A

1 I was so fed up.

2 Just listen to me.

3 Get it right from now on.

4 That's what you say but it's a lie!

B

a You should be less misleading in future.

b I would just like to point out that...

c We were assured that that is the case but it turns out not to be true.

d I was very disappointed.

c Complete some of the phrases in the box in an appropriate way for your letter.

I am writing to complain about/to say that I am not happy with … .	*To my surprise/horror/disappointment … .*
	Furthermore … .
You say/said that … . In fact, … .	*Even worse, …/Even more worrying, … .*
You do not seem to realise that … .	*When it comes to the question of … .*
My first/second complaint is that … .	*I must insist that/you … .*
The problems do/did not stop there.	*I must ask you to … .*

d Match the sentence halves in A and B.

A

1 *If I had known*
2 *I think it is awful that*
3 *I would rather have*
4 *I really feel you should*

5 *I was very surprised*

B

a when I found out there was only one prize.
b be more careful what you say in future.
c you charge so much for a single game.
d that there was only one big prize, I would not have entered.
e sent my money directly to the charity.

e Complete one of the phrases below to finish your letter.
I hope that in future … .
If I do not get a satisfactory reply, I will have no alternative but to … .
Please can you assure me that … .

Write your letter 5 Now write your letter using the ideas and some of the language above. Avoid copying whole phrases from the question.

Check and improve your letter 6 Edit your work.

▶ Writing reference page 206

LANGUAGE SPOT: spelling

a Which words in English do you commonly misspell?

b Correct the incorrect spellings of these words:

surprized   seperate   recomend   unneccesary   comittee   imediately
sincerly   recieve   begining   embarassed   advertisment   writting

c Correct the spelling mistakes in these sentences. The number in brackets tells you how many mistakes there are in each sentence.

1 When I tryed the jeans on at home I found they were too lose. (2)
2 The casette does not help foriegn students with pronounciation. (3)
3 The college principle refused to give us there acomodation adress. (4)
4 Unfortunatly the medecine had no affect at all. (3)
5 I am definately not going to buy your products again untill you have developped a more responsable approach. (4)

18 Spending money

Speaking (Paper 5 Part 2)

Lead-in

1 a Look at the photos. What do they show?

b What are the advantages and disadvantages of each type of shopping?

Paraphrasing

2 Talk about things you can see in the photos using these expressions.

Speaking strategy

If you don't know the exact word for something, try to say it in another way.

It's/They're like (a)	It's something you need when ... .
It's a kind of	It's when you ... .
You use it/them to	

Individual long turn

▶ Task strategy Unit 6 page 45

3 a Work in groups of three.

Task 1

STUDENT 1: You are the examiner. Follow the instructions for Task 1 on page 220.

STUDENTS 2 AND 3: You are Candidates A and B. Look at the photos on this page. Follow the examiner's instructions. Candidate A: pretend you don't really understand the task, and ask the examiner to repeat the instructions.

b Work in groups of three again.

Task 2

STUDENT 2: You are the examiner. Follow the instructions for Task 2 on page 221.

STUDENTS 1 AND 3: You are Candidates A and B. Look at the photos on page 220. Follow the examiner's instructions. Candidate B: pretend you don't understand the question, and ask the examiner to repeat it.

c Discuss the two tasks you have done.

1 Were you able to keep going without too many hesitations, and paraphrase when necessary?

2 Were you reasonably accurate? Could you be understood easily?

3 Did you complete the task according to the instructions?

Listening (Paper 4 Part 1)

Before you listen   **1** Look at the listening task below. Decide what you have to listen for in each case. Mark key words. Question 1 is done for you.

Extracts (multiple choice)

▸ Task strategy Unit 12 page 89

2 🔲 You will hear people talking in eight different situations. For questions 1–8, choose the best answer A, B or C.

1 You hear an advertisement on the radio. What is being advertised?
  A a television game show
  B a computer game
  C a board game ▢ 1

2 You overhear a man talking to a shop assistant.
  What is the man doing?
  A returning faulty goods
  B asking for his money back
  C trying to get some goods delivered ▢ 2

3 You hear a radio phone-in programme on the subject of cars.
  What is the caller doing?
  A blaming someone for something
  B asking for advice about something
  C making a suggestion about something ▢ 3

4 You hear part of a radio play. Where is this scene taking place?
  A in a bus station
  B in a shop
  C in a library ▢ 4

5 You overhear a woman talking in a travel agency.
  What is she complaining about?
  A the attitude of the staff towards her
  B the accuracy of the information she was given
  C the fact that her holiday arrangements were changed ▢ 5

6 You overhear a man talking on his mobile phone.
  Who is he talking to?
  A a hotel receptionist
  B a conference organiser
  C his secretary ▢ 6

7 You hear a radio announcement about a new service that's being offered in London.
  In which sector has the service been most successful so far?
  A travel
  B health
  C entertainment ▢ 7

8 You hear the beginning of a radio programme on shopping.
  What is the programme going to be about?
  A the disadvantages of e-commerce
  B a new idea that will help e-commerce
  C research into the success of e-commerce ▢ 8

Discussion   **3** Answer these questions.

1 Have you taken *faulty goods* back to a shop? What was the problem? Did you get a *cash refund* or *credit note* for goods?

2 Have you ever felt you were being *ripped off* by a shop or service provider?

3 In what sort of situations should travel agents or airlines *pay compensation* to travellers?

4 Do you ever make purchases from *mail-order catalogues*? Do you think it's a useful service?

Use of English 1 (Paper 3 Part 2)

Lead-in

1 Discuss these questions.
  1 When you buy something, do you always try to get the lowest price?
  2 What do you think is the best way to get the lowest price? Bargaining, comparing catalogues, window shopping?

Structural cloze

▶ Task strategy Unit 4 page 30

2 a What advice would you give someone doing the exam task below? Check your answer with the task strategy on page 30.

  b Read the title and text below and correct the information in these statements.
   1 The *Good Deal Directory* tells you where to buy expensive, high quality items.
   2 Noelle Walsh doesn't visit many shops, but she knows where to buy the cheapest things.
   3 She hates shopping at weekends, but she always does the family shopping.
   4 Noelle believes her work makes a big difference to people.

HELP

➤ Questions 1, 4, 7, 9, 13
Singular or plural?
➤ Question 12
They or *there*?

  c Do the task. Follow the task strategy and use the Help clues if necessary.

  Read the text below and think of a word which best fits each space. Use only **one** word in each space. There is an example at the beginning (**0**).

The Professional Shopper

Noelle Walsh publishes the *Good Deal Directory*, which tells you where you can buy things at (**0**) ...the... lowest prices, so her job is to go shopping. An amazing total of 100 shopping trips in eight hours (**1**).............. not uncommon for her, and she usually manages to get to more than 1,400 different shops a year. (**2**).............. even the most addicted shopper, visits as many shops (**3**)............ she does.

One of her main strengths (**4**)............ that she knows where to find any item without too (**5**)............ effort, and she knows where to get it more cheaply than anyone (**6**)............ . The majority of people (**7**)............ too little

stamina and patience to be great shoppers. Noelle may be a shopaholic, but she's a very discerning one (**8**)............ never buys rubbish. However, she hates shopping in her spare time, and her family (**9**)............ the shopping at the weekends.

According (**10**)............ Noelle, people think she's richer than she is because her house is so well-furnished, but really it is all (**11**)............ knowing where to buy things. Of course, she knows (**12**)............ are many more important jobs than hers. No one (**13**)............ going to live or die on (**14**)............ she finds out, but she feels her job (**15**)............ help improve other people's lives just a little.

Discussion

3 Discuss these questions.
  1 Would you like to do what Noelle does? Why/Why not?
  2 Do you think her job is important?

Language development 2

Number and concord

Verbs and their subjects should always 'agree':
She hates shopping. (singular subject, singular verb)
They think she's rich. (plural subject, plural verb)

But it's not always easy to know whether to use a singular or plural verb form!

A Nouns which are followed by a singular verb form:
   ***The news** is boring.* (athletics, politics, the United States)
   ***Ninety dollars** is a lot of money.* (two weeks, thirty miles)
   ***Neither of** these shops sells what I want.* (each of, none of)
   ***Hardly anyone** goes to the market now.* (almost nobody)
   ***Everyone** uses the supermarket.* (everybody, every + noun)
   ***More than one** small shop has closed.* (one of, every one of, a total of)

B Nouns which are followed by a plural verb form:
   ***People** do their shopping on the Internet.* (the police, the military)
   ***Glasses** are becoming cheaper.* (scissors, trousers, jeans)
   ***A number of** chain stores have opened.* (both of, all of, the majority of, a couple of, a group of)

(LOOK) **at Questions 1, 4, 7, 9, 13 in the Use of English text opposite. How many answers did you get right?**

C Some nouns can be followed by a singular **or** plural verb:
   the bank, the government, the family, the team, the school, the public

   *The staff **is getting** bigger.* (the staff as a single body.)
   *The staff **are** not very happy with their pay.* (the staff as a collection of individuals)

1 Tick (✓) the correct sentences. Correct the incorrect ones.

   1 Everyone think it's a good idea.
   2 The majority of us agrees.
   3 The police are coming.
   4 Neither of them know what to buy.
   5 These jeans doesn't fit.
   6 The news about the market wasn't good.
   7 Ten euros aren't very many.
   8 The company has a great future.
   9 This scissors doesn't cut very well.
   10 The United States have a new President.

2 Complete the text with the correct present simple form of the verb in brackets.

VARIETY – THE SPICE OF LIFE?

Every supermarket **(1)**............. (*sell*) up to 40,000 products but, according to recent research, many people **(2)**............. (*feel*) that greater choice **(3)**............. (*cause*) unnecessary stress. Hardly anyone **(4)**............. (*want*) 600 kinds of coffee! Both men and women **(5)**............. (*seem*) to want less choice when shopping.

And none of us **(6)**............. (*be*) happy to have more choice in other aspects of our lives; a significant number of people **(7)**............. (*say*) they find it hard to decide what to eat. But whereas only ten per cent of men **(8)**............. (*admit*) that deciding what to wear is difficult, nearly all of the women **(9)**............. (*confess*) that this is a major problem for them.

However, none of those interviewed really **(10)**............. (*want*) to change things. Too much choice is better than no choice at all!

it/there

A *There + be* = something exists:
   ***There are** many more important jobs than hers.*

B *It* replaces a noun:
   *What's her job like? **It's** quite interesting.*

C *It* is also used as an 'empty' subject to talk about time, weather and distance:
   It's nine o'clock. It's warm today. It's 24 km. to L.A.

3 Complete the sentences with *it* or *there* and the correct form of *be*.

Money-saving tips

(1)......................... lots of easy ways to save money. Here are just a few.

• When you go food shopping, **(2)**........................... important to write a list, and only buy what you need.

• When choosing a restaurant, see if **(3)**........................... a 'set meal'. **(4)**........................... usually a lot cheaper.

• These days **(5)**........................... many phone companies which offer cheap calls, so **(6)**........................... a good idea to compare different companies.

4 Answer these questions with *it* or *there*.

   1 What's the date today?
   2 How far is it from your house to where you work or study?
   3 What shopping tips can you think of for your town?
      EXAMPLE: *There's a great market … .*

Use of English 2 (Paper 3 Part 5)

Lead-in

1 Discuss these questions.
  1 What features and facilities do you appreciate most in a shop?
  2 What things frustrate you when shopping?

Word formation (A)

▶ Task strategy Unit 4 page 32

2 Do the task. Follow the task strategy and use the Help clues if necessary.

Read the text below. Use the word given in capitals at the end of each line to form a word that fits the space in the same line. There is an example at the beginning (**0**).

HELP
➤ Question 3
  Do you need a prefix, suffix or both?
➤ Question 5
  Be careful with your spelling!
➤ Question 9
  Is this an adjective or a noun?

KEEPING CUSTOMERS HAPPY

For years, there has been a (**0**) .disturbing. trend in stores to cut   **DISTURB**
costs, by reducing staff to the (**1**)............. possible number. Many   **SMALL**
stores, however, now realise that when employees are (**2**).............   **EXHAUST**
from overwork they become (**3**)............. with their customers.   **PATIENCE**
Nordstrom, an (**4**)............. well-respected US department store,   **EXTREME**
knows that customers find poor service (**5**)............. . The company   **STRESS**
believes that the helpfulness and (**6**)............. of its staff contribute   **FRIEND**
to customer (**7**)............. . One of Nordstrom's customers was about   **SATISFY**
to take a (**8**)............. recently and left her ticket on the counter.   **FLY**
The assistant was so worried when he caught (**9**)............. of it that   **SEE**
he took a taxi to the airport and, to the woman's (**10**)............. ,   **AMAZE**
delivered the ticket himself. Now that's service!

Discussion

3 Do you think service in stores is getting better or worse these days?

Word formation (B)

4 Do the task. (See the instructions above.)

When most European countries first adopted the euro, the UK still used pounds sterling. However, some stores accepted the euro as payment.

HELP
➤ Question 6
  Do you need a prefix, suffix or both?
➤ Question 7
  Is this an adjective or an adverb?

TEENAGER STRIKES LUCKY

During the (**0**) introduction of the euro in Europe, one teenager   **INTRODUCE**
in Britain did very well. He changed £10 into the new (**1**)............. ,   **CURRENT**
took it into the (**2**)............. department store he could find, and left **NEAR**
with £130 worth of (**3**)............. goods plus £10 change in sterling.   **DESIGN**
The reason was the staff's (**4**)............. to realise that, in all the   **FAIL**
(**5**)............. , the wrong exchange rate had been put into their computer **CONFUSE**
system, so that instead of 1.6 euros, the store charged an (**6**)............. **BELIEF**
0.6 euros to the pound! (**7**)............. , when the boy realised what had   **NATURE**
happened, he turned his (**8**)............. into more euros and bought   **WIN**
more luxury goods. And he has all the (**9**)............. to prove it! 'We   **RECEIVE**
will be carrying out a thorough (**10**)............. ,' said an embarrassed   **INVESTIGATE**
company spokesperson yesterday.

Discussion

5 Discuss these questions.
  1 Do you think the teenager was right to do what he did?
  2 What would you have done in that situation?

Language development 3

Money and banks

1 Work with another student and complete this quiz. You might want to use a dictionary to help you.

Money Vocabulary Quiz

1 Write A (= have money) or B (= not have money) next to each of these expressions.

1 I'm *a bit short of* cash today.
2 The Jacksons *live from hand to mouth*. They simply *can't make ends meet*.
3 Lucinda's *very well off*.
4 Peter *can't afford* to pay the rent this month. He's very *hard up*.
5 We're *quite comfortable*.
6 Are you *in debt*?
7 Mr and Mrs Johnson are very *wealthy*.

2 Mark the correct preposition in each pair.

1 Asha borrowed a camera *to / from* Alex.
2 Will you lend the car *to / from* us for the weekend?
3 The company owes its success *to / from* its excellent training programme.
4 You're spending too much money *to / on* food.
5 Mike's wasting most of his money *on / into* clothes.
6 Ella paid some money *on / into* her bank account.
7 Carl changed his money *in / into* euros.
8 We've made a lot of money *from / by* computer games.
9 I've got no money *by / on* me.
10 When Sue died, she left her money *at / to* her brother.

3 a In each of these groups, three of the noun phrases do not combine with the verb given. Cross them out.

1 pay:
by cheque   the tickets   a deposit   you back   in cash
by credit card   a fine   a big profit   a bill   a discount

2 earn:
a fortune   a living   a refund   your keep   a receipt
a good salary   interest   a loan

b Replace the incorrect word in italics with a word from question 3a.

1 You get a huge *account* if you book in advance so you'll save a lot of money.
2 Investors made a big *salary* of ten per cent when their shares went up in value.
3 Don't worry! You'll get a full *withdrawal* if you cancel the holiday.
4 I see from my bank statement that rates of *investment* are very low at the moment.
5 We've just had a huge electricity *receipt*; I don't know how we're going to pay it.
6 Tara may earn *a good profit* every month but she's always in the red.
7 Mike got a £60 *cost* when the police caught him speeding.
8 How soon do you have to pay back that *lend* that you got from the bank?

2 How do you record topic vocabulary? For example, you could record money expressions in your vocabulary book under different 'money' headings, such as:
Banks   Shopping   Money Problems.

3 Discuss whether these statements are true for you.
1 I like shopping for bargains.
2 I think credit cards are dangerous.
3 I'm happy to lend people money.
4 I believe in living – and spending – for today.
5 I think online banking is convenient but not secure.

Forming verbs

4 a Look at the four ways of forming verbs shown in the table.

No change	Internal change
clean (adj.) → clean (v.)	hot (adj.) → heat (v.)
'record (n.) → rec'ord (v.)	
Prefix	**Suffix**
large (adj.) → enlarge (v.)	modern (adj.) → modernise (v.)

b Decide what changes, if any, to make to these words to form verbs, and complete the table above. Use a dictionary if necessary.
critic (adj.)   dry (adj.)   strength (n.)
fat (adj.)   import (n.)   wide (adj.)
choice (n.)   danger (n.)   calm (adj.)
length (n.)   name (n.)   blood (n.)

5 a Match these definitions with verbs in Exercise 4.
1 ....: to talk about someone's faults
2 ....: to bring goods into a country
3 ....: to make someone unsafe
4 ....: to decide which thing

b Which of the verbs in Exercise 4 would you use to talk about:
• *making* a road *bigger*?
• *renovating* an old house?
• *making* a class *quieter*?
• *making* a bridge *stronger*?

Module 9: Review

1 Match the sentence halves in A and B.

A

ADVICE TO ONLINE SHOPPERS

1 Only buy from an online company if
2 Unless you're confident about the company,
3 Provided that you keep a record of your order,
4 Don't place an order from an Internet café even if
5 You can always return your goods if
6 Internet shopping is perfectly safe

B

---

a you should get your money back if things go wrong.
b as long as you use your common sense.
c don't send them your personal details.
d you're not happy with them.
e you know something about them.
f you're sitting by yourself.

---

2 Complete the second sentence so that it has a similar meaning to the first sentence.

1 This car's too expensive for me to buy.
I'd buy this car if ....

2 I didn't know the computer had a fault when I sold it to you.
If I .... , I
.... sold it to you.

3 Mark spent a lot of money on a holiday so he hasn't got enough to buy a new TV.
If Mark .... , he
.... a new TV.

4 The shop won't reserve the bike without you paying a deposit.
Unless .... a deposit, the
shop ....

3 a Complete the sentences with one appropriate word in each space.

1 People .... all their shopping there because
.... is a very big store.

2 A large number of its customers .... been going there for years.

3 Nearly .... uses a credit card and ....
anyone pays in cash.

4 .... are lots of bargains every day so .... is best to get there early.

5 .... takes a long time to get served because
.... aren't enough shop assistants.

6 Every member of staff .... very pleasant to the customers.

b Think of a shop that you often use. Which sentences in Exercise 3a are true for that shop?

4 Mark the correct word in each pair.

1 A: I'm *well off / hard up* at the moment. Can you lend me some money?
   B: Why don't you borrow some *from / to* your brother?

2 A: Do I get a *discount / profit* if I pay the bill immediately?
   B: No, but you have to *pay / earn* interest if you pay it late.

3 A: I'm earning ten per cent *interest / refund* on my latest investment.
   B: Lucky you! You'll make a good *salary / profit* by the end of the year.

4 A: My father's just paid some money *on / into* my bank account.
   B: I hope you don't waste it all *on / into* CDs.

5 A: I'm getting a *loan / debt* from the bank.
   B: When will you *earn / pay* it back?

5 a Complete the text with verbs formed from the words in italics.

I'd really like to **(1)**.............. (*modern*) my family's flat. First I'd like to **(2)**.............. (*long*) the passage and **(3)**.............. (*large*) the kitchen. To do that, I'd have to make the living room smaller and **(4)**.............. (*strong*) the walls so they wouldn't **(5)**.............. (*danger*) anybody. Also, it would probably be a good idea to **(6)**.............. (*wide*) the door.

Then I'd **(7)**.............. (*clean*) all the walls, paint them white and **(8)**.............. (*choice*) some stylish furniture to put in.

But whenever I mention it to my parents, they **(9)**.............. (*critic*) my plans. They get angry and I have to **(10)**.............. (*calm*) them down. They obviously like our flat just the way it is!

---

b In what ways would <u>you</u> like to change your house/flat?

MODULE 10
Out and about

Overview

- **Reading:** multiple matching: headings (Paper 1 Part 1)
- **Language development 1:** passives
- **Writing:** report (Paper 2 Part 2)
- **Listening:** matching statements (Paper 4 Part 4)
- **Speaking:** individual long turn (Paper 5 Part 2)
- **Language development 2:** past tenses and other expressions for hypothetical situations
- **Use of English 1:** key word transformations (Paper 3 Part 3)
- **Use of English 2:** structural cloze (Paper 3 Part 2)
- **Language development 3:** verbs and participles + prepositions; verbs with similar meanings

Lead-in

- How far do you have to travel to your place of work/study? to take part in leisure activities?
- What method of transport do you use to get there?
- How often do you travel abroad? How do you travel?
- Read this quote by the contemporary travel writer, Paul Theroux. How far do you agree or disagree? 'Travel is only glamorous in retrospect.'

19 Travel

Reading (Paper 1 Part 1)

Before you read

1 Look at the title and subheading of the article opposite and at the photos.

  1 What groups of people do you think are choosing to take a 'year out'?

  2 What kind of preparations would you need to make before going away?

  3 How do you think these travellers pay for their year out?

Skimming and scanning

2 Skim and scan the text to check your answers to Exercise 1.

Multiple matching: headings

▶ Task strategy Unit 13 page 98

3 Choose the most suitable heading from the list A–I for each part (1–7) of the article. There is one extra heading that you do not need to use. There is an example at the beginning (0).

  a Look at the example (0–I). Which words in the heading match the key phrases in the text? Mark them.

  b Do the task. Use the Help clues if necessary.

HELP
➤ Heading A
  Initial means *at the beginning.*
➤ Heading D
  Only one paragraph refers to local laws that travellers should obey.
➤ Heading E
  Which paragraph refers to an *increasing range* of destinations?
➤ Heading G
  Which paragraph refers to problems that could happen unexpectedly?

> **A** Initial investments
>
> **B** Not such an easy option
>
> **C** Having realistic goals
>
> **D** Keeping within the regulations
>
> **E** Ever-expanding horizons
>
> **F** Good timing is needed
>
> **G** Planning for the unexpected
>
> **H** Employees join the trend
>
> **I** An idea is established

  c Compare and justify your answers.

Discussion

4 Work in pairs. You have the opportunity to take a year out to travel with a friend.

  1 Decide what countries you want to visit. Plan your itinerary.

  2 Make a list of the things you need to do in advance (e.g. book tickets, arrange insurance, etc.).

  3 Make a list of clothing and equipment you will need to take with you. Bear in mind you will need to carry everything with you. Think about the problems you might need to deal with (e.g. getting bitten by insects, etc.).

Go for it

We all need holidays, but a standard two or three-week break isn't enough if you really want to experience a different culture and way of life. That's why so many people are opting to take a 'year out' and go on much longer trips. Dan Shaw reports.

0 | **I**

It was 'hippy' student types who first discovered the so-called 'backpacker trail' in the 1960s and 1970s. This
5 was a new kind of cheap extended holiday which involved travelling on local public transport, avoiding tourist resorts and carrying all you needed in a rucksack on your back. In subsequent decades, it became a
10 must for the more adventurous type of student. Up to 20,000 British youngsters take time out for travel before going to university, with similar numbers opting to go after
15 their course has finished.

1 |

In some ways, this 'year-out' boom can be seen as an effect of the wider general availability of travel. What is surprising, however, is the way that
20 what were once exotic long-distance destinations have now become commonplace. Young people today are undertaking journeys which, in an earlier age, might have made them
25 famous explorers. Global adventure, it seems, is no longer just for the brave few.

2 |

Don't be put off by thinking you have to be a student in order to make
30 the leap: being in a secure job isn't the barrier that it once was. A growing number of working people are opting to clear their desks and head for the open road. Those who
35 are lucky enough to be with a

progressive company may even find that their positions can be held open for them for a given period of time.

3 |

Indeed, those in employment are
40 arguably in a better position than humble students; at least they have a regular income and access to some ready cash. All trips will require a certain amount of money up front to
45 get you on the road. New gear, outward flights, visas, inoculations and a good travel book are all things that must be obtained before you set off.

4 |

50 In the old days, travellers were encouraged to take photocopies of their passport, visas, tickets etc. in case they were lost or stolen. This meant quite a bundle of papers to add
55 to the weight of your kit. Now, with worldwide access to the Internet, you can scan copies of all your paperwork onto a PC and then email it to a Hotmail account before you leave
60 home. Then, if you lose any vital documents, you can get hold of them easily, saving a lot of time and hassle.

5 |

With the average gap year costing around £2,000, a lengthy multiple-
65 destination trip may only be possible if you can earn your keep along the way. An estimated 40 per cent of people on a gap year undertake paid employment during their trip. Even
70 in countries where foreign visitors

are entitled to earn money, this will only be possible if you apply for work permits and other documents. Without these, you lose your rights.
75 If you suffer an accident in the workplace, for example, or should your employer decide not to pay you, you're not covered by the law.

6 |

Farm work is popular amongst
80 backpackers, but be warned: it's not all about lazy afternoons picking fruit in the sunshine. The days are often long and the work physically demanding. Don't underestimate the
85 weight of a sack of grapefruit around your neck or a huge bunch of bananas on your shoulder. I picked both on a year out a few years ago and I'm still feeling the effects!

7 |

90 Although farms do provide plenty of work for travellers every year, hostels are often packed to capacity with backpackers all after the same jobs. This type of work is usually given on
95 a first-come-first-served basis, so arriving at the right moment could be essential. But once you've got it, the work's usually fairly well-paid, good fun and a great way to get to know
100 the local community while saving enough money to pay for the bus fare to your next adventure.

Now you know where to begin, all that's left is to start your research
105 and plan which country or countries you want to visit.

Language development 1

Passives

1 a What type of holiday accommodation do you prefer? For example, a hotel, a self-catering apartment or a campsite? Why?

b Read the text and answer the questions.
1 What are the advantages of these self-catering apartments?
2 What possible disadvantages are there?

These high-quality self-catering apartments are grouped around a central garden. They were built in traditional Ottoman style by a team of highly skilled workers and have been designed to stay cool in summer. The rooms have all been decorated to a very high standard. A buffet breakfast is served around the pool for a small charge, and a patio barbecue area is now being constructed. This will soon be completed and available for use by guests. Shops can be found within ten minutes' walk. We are sure you will have a wonderful holiday.

c Mark examples of the passive in the text. Why is the passive used here?

d Complete the table with examples from the text.

Passive form	Examples
Present simple	1 ....
	2 ....
Present perfect	3 ....
	4 ....
Past simple	5 ....
Present continuous	6 ....
will future	7 ....
Modal	8 ....

▶ Grammar reference page 203.

2 a Correct the mistakes in the text below.

Our apartments **(1)** *be situated* on the Bosphorus and have excellent views. Last winter they **(2)** *was redecorated*. Internet facilities **(3)** *can been supplied* by our local representative on request and fire safety equipment **(4)** *have be installed* by the time you arrive.

Smaller apartments **(5)** *are been built* at the moment and will be available next year. Also, permission **(6)** *has be given* to build two all-weather tennis courts.

Availability **(7)** *must checked* with our Booking Service before making a reservation and guests **(8)** *will asked* to pay a deposit.

b Rewrite the sentences below to make them more formal, beginning with the words in italics.
1 We are always improving *our facilities*.
2 We have modernised *all our flats* in the last two years.
3 We have equipped *our kitchens* to the highest standards.
4 Maids will make *the beds* daily.
5 You can find *the holiday village* two kilometres outside the town.
6 The village offers *a full programme of sports activities*.
7 We received *very few complaints* last year.
8 Guests may accommodate *extra people* on the sofa beds.
9 Our brochure indicates *the maximum number of people allowed in each caravan*.
10 You must return *keys* to reception on departure.

3 Read the information in the box and answer the questions.

A The passive is sometimes used to put new information at the end of the sentence for emphasis. Mark the correct form:
*The telescope is very useful. It was invented **by / from** Galileo.*

B Some verbs (e.g. *give, lend, send, show, promise*) can have two objects – a person and a thing.
Active: *The rest of the class gave **Tania a present**.*
Which passive structure below do you think is more common, 1 or 2?
Passive:
1 ***Tania was given a present** by the rest of the class.*
2 ***A present was given to Tania** by the rest of the class.*

C In news reports, passive structures are often used with *say/believe/consider/think*, etc. Complete these sentences with an appropriate verb.
1 *We think Filton is planning ten new hotels.* (active)
*Filton **is** .... **to be planning** ten new hotels.*
(passive + infinitive)
2 *Analysts say that SkyFly's profits are up.* (active)
*It **is** .... **that** SkyFly's profits are up.* (passive + *that* clause)

D Some verbs are followed by an infinitive without *to* when active but an infinitive with *to* when passive. Mark the correct forms.
Active: *They heard the crowd cheer a long way away.*
Passive: *The crowd was heard **cheer / to cheer** a long way away.*
Active: *They made me empty all my bags at Customs.*
Passive: *I was made **empty / to empty** all my bags at Customs.*

▶ Grammar reference page 203.

---

4 Complete the responses. Put the verbs in the most appropriate passive form.

1 A: Did Mozart compose the Unfinished Symphony?
B: No, I think (*Schubert / compose*)
....

2 A: Why was there so much confusion?
B: Some people (*give / two tickets*)
.... by mistake.

3 A: Why has that man been arrested?
B: I think he (*see / steal*) ....
some things.

4 A: When's the next election?
B: It (*believe / Prime Minister / call*)
.... one soon.

5 A: What's Megan doing next year?
B: She (*promise / place*) ....
at university.

6 A: Didn't Marie Curie discover penicillin?
B: No, I'm pretty sure (*Fleming / discover*)
....

7 A: Do the police know how the burglar got in?
B: Yes, he (*think / hide*) .... in the museum during the day.

8 A: What a lovely antique shop. Oh, no, I've broken a vase!
B: Oh dear, I think you (*make / pay*)
.... for that!

5 a Rewrite the text below to make it more formal, in the style of a report, using passives where appropriate.

The town has changed a lot in the last 30 years. They have pulled down all the old factories and replaced them with hi-tech science parks. Many of the residents feel it's unfortunate that they also demolished one of the older schools, as they will have to send their children by bus to the next town. Some people say that they will build a brand new school in the town in the next few years when the Government provides extra funding. The newer residents in particular will appreciate that.

---

b What changes have happened in your town? What changes are planned for the future?

Golders Green Parade, London, circa 1920

Golders Green Parade, London, 2001

Writing   Report (Paper 2 Part 2)

Lead-in
1 Discuss these questions.
  1 Which form of public transport do you prefer?
  2 What is good and bad about public transport where you live?

Understand the task
2 Read the task below and answer the questions.
  1 How many PARTS are there to the task?
  2 Decide how personal or formal your STYLE should be. (Remember your ROLE and who you are reporting to.)

▶ Writing reference page 214
  3 What will make the reader think it is a GOOD report?

> It is difficult for students to get to your college. Public transport is not very good and the college car park is very small. A committee has been set up by the Principal to analyse the problem and to recommend what the college should do. You are on the committee, and you have just had your last meeting.
>
> You have been asked to write a **report** for the Principal.
>
> Write your **report** in **120–180** words in an appropriate style.

Plan your report
3 a Make notes under these headings. Then choose the two most important points under each heading.

Public transport	Car park	Possible solutions
buses every hour	more students have cars	write to bus company

b Match these pieces of advice to the paragraphs below. Some go with more than one paragraph.

Paragraph 1: Introducing the report
Paragraph 2: Describing the first problem
Paragraph 3: Describing the second problem
Paragraph 4: Summarising and recommending

a Focus on a maximum of two points.
b State the purpose of the report.
c Give a clear summary of the situation.
d Describe how you got the information.
e Only give relevant information.
f Give just one or two recommendations.
g Give the facts briefly and clearly without strong personal opinions.

c Match your notes in Exercise 3a to the paragraphs (1–4).

d Choose the best subject heading for your report from the ones below.

A Cars, buses and trains   B To and from college   c Student transport

e Think of a suitable heading for each paragraph (1–4).

Note: You could number (1, 2, etc.) or use bullet points (•) within a paragraph to make your points clearer.

Language and content

4 **a** Complete these possible topic sentences for each paragraph.
   Paragraph 1: The report describes … .
   Paragraph 2: In recent years public transport … .
   Paragraph 3: Another problem is that … .
   Paragraph 4: On balance, it is recommended that … .

b Use these phrases to complete the sentences in the table below.
   1 … unwilling to walk far.
   2 … examine the problem of student transport.
   3 … the car park quickly becomes full.
   4 … the most realistic solution is to improve the bus service.
   5 … students we spoke to, the car park is used by a lot of visitors.
   6 … we interviewed students from all parts of the college.
   7 … cannot afford the taxi fare from the station.
   8 … that the car park is extended into the sports field.
   9 … the buses often run late.

Introduction	*The aim of this report is to … .*
	In order to prepare this report … .
Reporting findings	*It appears that the majority of students … .*
	The only problem is that … .
	Most students seem … .
	Not surprisingly, … .
	According to … .
Concluding and making recommendations	*All things considered, … .*
	We have no hesitation in recommending … .

c Mark the best word in each pair to complete this advice:
   Use *active / passive* verb forms in a report to make it *more / less* formal and *more / less* personal.

Write your report

5 Now write your report using some of the language above. Avoid copying whole phrases from the task. Use passive forms where appropriate.

Check and improve your report

6 Edit your report using this list.
   • Is the information relevant? (Have I included everything, but not too much?)
   • Is the style clear and neutral?
   • Does the report feel balanced? (Are different viewpoints presented fairly?)

▶ Writing reference page 214

LANGUAGE SPOT: passive report structures   ▶ Grammar reference page 203

a Complete the second sentence so that it has a similar meaning to the first.

1 The Principal is thought to be in favour.
   It is thought ....
2 About 50 students are expected to attend.
   It is expected ....
3 Many of the students are reported to have had difficulties getting a visa.
   It is reported ....
4 Some of them are said to have left early.
   It is said ....

b Now do the same with these sentences, using *supposed to*.

1 People say that good public transport reduces the number of private cars.
   Good public transport ....
2 People say that air travel is becoming easier and cheaper.
   Air travel ....
3 People say that we travel further on holiday these days.
   We ....
4 People say that travel broadens the mind.
   Travel ....

20 Going out

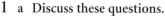

Listening (Paper 4 Part 4)

Before you listen

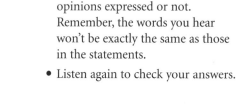

1 a Discuss these questions.

1 What do you like doing on a night out? Do you do any of the things in the pictures?

2 Are the leisure facilities in your area good or do you have to travel to another town for entertainment?

b Look at the listening task in Exercise 2a.

1 How many speakers will you hear? What will they talk about?

2 Think about your own town. Which of the statements 1–7 would you agree with?

Matching statements

▶ page 191

Task strategy

• Check carefully if statements have a positive or negative meaning. Mark key words.

• During the first listening, decide if the statements exactly match the opinions expressed or not. Remember, the words you hear won't be exactly the same as those in the statements.

• Listen again to check your answers.

2 a 🔊 You will hear two people discussing facilities in the small town where they live. For questions 1–7, decide which views are expressed by either of the speakers and which are not. Write YES next to those views which are expressed and NO next to those which are not expressed.

1 Employment opportunities in the town seem to be on the decline. ☐ 1

2 It's easy for people to travel to the nearest city for free-time activities. ☐ 2

3 The leisure centre provides facilities for all age groups. ☐ 3

4 Public transport to nearby towns is inadequate. ☐ 4

5 Entertainment facilities in the town were better in the past. ☐ 5

6 The existing shopping area should be expanded to provide extra leisure facilities. ☐ 6

7 Improved leisure facilities may cause some social problems to increase. ☐ 7

b Compare and justify your answers. Listen to the recording again if necessary.

Discussion

3 If your town had money to develop <u>one</u> of the following amenities, which would you choose? Why?

• indoor shopping mall with Food Hall (food outlets)
• multiplex cinema with car park
• arts centre including theatre and workshops
• sports stadium
• lending library with multi-media facilities
• community college
• park with boating and leisure facilities

Vocabulary: get

4 Replace the phrases with *get* from the recording with another word or expression.

1 How do they *get there* (e.g. to the next town)?

2 The town is *getting* too big.

3 … when large numbers of kids *get together* …

4 … that sort of behaviour is much more likely if they're just hanging around *getting* bored …

Speaking (Paper 5 part 2)

Lead-in

1 a **Look at the statements below about Paper 5 Part 2 and discuss whether they are *True* or *False*.**

1 You each have a minute to talk about the photos.
2 The task has two parts.
3 You should describe each photo separately.
4 You will be asked for your opinion.
5 You can interrupt while the other candidate is speaking.
6 You each give a short response after the other candidate's long turn.

b **Look at the list of things (1–7) you might have to do in the exam. Match them to the expressions (a–g) below.**

1 talk about similarities
2 talk about differences
3 speculate about a picture
4 give opinions on something
5 ask for clarification/check information
6 paraphrase
7 correct what you say

---

a *It could be a ... . It looks ... .*
b *So, do you want me to ... ?*
c *The one on the left looks ... while the other one ... .*
d *It's like a ... .*
e *What I meant was ... .*
f *As far as I'm concerned, ...*
g *Both of these ... .*

---

c **Add any other expressions you can think of.**

Individual long turn

▶ Task strategy unit 6 page 45

2 a **Work in groups of three.**
Task 1
STUDENT 1: You are the examiner. Follow the instructions for Task 1 on page 221.
STUDENTS 2 AND 3: You are Candidates A and B. Look at the photos on this page. Follow the examiner's instructions.

b **Work in groups of three again.**
Task 2
STUDENT 2: You are the examiner. Follow the instructions for Task 2 on page 220.
STUDENTS 1 AND 3: You are Candidates A and B. Look at the photos on page 221. Follow the examiner's instructions.

c **Discuss and compare your answers. Did you:**

- follow the instructions?
- speak clearly and accurately?
- use appropriate vocabulary?
- communicate what you wanted to say?
- use the full minute?

Language development 2

Past tenses for hypothetical situations

1 Read the comments in the thought bubbles and answer the questions below.

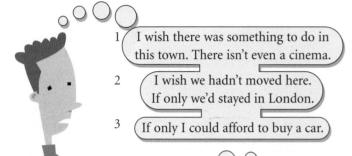

1 I wish there was something to do in this town. There isn't even a cinema.

2 I wish we hadn't moved here. If only we'd stayed in London.

3 If only I could afford to buy a car.

4 John is always complaining. I wish he would stop being so negative.

5 If only the Town Council would provide more facilities for young people.

1 Which comments refer to a situation in:
   • the present   • the past   • the future?
2 What verb form is used in each case?
3 What's the difference between *wish* and *if only*?

---

wish + **past versus** *wish* + *would*

A We use *wish* + past when we want our own situation to be different.
   I wish I ~~**would have**~~ *a fast car.* ✗
   I wish I **had** *a fast car.* ✓

B We use *wish* + *would* when we want another person or thing to be different.
   I wish you ~~**changed**~~ *your mind about moving.* ✗
   I wish you **would change** *your mind about moving.* ✓

▶ Grammar reference page 205.

2 What would you say in these situations? Use *I wish* or *If only.*
   EXAMPLE: Your friend has invited you to go out tonight, but you have too much work to do.
   I wish I could go out tonight. If only I didn't have so much work to do.
   1 You regret dyeing your hair bright red. Blonde suits you better.
   2 Your brother is always borrowing your car without asking. You want him to stop.
   3 It's late, but you can't afford to get a taxi home, so you'll have to take the bus.
   4 You're watching a film at the cinema but you don't like it at all.
   5 Your flatmate has been in the bathroom for a long time and you want to use it yourself.

3 Complete these sentences about yourself.
   EXAMPLE: I wish ...I was taller... but I'm not.
   1 I wish .... but I'm not.
   2 I wish .... but I haven't.
   3 If only .... but I can't.
   4 I wish .... but I didn't.
   5 If only .... but he/she won't.
   6 I wish I could ....

Other expressions for hypothetical situations

A *It's (about/high) time* + object + past
   It's (about) time we **went** *home.* (we should go now)
   Don't you think it's time you **got** *a job?* (implies criticism)

B *would rather* + object + past or past perfect
   I'd rather you **didn't smoke** *in the house.* (I don't want you to)
   I'd rather you **hadn't gone out** *last night.* (but you did)

C *as though/as if* + past or past perfect
   You're looking at me as if/as though I **was/were** *crazy.* (but I'm not)
   You look as if you **had seen** *a ghost.* (but you haven't)

---

4 Decide which option A or B best shows the meaning of each sentence.
   1 It's time you learned how to drive.
      A You haven't learned yet.
      B You don't have time to learn.
   2 I'd rather you hadn't invited him to the party.
      A You didn't invite him.
      B You invited him and I'm annoyed.
   3 You talk as if you had done all the work yourself.
      A You did all the work.
      B You didn't do all the work.

5 Complete the sentences with an appropriate verb in the correct form.
   1 It's about time you .... how to use that computer properly. You've had it long enough.
   2 My brother treats me as if I .... a child, even though I'm only two years younger than him!
   3 No, I don't want to phone her. I'd rather you .... her.
   4 He talks as though he .... her but he hasn't. He's only seen her on TV.
   5 Why did you buy me such an expensive gift? I'd rather you .... something cheaper.

6 Complete the sentences in an appropriate way.
   1 The film was awful, wasn't it? I wish ... .
   2 My room's in a complete mess. It's about time ... .
   3 My best friend sometimes acts as if ... .
   4 I don't have any money left! If only ... .
   5 My brother has gone to work abroad. I'd rather ... .

Use of English 1 (Paper 3 Part 3)

Lead-in 1 What advice would you give to these two candidates?

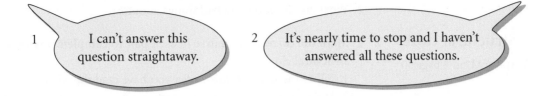

1 I can't answer this question straightaway.

2 It's nearly time to stop and I haven't answered all these questions.

Key word transformation

▶ Task strategy Unit 2 page 17

2 a Do the task below. Remember – you usually have to make more than one change to the original sentence.

Complete the second sentence so that it has a similar meaning to the first sentence, using the word given. **Do not change the word given**. You must use between **two** and **five** words, including the word given. Write **only** the missing words.

1 I'm sorry I didn't go to the party last night.
   wish
   I .... to the party last night.

2 I would prefer you to phone Jane.
   rather
   I .... Jane.

3 Tim advised Sarah to book a table at the Indian restaurant.
   you
   'If I .... a table at the Indian restaurant,' Tim said to Sarah.

4 I live quite near the cinema.
   far
   The cinema .... my house.

5 I regret lying to my brother.
   had
   I .... my brother the truth.

6 The theatre was practically empty.
   hardly
   There .... the theatre.

7 If we'd arrived a moment later, we would have missed the film.
   in
   We arrived .... the film.

8 People say that dancing is good for your health.
   supposed
   Dancing .... good for your health.

9 You should stop going to late night concerts.
   time
   It's .... to late night concerts.

10 I'd rather you didn't use my car.
   mind
   Would .... my car?

b Answer these questions about the task.
   1 Which questions test language from the opposite page?
   2 How does question 10 require you to make more than one change?

Use of English 2 (Paper 3 Part 2)

Lead-in

1 Discuss these questions.
   1 Is clubbing popular with young people in your country?
   2 What are the good and bad things about it?

Structural cloze

▶ Task strategy Unit 4 page 30

2 a Mark the correct alternative in each pair to complete this advice on the structural cloze.
   1 Fill in the spaces *before / after* you have read the whole text.
   2 Spend a *short / long* time on each space.
   3 Put *one / more than one* word in each space.

   b Read the title and text and find out:
   1 how clubs have changed in recent years.
   2 why they are successful.

   c Do the task.

   Read the text below and think of a word which best fits each space. Use only **one** word in each space. There is an example at the beginning (**0**).

Clubbing

Nightclubs have changed (**0**) ..from.. something enjoyed by the few (**1**)............ a way of life for the young. A few years ago, no one had heard (**2**)............ most nightclub DJs. Now they are celebrities and can earn up to £25,000, which (**3**)............ big money for a two-hour session. Superclubs like London's *Ministry of Sound* (**4**)............ once only known locally. Now they are well-known nationally and they have even set (**5**)............ dance festivals around the world. Clubs in the Mediterranean, popular with teenagers from all over Europe, have become more respectable compared (**6**)............ those that were active in the 1990s. These are clubs (**7**)............ rely on the quality of the music and the DJ.

One top DJ, Judge Jules, thinks seriously (**8**)............ what he does and why he does (**9**)............ . For him, the success of the music depends (**10**)............ a number of things. The beat must (**11**)............ linked to the beat of the human heart and the crowd must come together as a group; it is not just about listening to music. He believes strongly (**12**)............ the social value of clubbing. He says that in today's society we are more afraid of meeting (**13**)............ neighbours than we used to be. So there is less opportunity to meet new people and people who differ (**14**)............ us. Clubs give us a wonderful opportunity to do that, (**15**)............ if it may be difficult to hear each other!

HELP
➤ Question 3
   Singular or plural?
➤ Question 5
   A phrasal verb.
➤ Question 11
   Active or passive?

   d Which questions test verb + preposition combinations?

Discussion

3 Discuss these questions.
   1 Do you agree with Judge Jules about today's society?
   2 Do you think clubs are a good place to meet new people? Why/Why not?

Language development 3

Verbs and participles + prepositions

> **(LOOK)** at these examples from the Use of English text opposite.
>
> A Verb + preposition
> *A few years ago no one had heard **of** the DJs who work in nightclubs.*
> *The DJ Judge Jules believes **in** the social value of clubbing.*
>
> B Participle + preposition
> *Clubs have become more respectable compared **to/with** those in the 1990s.*

1 Mark the correct prepositions in each sentence. Use your dictionary if necessary.

Do you belong **(1)** *to / at / on* that new nightclub? It's situated **(2)** *in / at / on* the town centre, where the cinema used to be. I thought they would be prevented **(3)** *to / from / at* building a nightclub there; a lot of people objected **(4)** *at / for / to* it because they said the town couldn't cope **(5)** *by / at / with* so many people late at night. But there haven't been too many problems, and it's helping the town's economy recover **(6)** *to / from / by* the closure of the cinema.

2 Complete the sentences with the correct prepositions.

1 *for/on*
   We had to wait half an hour .... a table, but it was nice to eat out and be waited ....

2 *about/of*
   We're thinking seriously .... starting a band. I suppose we'll have to think .... a name for it!

3 *from/to*
   The manager seems resigned .... the fact that the leisure centre is losing money; I expect he'll resign .... the job quite soon.

4 *as/for*
   He's always been known .... a singer more than an actor. He's best known .... his love songs.

5 *of/from*
   I turned down Andy's invitation to the cinema last week, because I hadn't heard .... the film. I haven't heard .... him since then.

6 *for/to*
   It was a great party, but I'll have to apologise .... the neighbours .... making so much noise.

3 Complete the text with the correct prepositions.

The rise of the Internet café

easyInternetCafé is a company that believes **(1)**............ itself. When it opened its first *easyEverything* Internet cafés in 1999, few people believed it would succeed **(2)**............ making a profit. The company Chairman, Stelios Haji-Ioannou, firmly believed that people would be keen to communicate **(3)**............ each other on the Internet, but at that time not many people agreed **(4)**............ him.

Today, however, his Internet cafés are crowded **(5)**............ up to 800 surfers at any one time. In fact, they're busier than ever, even compared **(6)**............ the exciting early days when they first opened. Customers have to pay separately **(7)**............ instant coffee, which is the only thing that people sometimes complain **(8)**............ .

No matter what you think **(9)**............ the Internet, no one can deny that many people around the world now depend **(10)**............ it in their daily lives. *easyInternetCafé* already has sites in New York and several European cities and has plans to concentrate **(11)**............ South America. It's also looking forward **(12)**............ extending its business in Africa.

Verbs with similar meanings

> Some verbs of perception have similar meanings, but are easily confused:
> *It is not just about **listening to** music.*
> *... it may be difficult to **hear** each other.*

4 Complete the sentences with the verbs in the correct form.
1 *look/see/watch*
   a I've .... everywhere for my sunglasses. Have you .... them?
   b Do you want to dance? No, I'd rather just sit and ....

2 *gaze/peer/stare*
   a You shouldn't .... at people. It's rude.
   b I .... at the stage, but I was too far away to see much.
   c We stood and .... at the wonderful view.

3 *hear/listen*
   a I .... hard but I couldn't .... what she was saying.
   b I could .... to his songs all day – he's got a beautiful voice.
   c We're going to .... that new band at the weekend.

4 *feel/touch*
   a I could .... something .... my shoulder.
   b .... how soft this material is.
   c My brother doesn't let anyone .... his CDs.

Exam practice 5

Paper 1: Reading

Part 1: multiple matching (headings)

You are going to read a magazine article about supermarkets in Britain. Choose the most suitable heading from the list **A–H** for each part (**1–6**) of the article. There is one extra heading which you do not need to use. There is an example at the beginning (**0**).

A Making the shopping trip even easier

B Keeping the customers moving

C Feeling a little less welcome

D Tempting customers to return

E Taking advantage of changing lifestyles

F Appealing to the senses

G Paying the price of expansion

H Identifying key locations

Supermarket Secrets

In Britain, supermarkets have a huge influence on everyday life. Sonia Putnell reveals how they keep people shopping.

0	H

The most important place in a supermarket is at the end of each row. Just moving a particular product to these shelves can easily double its sales, so manufacturers pay big money to have their products displayed there. In the same way, luxury goods are placed at eye-level, where people tend to look first, while cheaper items, which don't make so much money for the supermarket, are put nearer the floor.

1	

Every detail of a supermarket is planned carefully to encourage people to part with their money. Bright blue lighting is often used to show off the colour and freshness of vegetables, and particularly attractive fruit may be piled under a spotlight near the entrance. In areas where there are tins and packets, softer lighting encourages people to spend more time looking. Drinks, often an unplanned purchase, may have dramatic lighting behind them to suggest a nightclub atmosphere. Smells play their part too. When supermarkets bake bread on the premises, they tend to sell more of it.

2	

Each supermarket manager has a diagram which shows every aspect of the store layout. Not a trick is missed. Essential food such as bread, eggs and milk are always positioned a long way apart so that shoppers have to visit other parts of the shop in order to get to them. These products are often shifted about, too; the longer shoppers spend in the store finding what they came in for, the more money they might be tempted to spend on something else.

3	

Even when they eventually reach the checkout, customers are not safe. While they wait, they might pick up leaflets about the store's services, or look through magazines promoting the store's products. The checkout operator may also offer them what's called a 'loyalty card'. This allows regular customers to take advantage of future special offers, but in fact it is the store which benefits more. By scanning in the card at the checkout, the store can build up information about its customers' regular purchases and see who is responding to promotions and offers, which helps it plan how to appeal to them more effectively in the future.

4	

Even checkouts might not actually exist for much longer, as new microchips placed on food wrapping will soon make it unnecessary for shoppers to unload their trolleys in order to pay. Within a few years, the trolley may just have to be pushed through an electronic 'door' where a computer calculates the bill automatically. On arrival at the store, shoppers may also be able to put their loyalty card into a special trolley, with a screen which greets them by name and gives information about special offers of interest to them personally.

5	

British supermarkets also work hard to be at the centre of local life by providing services such as cafés, dry-cleaning and photo-processing. This has not been without cost to the local economy, however, for 100,000 local shops have closed down since the rapid spread of large supermarkets across the country a generation ago. The environment has also suffered; deliveries round the clock to supermarkets from both within the country and overseas have played their part in increasing pollution and wasting the world's resources.

6	

It is not surprising then that feelings against supermarkets are strong in many places. When a new store is planned, supermarkets often offer money to local communities, which can be spent on schools and roads. Despite these inducements, it has recently become much more difficult for new supermarkets to get permission to build. Are supermarkets beginning to lose favour? Possibly, but there is no doubt that they will be thinking up new ideas to make sure people don't buy their eggs and bread elsewhere.

Paper 3: Use of English

Part 1: lexical cloze

Read the text below and decide which answer **A, B, C** or **D** best fits each space. There is an example at the beginning (**0**).

MEN AND SHOPPING

Normally, a crèche is where children are (**0**)....A.... while their parents work, but recently a shopping centre opened a 'crèche' which (**1**)............. men to play computer games while their partners go shopping. The aim is to (**2**)............. men to feel that shopping is fun. You only have to (**3**)............. at men's faces in a shopping centre in the UK to realise that they find shopping less (**4**)............. than women. Whether they are well off or (**5**)............. up, the effect is the same: they are so anxious before they go shopping that their stress levels increase to a truly (**6**)............. extent, comparable to those felt by (**7**)............. fighter pilots or riot police. According to one psychologist, women are much more (**8**)............. in the shops and men get so impatient because men are less used to shopping than women. She adds that, quite (**9**)............. , over the years, women have developed a laid-back (**10**)............. to shopping, but that men's negative feelings (**11**)............. when they are buying things for people other than themselves. It's understandable, then, that women (**12**)............. men for not (**13**)............. an effort when it comes to buying things for the family. She notes that, in the UK, many men (**14**)............. to go shopping at all, or claim to feel (**15**)............. out after only five minutes. Let's hope the crèche makes a difference!

	A	B	C	D
0	looked after	cared about	set up	put away
1	makes	opens	enables	removes
2	support	encourage	let	convince
3	catch	spot	watch	glance
4	funny	enjoyable	silly	capable
5	hard	short	weak	poor
6	astonished	influential	easy	amazing
7	taught	experienced	tested	prepared
8	comfortable	convenient	relaxing	restful
9	naturally	physically	biologically	environmentally
10	acceptance	appeal	agreement	approach
11	exaggerate	lengthen	add	increase
12	complain	criticise	object	argue
13	doing	taking	making	giving
14	refuse	cancel	reject	deny
15	broken	fed	tired	paid

Part 3: key word transformation

Complete the second sentence so that it has a similar meaning to the first sentence, using the word given. **Do not change the word given.** You must use between **two** and **five** words, including the word given. Write **only** the missing words.

EXAMPLE:

0 You must do exactly what the manager tells you.
   carry
   You must ~~carry out the manager's~~ instructions exactly.

1 Everything I know about music I learnt from my music teacher.
   was
   I .... about music by my music teacher.

2 I really think you should get a new car.
   time
   I really think it's .... a new car.

3 When I was at school, I had no choice but to wear a uniform.
   made
   I .... a uniform when I was at school.

4 They say the new computer program is very easy to use.
   said
   The new computer program .... very easy to use.

5 I couldn't have cooked such a big meal without your help.
   had
   If I .... help, I couldn't have cooked such a big meal.

6 Mary regretted selling her house.
   wished
   Mary .... her house.

7 I would prefer you not to get up if you are ill.
   rather
   I .... get up if you are ill.

8 Only a very small number of people think he is a good president.
   hardly
   There's .... he is a good president.

9 Sarah isn't living in London now because she didn't get the job.
   she
   If Sarah had got the job, ... in London now.

10 We weren't allowed to go into the club.
   let
   They .... go into the club.

Part 4: error correction

Read the text below and look carefully at each line. Some of the lines are correct, and some have a word which should not be there.
If a line is correct, put a tick (✓) by the number. If a line has a word which should not be there, write the word in the space. There are two examples at the beginning (**0** and **00**).

A HOLIDAY IN WINTER

Last December, I drove northwards across Europe to visit friends	**0** ✓
in Sweden. I must to admit that I really wasn't very well prepared	**00** to
for the trip. When I got off the car ferry, I immediately felt myself	**1**
very cold. I soon realised that I had not brought enough and layers	**2**
of warm clothes with me. So, before continuing my journey, I was	**3**
parked the car and went shopping. When I came back, however, the	**4**
car wouldn't start, because the water in my radiator had been frozen.	**5**
If I had taken my car to a garage and have had special anti-freeze	**6**
liquid put in before I'd come, then I wouldn't have had this problem.	**7**
Anyway, after a few hours I got it fixed and I drove to the my friend's	**8**
house just outside Stockholm. I was amazed at these how well the	**9**
majority of Swedes seem cope in difficult weather conditions. The	**10**
roads are cleared of any kind ice and snow very quickly and people	**11**
is drive vehicles which are designed to perform reliably in bad	**12**
weather. I wish that when it snowed in my country, all of any the	**13**
buses ran on time and that the traffic moved as freely as it so does in	**14**
Sweden. But then, I guess they're more used to the snow than we are.	**15**

Part 5: word formation

Read the text below. Use the word given in capitals at the end of each line to form a word that fits the space in the same line. There is an example at the beginning (**0**).

NO MORE HAPPY ENDINGS

Some people like (**0**) _romantic_ films with happy endings, but others	**ROMANCE**
find them (**1**)............. , saying that real life is complicated and sometimes	**IRRITATE**
(**2**)............. and that this should be reflected more in the films we watch.	**PLEASE**
Indeed, it is Hollywood's (**3**)............. to make films which are true to life	**FAIL**
that led to the setting up of the (**4**)............. successful Sundance Institute	**HIGH**
by the American actor, Robert Redford. His aim has been to (**5**).............	**WIDE**
the horizons of film-makers who dislike the (**6**)............. imposed by large	**RESTRICT**
studios, and help them make films that are more (**7**)............. . For example,	**REAL**
he doesn't let any of his directors use (**8**)............. special effects for their	**CREDIBLE**
own sake, and his (**9**)............. to accept scripts with happy endings means	**REFUSE**
that the plots of these films grow (**10**)............. out of the characters' lives.	**NATURE**

Well-being

Overview

- **Reading:** gapped text (Paper 1 Part 3)
- **Language development 1:** clauses of reason, purpose and contrast
- **Writing:** transactional letter (Paper 2 Part 1)
- **Listening:** note completion (Paper 4 Part 2)
- **Speaking:** collaborative task, discussion (Paper 5 Parts 3 and 4)
- **Language development 2:** *so/such*; *too/enough/very*; *as/like*
- **Use of English 1:** key word transformations (Paper 3 Part 3)
- **Use of English 2:** lexical cloze (Paper 3 Part 1)
- **Language development 3:** idiomatic expressions and phrasal verbs to do with health and fitness

Lead-in

- How do you think the photos illustrate the theme of well-being?
- Choose two or three photos which you think go together, and explain how they are related.
- What is most important to **your** well-being?

Happiness

Reading (Paper 1 Part 3)

Before you read

1 a Look at the photo.
1 Would you say this glass is half empty or half full?
2 Do you think your answer reflects your character? How?

b Look at the title of the article opposite and discuss the questions.
1 What do **you** think are 'the secrets of true happiness'?
2 Is it possible to learn how to be happy?

Skimming

2 Skim the text. (Ignore the gaps at this stage.) What answers does the article give to the questions in Exercise 1b?

Gapped text: sentences

▶ Task strategy Unit 7 page 52

3 Eight sentences have been removed from the article. Choose from the sentences A–I the one which fits each gap (1–7). There is one extra sentence, which you do not need to use. There is an example at the beginning (0).

a Look at the highlighted words in the example sentence I. What words in the first paragraph of the base text do they link to?

b Do the task. Follow the task strategy and use the Help clues if necessary.

c Compare and justify your answers. What grammatical and lexical links helped you?

HELP

➤ Gap 2
The writer says *we always return to our own fixed level of happiness whatever happens*. So this means other levels of happiness or unhappiness don't last.

➤ Gap 3
Look for an expression meaning the opposite of *The former*.

➤ Gap 4
Read the last sentence of the previous paragraph as well.

Discussion

4 Discuss these questions.
1 What did you find most interesting about the article? From your own experience, is there anything you strongly agree or disagree with?
2 What advice in the article do you think you would like to try?

Vocabulary: word formation

5 a Change the nouns below into adjectives using one of the suffixes in the list. Check the spelling in your dictionary if necessary.
-able   -(i)ous   -(i)ed
1 contentment   2 satisfaction   3 frustration   4 anxiety
5 depression   6 stress   7 misery

b When and why have you experienced any of these feelings?

The Secrets of True Happiness

Lollie Barr reviews some recent research.

A happy nature is a gift we all wish we'd been born with. Everybody knows someone with this gift: the cheerful type of person with a positive attitude who will always say a glass is half full rather than half empty. It's the person who is not easily put off when things go wrong and who appears to lead a happier life as a result. [0 I] But what is the secret of happiness? And how can we achieve it?

Psychologists define this feeling of well-being as 'when thoughts and feelings about one's life are mainly positive'. The key seems to be contentment with what you already have, emotionally, materially and professionally. The more people try to keep up with others, for example, the more likely they are to be dissatisfied with life. [1]

David Lykken, Professor of Psychology at the University of Minnesota, is a leading specialist in happiness. As a result of studying 300 sets of twins, he now believes that happiness is more than 50 per cent genetically determined. He also believes that we each have our own fixed 'happiness point', a level we always return to, whatever happens to us in life. [2]

But does this mean we are stuck with the level of happiness we were born with? Dr. Michael Issac, a psychiatrist, believes this is not necessarily the case. This is because although a person's temperament is not easily changed, their character can be. The former determines what kind of things will make someone happy, but not how much pleasure that person obtains from them. [3] This is why Dr Isaac believes we need to study happy people and learn how to be like them.

[4] They also tend to be interested in things other than themselves. This could be through their day-to-day work, for example, or by caring for others less fortunate, or by having some kind of spiritual focus to their life.

Happy individuals also tend to relate to other people and are able to give and receive affection. [5] They are, therefore, more likely to belong to things like sports teams, choirs and political parties. Researchers at Harvard University have found that people involved in such activities were happier than those who were not, and that this had nothing to do with how well-off people were financially.

Another factor in happiness appears to be physical activity. Exercise improves a person's mood and gets rid of tension. But there must be a balance between activity and rest, because stress results in unhappiness. [6]

But mental activity can be just as important. Psychologists believe it's possible to train yourself to recognise happiness and, therefore, feel the benefits of it more often. [7] One way of doing this is to set yourself the task of noticing, say, five different happy moments in the day. The more you recognise when there's a decision to be made about how you feel, the better you'll become at choosing happiness over misery, it is claimed.

A That's why being part of a social group, such as a family, a community or a club adds to their overall sense of well-being.

B Such people, for example, seem to find satisfaction in activities which are meaningful and give a feeling of personal achievement.

C The latter develops in response to the experiences a person has during his or her life.

D There will always be someone else with more than you, so trying to compete can often lead to frustration and anxiety.

E To avoid this, it is important to pick a sport or activity you enjoy and which you do when you want to, rather than when you think you should.

F In other words, no matter how happy or unhappy an individual event may make us, this is just a temporary state.

G The key, apparently, is not taking your feelings for granted, but rather learning to celebrate them.

H Other scientists, however, maintain that happiness is not so difficult to achieve.

I Such people may be healthier too, since there seems to be a link between happiness and good health.

Language development 1

Clauses of reason

1 **a** What do you do to relax?

b Read about Sally Gunnell, a former Olympic athlete, and answer the questions.
1 Why do professional athletes have little time to relax?
2 What does Sally Gunnell do to relax?

A
Many people never find time to relax *owing to* their busy lifestyles.

B
This is certainly true of professional athletes *due to* the fact that they have to travel the world to compete and do a lot of promotional work.

C
Sally Gunnell explains: 'It's important to look after yourself *because of* the risk of illness brought on by stress.'

D
'I put more strain on my body than most people *because* I'm a professional athlete.'

E
'*Since* I have to train very hard, it's important for me to find time to rest.'

F
'I took up yoga *as* I needed to learn to unwind.'

c The expressions in italics in the text extracts introduce an answer to the question *Why*? Which expressions can go in each sentence below?
1 Mark left his job .... it was stressful. (+ subject + verb)
2 Mark left his job .... the stress. (+ noun)
3 Mark left his job .... the fact that it was stressful. (+ *the fact that* + subject + verb)

2 **a** Complete these sentences about Joe with the words or expressions from Exercise 1b.
1 Joe put on some music .... he wanted to relax.
2 He had lost his job .... his age.
3 The club had reduced its staff .... the fact it was losing money.
4 But .... he was a talented trainer, he knew he'd get another job.
5 .... his many interests, he was never bored.
6 A lot of unhappiness is .... boredom.

b Complete the sentences in three different ways, using the word in brackets.
1 Dave was late for the meeting … (*snow*)
a because it ....
b because of ....
c due to ....
2 Marta decided to drive to work … (*rain*)
a as it ....
b because of ....
c since ....

Clauses of purpose

The expressions in **bold** all express purpose. They introduce an answer to the question *what for?*

The office closes early on Fridays	*in order that* *so that*	*we can have a longer weekend.*
	in order to	
I like to go away	*so as to* *to*	*have a break.*

I take my mobile phone **in case** *anyone needs to contact me.*

3 a Which expressions in the box above can go in each sentence below?

1 I have a sauna once a week .... relax. (+ verb)

2 The fitness centre stays open late .... people can go after work. (+ subject + verb)

3 I usually call before I go, ... they're closed for any reason. (+ subject + verb: precaution)

b Mark the correct alternative in each pair.

1 Get regular exercise *to / so that* keep yourself fit.

2 Take food and drink to work *in order that / in case* you can't stop for lunch.

3 Breathe deeply *in case / so that* your whole body relaxes.

4 Read an amusing book *in order to / in order that* reduce tension.

5 *In order to / In order that* you can see a problem clearly, change your routine.

6 Allow plenty of time for journeys, *in case / so that* there are delays.

7 Leave work on time *so as to / so that* spend time with your friends and family.

8 Only drink one cup of coffee a day *so as not to / not to* overstimulate your body.

Clauses of contrast

The expressions in **bold** connect contrasting ideas:

I ran all the way	**despite** **in spite of**	*being exhausted.* (+ -ing) *my exhaustion.* (+ noun) *the fact that I was exhausted.* (+ the fact that)
I ran all the way	**even though** **although** **though**	*it was very cold.* (+ subject + verb)
Tom loves judo,	**whereas**	*Mary prefers swimming.* (+ subject + verb: contrasting but not contradicting ideas)

4 Look at the examples in the box above and match the sentence halves.

1 My mother goes out to work whereas
2 He's still out of work despite
3 Jo is very active although
4 David isn't getting better even though
5 They always seem happy despite
6 He's unhappy in spite of the fact that
7 Sam gets a huge salary while
8 I'm feeling really tired in spite of

a his appetite has returned.
b he makes a lot of money.
c going for three interviews a week.
d having slept well last night.
e my father stays at home.
f his assistant hardly earns anything.
g their poverty.
h she hasn't been feeling well lately.

5 Complete these sentences in a logical way.

1 Unfortunately, I can't give up smoking even though ... .
2 She couldn't sleep last night because of ... .
3 I must call Mike so that ... .
4 Despite ... , she was wearing a heavy coat.
5 Sheila phoned the restaurant to ... .
6 He left his mobile phone behind in spite of ... .

▶ Grammar reference page 196.

Writing   Transactional letter (Paper 2 Part 1)

Lead-in   1   Discuss this question, giving examples.

Do you think people nowadays are more or less polite than they used to be?

Understand the task   2   Read and analyse the task below. Was the letter written by an older or a younger person?

You read this letter in a local newspaper and you think that some of the things the person says in it are untrue. Read the letter and the notes you made beside it. Then, using all your notes, write a letter to the editor of the newspaper giving your opinion and correcting the information.

Not true! Most young people are polite.

People have to hurry to get to work, don't they?

Why is it that these days young people in our city are so noisy and aggressive and always in such a hurry? Every time you get on a bus or go shopping, they seem to be having an argument with someone or trying to push past you. You walk down the street and even young children are <u>shouting</u> at each other, making an awful noise.

Children have always been noisy – they have to play.

Older people, particularly those over 50, are much calmer and quieter. When we were young, we were patient and polite. That's why life was much more pleasant then.

I've seen old people get aggressive and impatient in shops.

Write a **letter** of between **120** and **180** words in an appropriate style. Do not write any postal addresses.

Plan your letter   3   a   Decide on the best order for the points discussed in the letter. Can any of them be grouped together?

b   Make a paragraph plan for the letter.

Language and content

4 Replace the underlined phrases in this student's letter with more appropriate ones from the table below.

> Dear Sir or Madam,
>
> <u>About that letter</u> about young people's behaviour in last week's Courier. <u>I just can't get on with</u> the points the writer makes.
>
> Firstly, <u>it's total rubbish that</u> all young people are noisy and aggressive. <u>Round my way</u>, most young people are polite. <u>And OK, maybe</u> they are sometimes in a hurry, <u>but come on</u>, they need to get to work, school or college.
>
> <u>And I can't go along with</u> the generalisations about younger and older people. Children are no noisier today than they used to be. They have always had to play. <u>And you'd say</u> older people are more polite? I have seen older people being aggressive and impatient in shops, for example.
>
> <u>In the end</u>, while we should all have consideration for others, <u>I reckon</u> we should all try to be more patient and tolerant of each other. We were all young once!

Opening	I am writing in response to the letter … .
Disagreeing	I have to disagree with … . It is simply not true that … . I also disagree with … . And do you really think … ?
Tentatively agreeing	And whereas it may be true that … . We have to accept that … .
Describing your experience	In my experience, … .
Summarising	In conclusion, … . I think … .

Write your letter

5 Now write your letter using the ideas and some of the language above. Avoid copying whole phrases from the question.

Check and improve your letter

6 Edit your work.

▶ Writing reference pages 207–208

LANGUAGE SPOT: attitude phrases

Mark the correct alternative in each sentence.

1 *To be honest / As far as I know*, I think young people are more polite than older people.
2 *Actually / Presumably*, the person who wrote the letter doesn't meet many young people.
3 *As a matter of fact / Clearly / Naturally*, last Saturday there was a fight between a group of youths in the town.
4 *Frankly / Certainly / Surely*, some young people create a lot of trouble, that's true, but … .
5 *Strictly speaking / Roughly speaking / Generally speaking*, the writer has a point. Young people seem to shout at each other, even when they're joking.
6 *In my opinion / Admittedly / At least*, I don't meet many young people, but I see them on TV.
7 *As far as I'm concerned / According to me*, older people can be just as aggressive.
8 *In person / Personally / Truly*, I think we should be more tolerant of each other.

Health and fitness

Listening (Paper 4 Part 2)

Before you listen

1 a How healthy are you? How far are these statements true for you?
    1 I usually eat and drink things that are good for me.
    2 I try to get plenty of sleep every night.
    3 I take regular exercise.
    4 I try to balance work with a good social life.

b Look at the task in Exercise 2a. Can you guess the missing information?

Note completion ▶ page 190

2 a ▭ You will hear a radio programme about how to be healthy and live longer. For questions 1–10 complete the notes. Follow the task strategy.

Task strategy

- Read through the notes. The missing information is usually factual.
- Listen and complete the gaps with a word, number or short phrase from the recording (no more than three or four words).
- The notes must make sense, but you don't have to create correct grammatical sentences.
- Check your answers during the second listening. Guess if necessary.

THIS YEAR'S HEALTH TIPS

Food and drink: what should we be getting more of?
- .... **(1)** – to increase our breathing capacity.
- Chocolate   – to prevent .... **(2)** problems
- Tea without milk   – good for your .... **(3)**
- Coffee   – good for treating .... **(4)**

Rest and exercise: what should we be doing?
- Sleep   – .... **(5)** a night is enough.
- Regular exercise – .... **(6)** is better for you.
- Laughter   – exercises up to .... **(7)** different muscles.

Long life: what can we do to live longer?
- .... **(8)** – helps you make friends.
- .... **(9)** – to keep your brain active.
- .... **(10)** – increases your chances of living longer.

b Compare and discuss your answers.

Discussion

3 Discuss these questions.
    1 Were you surprised by any of the information you heard in the programme?
    2 Are there any aspects of your lifestyle you would consider changing as a result of listening to it?
    3 Do the government and newspapers in your country publish health advice? How much notice do people take?

Vocabulary: health and lifestyle

4 Make a list of things associated with an <u>unhealthy</u> lifestyle.
EXAMPLES: *eating junk food, having a lie-in every Saturday and Sunday …*

Speaking (Paper 5 Parts 3 and 4)

Lead-in

1 a Read the statements below about Paper 5 Parts 3 and 4, and discuss whether they are *True* or *False*.

Part 3:

1 Candidates speak for three minutes each.
2 The task has two parts.
3 You are not allowed to disagree with your partner.

Part 4:

4 You may be asked more than one question.
5 You should give short answers.
6 You should listen carefully to the other candidate.

b Look at the list of things (1–6) you might have to do in the exam. Match them to the expressions (a–f) below.

1 begin a discussion   4 ask for clarification
2 involve the other candidate   5 come to a conclusion
3 disagree politely   6 develop ideas

a	*I'm not quite sure what we have to do first.*	d	*Yes, but … .*
b	*Why don't we start by …?*	e	*I hadn't thought of that! We could also … .*
c	*Do you think we should …?*	f	*So are we agreed that …?*

c Add any other expressions you can think of.

Collaborative task

▶ Task strategy Unit 8 page 59

2 Work in groups of three.

STUDENT 1: You are the examiner. Turn to page 223 and read the instructions.
STUDENTS 2 AND 3: You are Candidates A and B. Look at the pictures on this page. Follow the examiner's instructions.

Three-way discussion

▶ Task strategy Unit 10 page 75

3 a Work in groups of three. Take turns at being the examiner and candidates.

EXAMINER: Ask some of the questions below.

1 What kind of food do you like?
2 What kind of 'convenience food' would you really hate to give up?
3 Whose responsibility should it be to educate children about health issues?
4 What do you do to stay healthy?
5 Do you think that people these days are healthier than they used to be?
6 Do you think we worry too much about our health?

b Discuss and compare your answers. Did you:

- put your ideas across clearly?
- keep closely to the task?
- work well with your partner to complete the task?
- use a range of vocabulary?
- use correct grammar and pronunciation?

Language development 2

so/such; too/enough/very

1 a Read the examples in the box and complete the rules.

- *so/such*
  *Why is it **so difficult** to lose weight?*
  *You shouldn't eat **so many** sweets – they're bad for you!*
  *He walks **so fast** (that) I can hardly keep up with him.*
  ***Such bad behaviour** is not acceptable.*
  *He's **such a nice person** – everyone likes him.*
  *There was **such a lot** of salt in the food (that) I couldn't eat it.*

  1 We use .... before adjectives, adverbs and quantifiers.
  2 We use .... before a noun phrase with an uncountable noun.
  3 We use .... + ... before singular countable nouns.

b Read the examples in the box and answer the questions below.

- *enough/too/very*
  *Five hours a night isn't **enough sleep**.*
  There aren't enough facilities for young people.
  *It isn't **warm enough** (for us) to go swimming.*
  ***Too much** red meat isn't good for you.*
  *That health club is so expensive! It's much **too expensive** (for me) **to** join.*
  *I'm **very tired** – but not **too** tired to go out!*

  1 *enough* goes in front of a .... and after an ....
  2 Match the words to the definitions below.
     1 *too* (+ adjective/quantifier)
     2 *very* (+ adjective)
     3 *enough* (+ noun/adjective)
     a a lot
     b as much as we want/need
     c more than is good, reasonable or acceptable

2 Correct the mistakes in the sentences.
   1 Jim's a so good doctor that everybody likes him.
   2 My yoga class is great; I'm always too relaxed afterwards.
   3 Paul has bought such an expensive fitness equipment!
   4 The food is too spicy for me to eat it.
   5 The vegetables in your diet aren't enough.
   6 I'm very tired to go jogging now.
   7 John is so unfit so he can't even run for a bus.
   8 The money isn't enough for us to buy a drink.
   9 You should be pleased with yourself for losing so weight.
   10 I'm not enough old for to join that club.

as/like

A Comparison: *like* + noun, *as if/though* + clause
  *He's just **like** his father.*
  *I wish I could sing **like** Pavarotti (does).*
  *This looks/seems **like** a nice place.*
  *It seems **as if/like** (informal) he's going to be late. (likely situation)*
  *They treat me **like** their daughter/**as though I was** their daughter. (imaginary situation)*
The following verbs are often followed by *like* + noun or *as if* + clause: *feel, look, seem, smell, sound, taste.*
*It **looks like** rain/**as if** it is going to rain.*
*He looks **as if** he had seen a ghost.* (See Unit 20, page 150)

B Role, function: *as* + noun; manner: *as* + clause
  *He's found a job **as** a barman.*
  *Please think of me **as** a friend.*
  *He arrived late, **as** he had warned us.*
  *Please do **as** I tell you.*
Other verbs followed by *as*: *describe, be known, recognise, regard, treat*

C Examples: *like/such as* + noun
  *Foods **like/such as** beans are a rich source of protein.*

3 Look at the information in the box above and complete the sentences with *as, like, such as* or *as if/as though*.
   1 I love sweet things .... chocolates.
   2 My friend Anna is looking for a job .... an au pair.
   3 Taking up yoga sounds .... a good idea.
   4 Foods .... oranges are full of Vitamin C.
   5 He looks .... he hadn't slept for a week.
   6 .... you can see, I've lost ten kilos!

4 Complete this extract from a letter with *as, like* or *such as*.

I'm working (1).................... a nurse in a clinic in the Himalayas and, since I live next to the clinic, people expect me to behave (2).................... a nurse all the time. (3).................... with any nursing job, my main task is to look after patients, but here I also do other things, (4).................... help prepare the food and take it to the homes of sick people. The views from my bedroom are spectacular – it looks (5).................... paradise! – and (6).................... you predicted, sometimes I feel I never want to go back home.

Use of English 1   (Paper 3 Part 3)

Lead-in

1 a What advice would you give someone doing the exam task below? Check your answers by looking back at the task strategy on page 17.

   b Look at the completed transformations below. Can you correct this candidate's mistakes?

---

1 I remember the first time I met my wife.
   meeting
   I remember <u>meeting my wife for</u> first time.
2 The tickets may be expensive so take plenty of money.
   case
   Take plenty of money <u>in case of the tickets are</u> expensive.
3 By eight o'clock, Tom was very tired so he went back to bed.
   that
   By eight o'clock, Tom <u>was too tired that he</u> went back to bed.
4 We'll get into the stadium if we arrive by eight.
   long
   We'll get into the stadium <u>as long as we will arrive</u> by eight.

Key word transformation

▶ Task strategy Unit 2 page 17

2 a Do the task below.

Complete the second sentence so that it has a similar meaning to the first sentence, using the word given. **Do not change the word given.** You must use between **two** and **five** words, including the word given. Write **only** the missing words.

1 We were told by the engineer what the problem with the TV was.
   explained
   The engineer .... problem was with the TV.
2 I'm just eating my dinner – do you mind if I phone you later?
   get
   I'm just eating my dinner – can .... later?
3 Sue was too unfit to take part in the race.
   enough
   Sue .... take part in the race.
4 You could stay with us next time you're in town.
   put
   We could .... next time you're in town.
5 If it were cooler, we could go for a walk.
   hot
   If it .... could go for a walk.
6 Jane had never eaten a meal that was as delicious as that one.
   such
   Jane had never eaten .... meal.
7 'Do you want to buy my car or not?' Alan asked Judy.
   whether
   Alan asked .... to buy his car or not.
8 This car is too small for any more luggage.
   enough
   There .... in this car for any more luggage.
9 Tom is not usually so bad-tempered.
   like
   It is .... so bad-tempered.
10 Jazz is less popular now than it was 50 years ago.
   not
   Jazz .... it was 50 years ago.

   b Compare and discuss your answers.

Use of English 2   (Paper 3 Part 1)

Lead-in

1 Look at the photo of Roman baths. Why do you think they were popular?

Lexical cloze

▶ Task strategy Unit 2 page 18

2 a Read the title and text quickly and answer the questions.

1 What is a spa?

2 Why were spas so popular in Roman times?

3 What other things could people do there apart from exercise and bathe?

b Do the task.

Read the text below and decide which answer **A**, **B**, **C** or **D** best fits each space. There is an example at the beginning (**0**).

| 0 | A sick | B wounded | C damaged | D unhealthy |

The Origin of Spas

Traditionally, spas were places which had a spring of mineral water, where people who were (**0**)....**A**.... went to recover from an illness or (**1**)............ a disease. Spas were developed by the (**2**)............ Romans, who built public bath houses over hot volcanic springs. Some Roman baths could (**3**)............ up to 6,000 bathers and had restaurants, sports centres, swimming pools, gardens and libraries. An extremely (**4**)............ entrance fee ensured the popularity of the baths.

There was no fixed (**5**)............ in which the rooms were used. People might begin with a (**6**)............ workout, before going to the Warm Room to relax, (**7**)............ a vigorous massage in olive oil and then (**8**)............ a good soak in a warm bath. Next, they could take a bath in the Hot Room, before (**9**)............ down in the Cold Room. After that, they might (**10**)............ for a swim, read some poetry in the library, have a (**11**)............ to eat, or talk about urgent matters of state in a private talk room.

In those days, the daily bath was a great social (**12**)............ . Today, spas, or 'day spas' as they are sometimes (**13**)............ , are rather expensive. They are for people with less time on their (**14**)............ than the Romans, who don't (**15**)............ paying a lot of money when they're feeling under the weather or need to unwind from stressful jobs.

1	A correct	B improve	C cure	D support
2	A antique	B dated	C historical	D ancient
3	A accommodate	B provide	C use	D involve
4	A poor	B low	C little	D short
5	A line	B queue	C route	D order
6	A tired	B solid	C hard	D high
7	A hold	B have	C admit	D possess
8	A enjoy	B like	C love	D satisfy
9	A cooling	B heating	C warming	D chilling
10	A take	B go	C spend	D use
11	A taste	B piece	C mouth	D bite
12	A chance	B circumstance	C occasion	D season
13	A called	B cried	C announced	D stated
14	A feet	B hands	C seat	D chest
15	A matter	B care	C bother	D mind

Discussion

3 Discuss these questions.

1 Do you think you would like to spend a day in a Roman spa?

2 What similar things do people do today?

Language development 3

Idiomatic expressions: health

 LOOK at the sentence from the Use of English text opposite and choose the correct meaning for the expression in bold.

Today, spas are for people ... who don't mind paying a lot of money when they're feeling **under the weather***.*

1 unhappy because it is cold
2 not very well

1 a Read the following text, then mark the correct alternative in each pair in the sentences below.

George was **(1)** *feeling his age*. He hadn't **(2)** *felt himself* for a while and he was **(3)** *off his food*, which was unusual for him. He went to see his doctor, who said he was **(4)** *run-down* and needed a rest. The doctor told George to take a holiday and **(5)** *recharge his batteries*. He also said George needed to change his lifestyle, stop smoking and take more exercise. So George went to the south of France for three months, and when he got back, he was **(6)** *in good shape*. His doctor gave him **(7)** *a clean bill of health*. That was 20 years ago. George is **(8)** *still going strong* today.

1 George was *middle-aged / very old* when he went to the doctor's.
2 He went to the doctor's because he felt *different / unwell*.
3 Also, he *had no more food / didn't want to eat*.
4 The doctor said he *was very tired / had run too much*.
5 The doctor told George to *get back his energy / get a new battery*.
6 When George got back from holiday, he *had a good figure / was physically fit*.
7 His doctor said he was *clean / healthy*.
8 Today George is *fit and healthy / strong*.

b Check your answers in the Longman *Dictionary of Contemporary English*. When you look up an idiomatic expression, look for the first noun, verb, adjective, adverb or preposition.

feel[1] /fiːl/ *v past tense and past participle* **felt** /felt/
15 feel your age to realize that you are not as young or active as you used to be: *It was only looking at his son that made him feel his age.*

Phrasal verbs: health

2 a Complete the sentences with the correct form of a phrasal verb from the list. Use each verb once only.

cut down on   get over   take up   give up
come down with   cut out   pick up   put on

1 I think you need to .... some weight after so long without food.
2 You ought to .... sweet things, and .... chocolate completely.
3 You've probably .... a bug – there's something going round.
4 Why don't you .... smoking altogether? You know it's bad for your health.
5 You must be .... a cold. You'll soon .... it though.
6 You should .... yoga to strengthen your muscles.

b Complete the dialogues with the sentences from Exercise 2a.

1 A: I've got backache.
  B: ....
2 A: How many cigarettes do you smoke a day?
  B: About 20.
  A: ....
3 A: I can't stop sneezing.
  B: ....
4 A: Do you think I'm overweight?
  B: Yes, I do. ....
5 A: I feel very weak and thin after my illness.
  B: ....
6 A: I've got a terrible stomachache.
  B: ....

3 Ask a partner these questions.
1 Have you taken up a sport recently, or in the past?
2 When did you last come down with something? Did you get over it quickly?
3 What do you think you should cut down on, or cut out?

Module 11: Review

1 Complete the dialogues with the words in the list.

miserable   anxious   satisfied   contented
depressed   stressed

1 A: I'm really not at all .... with these exam
    results!
  B: They're not so bad. Don't get .... by them.
    Cheer up!
2 A: I had an .... moment this morning. The car
    wouldn't start and I thought I'd be late for the
    meeting.
  B: That's why you looked so .... when you
    arrived!
3 A: Why are you sitting there with that big smile,
    looking so .... ?
  B: The weather's so .... that I can't work
    outside, so I'm enjoying a day off!

2 **a** Combine each pair of sentences, using <u>one</u> of the
expressions in italics, to make one complete
sentence. Add any necessary words.

1 I don't laugh very much. I'm a very cheerful
  person. (*even though/in case*)
2 I drink a lot of water. I don't want to get
  dehydrated. (*while/so as not to*)
3 I get plenty of sleep. I always seem to feel tired.
  (*owing to/in spite of*)
4 I warm up before doing any serious exercise. I
  don't want to pull a muscle. (*although/in case*)
5 There are many warnings about eating animal
  fat. I still eat too much of it. (*despite/due to*)
6 I often listen to classical music. It helps me
  relax. (*whereas/in order to*)
7 Shopping makes me stressed. I try to avoid it as
  much as possible. (*while/since*)
8 I have a busy work schedule. I don't have much
  time to take holidays. (*in spite of/owing to*)
9 I like a big breakfast. I don't want to feel
  hungry in the middle of the morning. (*because
  of/so that*)
10 I like to go swimming to keep fit. A lot of my
  friends prefer to go jogging. (*whereas/due to*)

b Which of the sentences in Exercise 2a are true for
you?

3 **a** Correct the mistakes in this student's story.

Danny is (**1**) *a such nice young man* that everyone in
my street likes him, but I don't think he's (**2**) *enough
considerate* to be seen (**3**) *like* a good neighbour.
(**4**) *Just as* all young people, his idea of happiness is to
listen to CDs of bands (**5**) *such like* Prodigy, with the
volume (**6**) *far enough loud*. In fact some nights there
is (**7**) *very much noise* that it (**8**) *seems such as* the
whole house will come down. But when I see him the
next day he is always (**9**) *too friendly* that I can't be
angry with him. He smiles pleasantly (**10**) *like if*
nothing had happened.

b Do you have any neighbours like Danny? Or are
you like him?

4 Decide which answer A, B, C or D best fits each space.
1 I've got a temperature. I feel under the ....
  A health   B weather   C shape   D age
2 I'm staying at home. I don't .... myself this
  morning.
  A feel   B go   C run   D mind
3 Some modern music makes me feel my ....
  A shape   B ache   C illness   D age
4 She's 70 years old and still going ....
  A fit   B healthy   C strong   D clean
5 I need a holiday to .... my batteries.
  A get back   B recharge   C take up   D change
6 Chris goes to the gym a lot. He's in good ....
  A shape   B exercise   C position   D muscle
7 I'm fine. The doctor's given me a .... bill of
  health.
  A fit   B good   C relaxed   D clean

5 Correct the mistakes in the phrasal verbs in this
conversation.

PATIENT: I think I'm (**1**) *going up with* something.
        Maybe I've (**2**) *picked out* a bug. Last time I
        had something like this it took me a long
        time to (**3**) *get round* it.

DOCTOR: Well, you have (**4**) *picked up* a lot of weight
        since I last saw you. You must be eating too
        much – you need to (**5**) *cut up* your food,
        and (**6**) *take on* some form of exercise.

MODULE 12
Getting your message across

Overview

- **Reading:** multiple-choice questions (Paper 1 Part 2)
- **Language development 1:** connecting ideas; participle clauses
- **Writing:** set book (Paper 2 Part 2)
- **Listening:** multiple-choice questions (Paper 4 Part 4)
- **Speaking:** complete paper (Paper 5 Parts 1–4)
- **Use of English 1:** error correction (Paper 3 Part 3)
- **Language development 2:** *needs + -ing/to be done*; causative: *have/get something done*
- **Use of English 2:** word formation (Paper 3 Part 5)
- **Language development 3:** word formation: review

Lead-in

- Which different methods of communicating information and ideas are shown in the photos?
- What is the main purpose of each medium?
- What positive and negative effects have they had on our lives?

The Talented Mr Ripley

PATRICIA HIGHSMITH

PENGUIN READERS

Reading (Paper 1 Part 2)

Before you read

1 a What do you read most/least often? For example: newspapers, magazines, fiction books, non-fiction books, technical manuals? Why?

   b You are going to read an extract from a novel by Patricia Highsmith, which was made into a film in 1999. Look at the cover and a still from the film above. What kind of novel do you think it is: romance, historical, crime thriller, science fiction, etc.?

Reading

2 Read the extract once fairly quickly. Do you think your answer in Exercise 1b was right? Give reasons.

Multiple-choice questions

▶ Task strategy Unit 11 page 82

3 a Read the extract again. For Questions 1–7, choose the answer A, B, C or D which you think fits best according to the text. Follow the task strategy. Question 1 has been done for you. The highlighted words show how the answer was found.

   b Compare and justify your answers.

Discussion

4 a Discuss the story.
    1 What do you think will happen next?
    2 Which character do you sympathise with most? Which one would you like to meet?
    3 Having read this extract, would you like to read the novel or see the film? Why?/Why not?

   b What are the advantages and disadvantages of making a film based on a novel? Give examples of films you have seen.

Vocabulary: feelings; idiomatic expressions

5 a Find nouns and adjectives in the text that express feelings, emotions and reactions. Then explain why Dickie or Tom experienced these feelings.
   EXAMPLES: nouns: *hate, affection*
              adjectives: *enthusiastic*

   b Look at the numbered expressions 1–4 in the text. Can you explain what they mean?

Dickie said absolutely nothing on the train. Under a pretence of being sleepy, he folded his arms and closed his eyes. Tom sat opposite him, staring at his bony, arrogant, handsome face, at his hands with the green ring and the gold signet ring. **It crossed Tom's mind**[1] to steal the green ring when he left. It would be easy: Dickie took it off when he swam. Sometimes he took it off even when he showered at the house. He would do it the very last day, Tom thought. Tom stared at Dickie's closed eyelids. A crazy emotion of hate, of affection, of impatience and frustration was swelling in him, hampering his breathing.

He wanted to kill Dickie. It was not the first time he had thought of it. Before, once, twice or three times, it had been an impulse caused by anger or disappointment, an impulse that vanished immediately and left him with a feeling of shame. Now, he thought about it for an entire minute, two minutes, because he was leaving Dickie anyway and what was there to be ashamed of any more? He had failed Dickie in every way. He hated Dickie because, however he looked at what had happened, his failing had not been his own fault, not due to anything he had done, but due to Dickie's rudeness! He had offered Dickie friendship, companionship and respect, everything he had to offer, and Dickie had replied with ingratitude and now hostility. Dickie was just **shoving him out in the cold**[2].

If he killed him on this trip, Tom thought, he could simply say that some accident had happened. He could — he had just thought of something brilliant: he could become Dickie Greenleaf himself. He could do everything that Dickie did. He could go back to Mongibello first and collect Dickie's things, tell Marge any story, then set up an apartment in Rome or Paris, receive Dickie's cheque every month and forge Dickie's signature on it. He **could step right into Dickie's shoes**[3]. He could have Mr Greenleaf Senior **eating out of his hand**[4].

The danger of it, even the inevitable temporariness of it, which he vaguely realised, only made him more enthusiastic. He began to think of how. The water. But Dickie was such a good swimmer. The cliffs. It would be easy to push Dickie off some cliff when they took a walk, but he imagined Dickie grabbing at him and pulling him off with him and he tensed in his seat until his thighs ached and his nails cut red into his thumbs. He would have to get the other ring off, too. He would have to tint his hair a little lighter. But he wouldn't live in a place, of course, where anybody who knew Dickie lived. He had only to look enough like Dickie to be able to use his passport. Well, he did, if he –

Dickie opened his eyes, looking right at him, and Tom relaxed, slumped into the corner with his head back and his eyes shut, as quickly as if he had passed out. 'Tom, are you OK?' Dickie asked, shaking Tom's knee. 'OK,' Tom said, smiling a little. He saw Dickie sit back, with an air of irritation, and Tom knew why; because Dickie had hated giving him even that much attention. Tom smiled to himself, amused at his own quick reflex in pretending to collapse, because that had been the only way to keep Dickie from seeing what must have been a very strange expression on his face.

1 What do we learn about Tom in the first paragraph?
A He has already tried to steal Dickie's ring.
B He is familiar with the details of Dickie's life.
C He has just had an argument with Dickie.
D He is unsure whether Dickie is asleep or not.

2 Why does Tom decide that he wants to kill Dickie?
A He feels unfairly treated by Dickie.
B He wants to get away from Dickie.
C He thinks that Dickie has failed him.
D He feels ashamed of Dickie's behaviour.

3 In the third paragraph, Tom plans how he will
A cause Dickie to have an accident.
B go and live in Dickie's apartment.
C leave Dickie and return to Rome.
D receive money intended for Dickie.

4 How does Tom feel at the thought of actually killing Dickie?
A terrified of the consequences
B unsure of what to do with the body
C thrilled by the risks involved
D confident of his ability to do it

5 The word *grabbing* (line 44) describes a way of
A holding somebody.
B looking at somebody.
C speaking to somebody.
D understanding somebody.

6 Why did Tom pretend to faint?
A to annoy Dickie and start an argument
B to distract attention from how he looked
C to make a boring journey more interesting
D to make Dickie more sympathetic towards him

7 What does the phrase *Tom knew why* (line 57) refer to?
A Tom's smile
B Dickie's attention
C Dickie's irritation
D Tom's expression

a I read this book in order to find out more about the American way of life.

b As it was written by an American, it gives an accurate picture of life there.

c I had to read a lot of it before fully understanding the humour.

d If I'd known more about the USA before I started, I would have understood the book better.

e It's about two people who decide to drive across the USA.

f While they are driving along, they meet all kinds of people.

g Each night they arrive in a different town and feel exhausted.

h Because they don't know anyone, they have to find somewhere to stay.

i When they have found a hotel, they usually go out to eat.

j Sometimes they are so tired that they sleep in the car.

k However, they don't realise that they are being followed.

Language development 1

Connecting ideas

1 a Read the student's sentences, which describe a book he has read. Answer the questions.
  1 Why did the student read the book?
  2 What made it more difficult to understand?
  3 Why do the characters sometimes sleep in the car?

b Mark the words in the student's sentences which are used to connect ideas, and use them to complete the table.

Type	Example	Example from Exercise 1a
Relative pronoun	*which, that*	1 ....
Conjunction + clause	*when*	2 ....
		3 ....
Conjunction + -ing	*after*	4 ....
Clause of result	*such a … that*	5 ....
Conditional	*unless*	6 ....
Linking conjunction	*but*	7 ....
	Nevertheless, …	8 ....
Clause of purpose	*… to …*	9 ....
Clause of reason	*because, since*	10 ....
		11 ....

▶ Grammar reference page 196.

2 Correct the mistakes in these sentences.
  1 The part what I liked best was the ending.
  2 The main character is an old man who he has never left his home town.
  3 It was a such good book that I couldn't stop reading it.
  4 During the police look for the main suspect, Holmes makes other enquiries.
  5 It is set in a town where there are a lot of factories in.
  6 It can be helpful to see the film before to read the book in English.
  7 If you will like science fiction, you'll probably like this book.
  8 It is a good story despite the main character is not very realistic.
  9 The police are called in for investigate the theft of a painting.
  10 I didn't like the ending because of I thought it was disappointing.

Participle clauses

Participle clauses can be used in writing to make sentences shorter.
Look at these examples of shortened sentences from Exercise 1a:

A Present and perfect participles (actions/situations at the same time or in sequence)
When they are driving along, they meet all kinds of people.
→ **Driving** *along, they meet all kinds of people.*

Because they don't know anyone, they have to find somewhere to stay.
→ **Not knowing** *anyone, they have to find somewhere to stay.*

When they have found a hotel, they usually go out to eat.
→ **Having found** *a hotel, they usually go out to eat.*

B Past participles (for passives)
As it was written by an American, it gives an accurate picture of life there.
→ **Written** *by an American, it gives an accurate picture of life there.*

C Past participles used as adjectives.
Each night they arrive in a different town and feel exhausted.
→ *Each night they arrive in a different town,* **exhausted**.

3 Look at the information in the box and complete the second sentence with a participle so that it means the same as the first.

1 Since Jackson is an immigrant, he decided to write about immigrants.
.... an immigrant, Jackson decided to write about immigrants.

2 As he writes in the first person, he brings the story to life.
.... in the first person, he brings the story to life.

3 Because he has experienced problems himself, he writes very realistically.
.... problems himself, he writes very realistically.

4 Although the book was criticised at first, it was a huge success.
Although .... at first, his book was a huge success.

5 Despite the fact that she has had many problems, the protagonist never gives up.
Despite .... many problems, the protagonist never gives up.

6 Now that I've read this one, I can't wait for his next novel!
.... this one, I can't wait for his next novel!

7 I got to the end of the book and felt completely satisfied.
I got to the end of the book, ...

4 Look at the cover of the book *Heat and Dust*. The sentences below explain what the book is about. Use language from Exercises 1–3 to connect the ideas in the sentences as suggested. In each case, combine the sentences to make one long sentence.

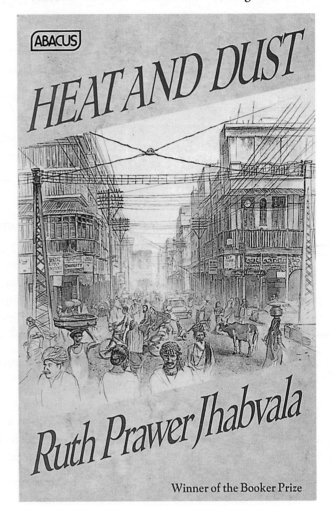

Winner of the Booker Prize

1 The book was written by a woman. She has lived in India for many years. It tells us a lot about life there. (*participle; relative*)
Written by a woman who has lived in India for many years, the book tells us a lot about life there.

2 It is about a young English woman. She goes to India with her child. She wants to find out the true story of her grandmother. (*relative; reason*)

3 Her English grandparents lived in India together. Her grandmother fell in love with an Indian man. (*contrast*)

4 She arrives there. Then she starts to follow the same life path as her grandmother. She falls in love with an Indian. (*perfect participle; conjunction + clause*)

5 It is set in two periods and tells two women's similar stories. It shows that lifestyles and attitudes change a lot over two generations. Love and relationships never change. (*participle; contrast*)

Writing   Set book (Paper 2 Part 2)

Lead-in   1   **Discuss these questions.**
1   What book have you read?
2   What kind of book is it?
3   What did you like most/least about it?

Understand the task   2   Read and analyse the task. What sort of writing are you being asked for in each task (e.g. a letter? a report?)?

> Answer **one** of the following two questions based on your reading of **one** of the set books.
>
> **Either a)** Your teacher has asked you to write a composition, giving your opinions on the following statement:
>
> *A good story should have a good beginning, a good middle and a good end.*
>
> Write your **composition**, explaining your views with reference to the book you have read.
>
> **Or b)** Your pen friend wants to buy a book in English for her father's birthday. He likes books with either interesting characters or an exciting story line. Your pen friend has written to ask whether you would recommend the book you have read. Write a **letter** in reply, giving your opinion and explaining the reasons.
>
> Write your **letter** in **120–180** words in an appropriate style.

Plan your answer   3   a   **Choose exam task a) or b) above, and answer these questions.**
1   What kind of story is your book?
2   Which aspects of the book are you going to focus on: plot, characters, general setting, a particular place?

b   Make notes under these headings. Make sure they relate to the question only.

Characters	Events	Setting (place)

c   Number the events you have listed (1, 2, 3, etc.) in the order they occur.

d   Choose the most important points for your answer.

e   Can you match your points from Exercise 3d to the paragraph plan below?
Paragraph 1: Reason for writing
Paragraph 2: General statements about the book + reasons
Paragraph 3: Statement(s) (about the story line) + reason + example
Paragraph 4: Statement(s) (about the characters) + reason + example
Paragraph 5: Conclusion + recommendation.

Language and content

4 a Put each of these adjectives under one of the headings for your notes in Exercise 3b. (There may be more than one possibility.) In context, would they be *Positive* (P) or *Negative* (N)?

lifelike   weak   unexpected   passionate   predictable   imaginative brave   disappointing   lovely   successful   interesting   convincing funny   clever   attractive   boring   sensitive   awful

b Can you think of any other adjectives you could use?

c How would you complete these expressions for your answer?

This is a story about … .
It is set in … .
The character(s) I like most/least … .
The reason I feel that … is … .
I think it is (written quite cleverly/extremely well-written) … because … .
It's full of … .
The best part of the book is when … .
I like/don't like the beginning/ending because … .

Write your answer

5 Write your answer using some of the language above.

Check and improve your answer

6 Edit your draft using this list.
Have you …
  • expressed yourself clearly?
  • given reasons for your opinions?
  • included enough detail, but not too much detail?
  • used a range of words, expressions and structures?
  • used appropriate linking expressions?

▶ Writing reference page 215

LANGUAGE SPOT: avoiding repetition

a **The words in bold below have been used to avoid repetition. What do they refer to?**

*No one writes better stories than Mike **does**, and **he's done so** for years. I like his early **ones**. Have you read any of **them**? If **so**, what do you think of **them**? If **not**, why don't I lend you **some**?*

b **Replace the phrases in italics in the sentences with one or more of these words in the correct form.**

so   not   one(s)   some   do

1 I think this is the first novel he has written. If *it is the first novel he has written*, it is an extraordinary achievement.
2 Most people who write novels *write novels* because they feel they have something to say.
3 They're very well-drawn characters, particularly the evil *characters*.
4 No one has written as many great plays as Shakespeare *wrote great plays*.
5 Have you got his latest book? If *you haven't got his latest book*, I'll lend it to you.
6 I like Chekhov plays. There's a good *Chekhov play* on at the Arts Theatre.
7 Have you got any good ideas? I need *good ideas* quickly.

24 The media

Listening (Paper 4 Part 4)

Before you listen

▶ Task strategy Unit 10 page 74

1 a Which newspaper do you usually read? What do you like about it? How does it compare with other papers?

  b Look at the listening task below. Read the questions but not the answers A–C.
    1 What personal qualities do you think are necessary to be a journalist?
    2 Discuss possible answers which you might hear.

Multiple-choice questions

▶ Task strategy Unit 10 page 74

2 ▭ You will hear an interview with a journalist. For Questions 1–7, choose the best answer A, B or C.

1 What convinced Mike to follow a career in journalism?
  A a course he took
  B his lack of success in business
  C the advice of a family member

2 What type of training did Mike have once he started work?
  A He studied for formal qualifications.
  B He worked closely with a more experienced colleague.
  C He received feedback on his work from newspaper readers.

3 When Mike first started working with the police, they
  A were unsure whether to trust him.
  B had little time to spend with him.
  C refused to accept drinks from him.

4 Why didn't Mike use the information he gained about Prince Charles?
  A It was against the law to do so.
  B He had promised that he wouldn't.
  C It was felt to be unfair to do so.

5 According to Mike, what is a journalist's most important quality?
  A being committed to the job
  B having good writing skills
  C feeling sure of your abilities

6 What does Mike say about modern journalism?
  A It's not as exciting as it used to be.
  B It's no longer as sociable as it was.
  C It's less demanding than in the past.

7 What disadvantage of journalism does Mike warn young people about?
  A the financial insecurity
  B the disruption of domestic life
  C the competitive atmosphere

Discussion

3 Now that you have heard Mike talking about his job, discuss these questions.
  1 Do you have the right qualities to be a journalist?
  2 What aspects of the job would you like/dislike?

Speaking   (Paper 5: parts 1–4)

Part 1: Interview

▶ Task strategy Unit 16 page 119

1 a Work in groups of three. One student is the examiner, the other two are Candidates A and B.

STUDENT 1: You are the examiner. Turn to page 223 for a list of questions to choose from. Stop after three minutes.

STUDENTS 2 AND 3: You are candidates. Look back at the task strategy for points to remember.

b Change roles so that everyone has a turn at answering the questions.

Part 2: Individual long turn

▶ Task strategy Unit 6 page 45

2 a Work in pairs. One student is Candidate A and the other is Candidate B. Respond to the examiner's instructions below.

Task 1

To Candidate A: Here are your two photos. They show people finding out about the news. Compare and contrast the photos, and say whether you prefer reading or listening to the news. You have one minute.

To Candidate B: Do you buy a newspaper?

b Work in pairs again. Respond to these instructions.

Task 2

To Candidate B: Look at the photographs on page 222. They show two different kinds of radio interview. Compare and contrast the photos, and say which you think makes the most interesting interview.

To Candidate A: Do you listen to the radio?

Part 3: Collaborative task

▶ Task strategy Unit 8 page 59

3 a Work in pairs. Look back at the task strategy for points to remember.

b Read the examiner's instructions below and do the exam task.

Look at the photos on page 222. They show different types of cars. First, talk to each other about what kind of people you think would buy each car. Then decide which car would be most suitable for a small family. You have about three minutes for this.

Part 4: Discussion

▶ Task strategy Unit 10 page 75

4 Now ask each other these questions. You have three or four minutes for this.

1 What do you think of car advertisements?

2 Do you drive a car?

3 If you could choose, what kind of car would you have?

4 Should governments do more to encourage people to use public transport?

5 What is the best way to travel around your country?

6 Which form of transport do you like least?

Use of English 1 (Paper 3 Part 4)

Lead-in

1 Are these statements *True* or *False*?
In Paper 3 Part 4, you should remove:
1 all words that can be removed.
2 one word that is incorrect.
3 words that appear twice on one line.

Error correction

2 a Read the text below and answer the questions.
1 What kind of adverts does the writer like and dislike?
2 In what way does advertising <u>not</u> give us a true picture of a product?

▶ Task strategy Unit 8 page 60
Unit 10 page 76

b Do the exam task. Follow the task strategy.

Read the text below and look carefully at each line. Some of the lines are correct, and some have a word which should not be there. If a line is correct, put a tick (✔) by the number. If a line has a word which should **not** be there, write the word in the space. There are two examples at the beginning (**0** and **00**).

DO YOU BELIEVE ADVERTS?

I like adverts that make me to laugh. Do you	**0** to
remember the one advertising long-life batteries? It	**00** ✔
showed a toy rabbit still was playing a drum while	**1**
all the other rabbits they collapsed one by one. I	**2**
thought so it was very funny. But I don't like adverts	**3**
that suggest me that what I have isn't good enough.	**4**
For example, ones that indicate that my house	**5**
needs improving but I needn't to spend a fortune	**6**
getting it fixed. If I listened to them, I'd have a	**7**
conservatory be added, a new shower installed and	**8**
all my furniture specially made out for me!	**9**
I have know that advertising tries to make us aware	**10**
of a product, and then it tries to get us for to buy it.	**11**
So we are only ever given by a positive image. We	**12**
are told us that a car goes fast, looks good and is	**13**
safe, but they don't mention that it will have to	**14**
have its bodywork repaired within the two years!	**15**

Discussion

3 Discuss these questions.
1 Do you think adverts are dishonest?
2 What things do you think should not be allowed in TV adverts, and why?

Language development 2

A *need + -ing/to be done*
  Active: *Someone **needs to** check the adverts.*
  Passive: *The adverts **need checking*** ⎫
       *The adverts **need to be checked*** ⎬ *to make sure they're legal.*

B *have/get something done*
  • We can use *have/get something done* when we arrange for someone to do something for us.
    *We think of the ideas ourselves, but we **have/get the adverts** made for us.*
  • We can also use *have/get something done* when someone else does something to us that we don't want.
    *We **had** our office **broken into** last night.* (had = not my fault)
    *I **got** my nose **broken** in a fight.* (got = my fault)

(LOOK) at the Use of English text opposite and find examples of *need + -ing* and *have/get something done.*

---

needs + -ing/to be(done)

1 a **Correct the mistakes in these sentences in two different ways.**
   1 The advert's too long. It needs shorten.
   2 Those posters are out of date. They need to replace.

  b **What needs doing? Respond to these sentences using *need +-ing* and a verb from the box.**

   rebuild   water   tidy up   cut   repaint   clean
   1 This garden's a mess.
   2 The grass is long.
   3 The plants all round the house are very dry.
   4 That wall's fallen down.
   5 Those windows over there are filthy.
   6 The paint on the doors is coming off.

  c **Look at these notes. Explain how to make a TV advert using *needs to be.***

   How to make a TV advert
   1 First raise money.
   2 Then write advert.
   3 Prepare script and bring to life.
   4 Find good production company.
   5 Hire experienced director.
   6 Recruit well-known actors.
   7 Shoot advert in studio you can afford.

have/get something done

2 a **Respond to the sentences using *have/get (done)* and any other language which is necessary.**
   1 A: Let's copy those pictures. Have you got a photocopier?
      B: No, I'll get them copied at the office.
   2 A: Where's your DVD player?
      B: I .... (*steal*).
   3 A: Let's repair your computer ourselves.
      B: No, ...
   4 A: Have you checked the tyres on the jeep?
      B: No, ...
   5 A: Shall we install the washing machine ourselves?
      B: No, ...
   6 A: These knives are very blunt.
      B: Yes, ... (*sharpen*).

  b **Why do we go to these places? Use *have/get (done).***
   1 a dentist's
   2 an optician's
   3 a dry cleaner's
   4 a hairdresser's
   5 a manicurist's
   6 a photographer
   7 a picture framer's
   8 a supermarket on the Internet

  c **Which of these things do you do yourself? Which do you have done for you?**
   • paint your room when it needs decorating
   • mend your TV when it's broken
   • tidy the house/apartment where you live
   • clean your car
   • service your car
   • clean your coat when it's very dirty
   • do the gardening

3 **Discuss these questions.**
   1 If you could have some of your clothes made especially for you by a tailor/shoemaker, etc. which ones would they be and what would you have done?
   2 If you could have a house built for you, where would you have it built and how would you have it designed?

Use of English 2 (Paper 3 Part 5)

Lead-in
1 **Discuss these questions about Paper 3 Part 5.**
   1 Is it better to read the text line by line or sentence by sentence?
   2 Should you answer the questions in order, or leave any you can't do and come back to them?

Word formation (A)
2 a **Read the text below and answer the questions.**
   1 What do some paparazzi do to get photographs?
   2 How do they defend what they do?

▶ Task strategy Unit 4 page 32

b **Do the task. Follow the task strategy.**

Read the text below. Use the word given in capitals at the end of each line to form a word that fits the space in the same line. There is an example at the beginning (0).

THE PAPARAZZI

Our interest in the private lives of celebrities seems **(0)** endless .	**END**
This has caused a **(1)**............. in the number of 'paparazzi', those	**GROW**
photojournalists who follow **(2)**............. celebrities around to	**GLAMOUR**
get **(3)**............. pictures of them, which they then sell to popular	**EMBARRASS**
magazines. There is a **(4)**............. large number of them, and some	**FRIGHTEN**
go to **(5)**............. lengths to get a picture. For example, they will	**BELIEF**
hire a helicopter in order to fly **(6)**............. close to the home of a	**DANGER**
celebrity and, much to his or her **(7)**............., peer into the bedroom.	**ANNOY**
But the paparazzi say that stars do not deserve **(8)**............., since	**PRIVATE**
they're only too happy to have their **(9)**............. weddings and	**ROMANCE**
the inside of their **(10)**............ homes photographed for huge fees.	**ORDINARY**

Word formation (B)
3 a **Read the text below and answer the questions.**
   1 What are special advisers?
   2 Why are some people in the UK concerned about them?

b **Do the task. (See the instructions above.)**

SPECIAL ADVISERS

Every **(0)** government likes to get its message across in the	**GOVERN**
best possible light. However, in the UK there has been a **(1)**.............	**WORRY**
increase in the number of advisers whose **(2)**............. it is to get the	**RESPONSIBLE**
public's **(3)**............. and to make sure that all news is good news.	**ATTEND**
These people tell **(4)**............. how they want a story to appear	**REPORT**
and have therefore become very **(5)**............. in politics. They also	**POWER**
write **(6)**............. sentences for speeches, which then get broadcast	**MEMORY**
on radio or TV. Nowadays, there is a **(7)**............. of ways of	**VARY**
getting news to people and **(8)**............. parties feel that the public	**POLITICS**
don't want to listen to long, careful **(9)**............. from their leaders.	**ARGUE**
However, some people think this reduces **(10)**............. of the press.	**FREE**

Discussion
4 **Discuss these questions.**
   1 Do you think politicians should present information in the best possible light?
   2 Should journalists always be free to say what they like? Why/Why not?

Language development 3

Word formation: review

1 a Look at the Use of English texts opposite and complete the table.

Adjective	Negative adjective	Noun	Adverb
responsible	....	....	....

b Complete the table, using a dictionary if necessary.

Adjective	Adverb	Noun	Verb
....	....	belief	....
....	worryingly	....	....
embarrassing	....	....	....
....	....	....	recognise
amazing	....	....	....
....	....	decision	....
....	....	....	think
legal	....	....	....
....	satisfactorily	....	....
....	....	....	astonish

c Use prefixes to make the opposites of these words.
legal *(adj.)*   satisfactorily *(adv.)*   romantic *(adj.)*
appear *(v.)*   accurate *(adj.)*   moral *(adj.)*
probable *(adj.)*   logical *(adj.)*   regular *(adj.)*
perfectly *(adv.)*

d Complete each sentence with a word from Exercises 1a, b or c above that has a similar meaning to the words in brackets. There may be more than one possibility.

1 The newspaper was .... to reveal secret information about the Queen. (*not thinking about the effects of their actions*)

2 It was an .... to the company that so many people complained about their adverts. (*something uncomfortable*)

3 Greenco says it is an environmentally friendly company, so it seems .... that its leaflets are not made of recycled paper. (*not based on careful thought*)

4 It is .... to make a false claim in an advert. (*against the law*)

5 To everyone's .... , our low cost advertising campaign was a big success. (*great surprise*)

6 The victim thanked the press for being so .... during the case. (*kind and considerate*)

7 News editors mustn't hesitate. They have to be .... (*able to make up their mind clearly and quickly*)

8 Many of the figures quoted in the newspaper were .... (*not correct*)

2 Complete the second sentence so that it is similar in meaning to the first sentence. Use the word in brackets, and the correct form of one of the words below.

use   lonely   fashion   relation   survive

1 The police and the media are getting on well these days. (*better*)
The police and the media have a .... these days.

2 This bag is no good at all – it's got a hole in it. (*absolutely*)
This bag is .... – it's got a hole in it.

3 I used to buy that music magazine long before everyone else bought it. (*became*)
I used to buy that music magazine long before it ....

4 The doctors said he would probably live. (*chance*)
The doctors said he had a good ....

5 When I left home, I had no friends. (*suffer*)
When I left home, I ....

3 a Complete these extracts from people talking about magazines with the correct form of the words in brackets.

1 I read a couple of great computer magazines each month. They're very .... (*profession*) produced.

2 Some men's magazines are quite .... (*entertain*) but I find others completely .... (*read*).

3 If I had to .... (*general*), I suppose I prefer magazines with .... (*stimulate*) articles about things that are happening in the world.

4 I have great .... (*admire*) for magazines about cooking. They are so .... (*create*) and I don't really like to .... (*critic*) them. However, sometimes I find their recipes a bit .... (*rely*).

5 I hate magazines that insult my .... (*intelligent*). So many of them are just about the .... (*relation*) of famous people. Not only are such articles extremely .... (*bore*), I find them rather .... (*offend*).

b Discuss these questions.
1 What kind of magazines do you read and why?
2 What kind of magazines do you dislike?

Exam practice 6

Paper 1: Reading

Part 3: gapped text (paragraphs)

You are going to read a newspaper article about the possibility of discovering life in space. Seven paragraphs have been removed from the article. Choose from the paragraphs **A–H** the one (**1–6**) which best fits each gap. There is one extra paragraph which you do not need to use. There is an example at the beginning (**0**).

Is ET out there?
We may soon have the answer.

Scientists believe it's only a matter of time before contact with aliens is made, says Michael Hanlon.

Nobody knows for sure what the future will bring. But one thing that seems certain is that some time between now and the year 3000, humans will discover that they are not the only intelligent beings in the universe. Aliens have been a dominant theme in science fiction and movies for a long time and millions claim to have seen UFOs.

0	H

This is despite the fact that in the 1970s they had become convinced of the opposite. The moon landings showed our nearest neighbour to be a dry sterile place, and further space investigations then established that Mars is a frozen desert and Venus is boiling hot.

1	

Now that this has been established, biologists believe that life in some form could probably exist elsewhere, too. Space scientists are organising missions to Mars in search of it.

2	

However, other people believe that finding such creatures is improbable, pointing out how difficult it is to get life started. You need water, a mild climate and a thick atmosphere to protect life forms from the sun. You also need a sun that will live long enough to get life started, a stable planet and a big moon to get rid of any passing asteroids.

3	

Those holding this view should, however, consider the enormous size of the universe. In our galaxy alone there may be 200 billion stars and there are about the same number of galaxies. There are about as many stars as there are grains of sand on all the beaches in the world.

4	

Finding alien bugs on any of these new discoveries would be the news of the century, finding intelligent life the biggest news in history. But we may now be able to discover alien civilisations for ourselves rather than just wait for them to appear to us in UFOs.

5	

By around 2010, these computers could come across the signal that would change history forever. Scientists are confident that we would have no problems understanding a message from aliens.

6	

However, a senior astronomer from the Californian Institute is confident that this will not happen. 'Being alone is the last possibility on my list.' he says 'If this is the only grain of sand where anything interesting is going on, that would be quite incredible.'

A This is more likely because computers are now so good at analysing signals from telescopes. This makes scientists believe they will soon pick up a radio message from aliens.

B Life could exist on other planets, too. For example, Europa, a moon of Jupiter, seems to have a giant ocean covered with ice. In these dark waters, warmed by volcanoes, some say strange sea monsters could be discovered by robot submarines within the next 30 years.

C These are no use without planets, of course. Ten years ago the only one that we knew had planets was our own – the sun. In the past few years, however, that number has gone up to about 30, as improved technology allows telescopes to spot more and more planets around stars.

D The efficiency of its work goes up by a factor of 100 every ten years. In astronomy, every time you improve something by a factor of 100, you find something.

E But then, of course, continuing silence could indicate that we actually are on our own – a more amazing possibility in a way than discovering a planet full of bug-eyed aliens.

F However, recent discoveries on our own planet have made scientists realise that life doesn't necessarily need an environment which is warm and earth-like. Creatures have been found in the most 'unfriendly' places imaginable – around undersea volcanoes a kilometre down, or even in rocks below the seabed.

G And even after all this, there still has to be the mysterious process that leads to life evolving. It is not surprising that many people think that life on earth was a unique event not repeated elsewhere.

H Clearly, therefore, many of us would like to believe there's something out there. Even scientists are now prepared to accept the possibility of finding something.

Paper 3: Use of English

Part 1: multiple choice cloze

Read the text below and decide which answer A, B, C or D best fits each space. There is an example at the beginning (0).

MIND OVER MUSCLES

If you're lazy and not in good physical (0) _C_ , then Dr Guang Yue, an exercise physiologist, has come up with a theory that might be of (1)............ to you. His (2)............ discovery is that the strength of our muscles can be improved without the need for physical activity. No longer do we have to (3)............ for long swims or have (4)............ workouts in the gym. It may seem (5)............ , but he says we can (6)............ up our muscles simply by thinking about exercise.

In Dr Yue's research, volunteers imagined they were moving their little fingers sideways, and found that the power of (7)............ was enough to increase strength in those finger muscles. Then he asked volunteers to (8)............ to themselves that they were moving their arm muscles in five training sessions a week. Remarkably, these volunteers experienced a rapid increase in the strength of their arms.

But sports psychologists say that, while this research is (9)............ , muscle strength is only one aspect of exercise, and we shouldn't (10)............ aerobic activity. We still need to (11)............ after our hearts, by taking exercise that (12)............ our heart rate to 70 per cent of its maximum for 20 minutes, three times a week. It would be (13)............ if people thought that exercise was (14)............ , and that they could (15)............ fit while slumped on a sofa just thinking about exercise.

0 A figure	B form	C shape	D body
1 A fascination	B appeal	C interest	D attraction
2 A extraordinary	B main	C individual	D clear
3 A take	B go	C stand	D get
4 A firm	B hard	C strong	D forceful
5 A insincere	B doubtful	C unsure	D improbable
6 A build	B grow	C spread	D develop
7 A idea	B mind	C thought	D brains
8 A persuade	B pretend	C expect	D convince
9 A significant	B chief	C principal	D leading
10 A throw away	B switch off	C look over	D cut out
11 A take	B look	C care	D run
12 A jumps	B climbs	C leaps	D raises
13 A worrying	B anxious	C concerned	D panicking
14 A helpless	B incapable	C useless	D minor
15 A make	B have	C put	D keep

Part 2: structural cloze

Read the text below and think of a word which best fits each space. Use only **one** word in each space. There is an example at the beginning (0).

BEHIND THE TV NEWS

Preparing for an evening TV news broadcast (0) _takes_ nearly all day. Early in the morning, yesterday's programme is played back, (1)............ that the producers can make sure it was (2)............ to their usual high standards.

Then, as (3)............ as everyone has arrived for work, the production team agrees (4)............ of the day's stories should be included in the programme. The producers then make decisions about the interviews that the journalists will go out and record. Whilst these (5)............ being filmed, the producers stay behind and (6)............ the rest of the scripts ready.

Meanwhile, the person (7)............ runs the studio, the director, checks on the cameras and lighting. If he or she (8)............ not do this efficiently, the broadcast could be a disaster.

Then, from early afternoon until the time of the broadcast, people (9)............ as the assistant producers and reporters are busy editing their stories. (10)............ people often don't realise is that even (11)............ some news teams are quite large, (12)............ is little time for rehearsals, because new stories are coming in all the time. Also, (13)............ the broadcast has to be exactly the right length, the producer always has to make last-minute changes.

Finally, in spite (14)............ the chaos, the time that everyone is looking forward to arrives and the programme goes (15)............ air.

Part 3: key word transformation

Complete the second sentence so that it has a similar meaning to the first sentence, using the word given. **Do not change the word given.** You must use between **two** and **five** words, including the word given. Write **only** the missing words.

EXAMPLE:

0 You must do exactly what the manager tells you.

carry

You must <u>carry out the manager's</u> instructions exactly.

1 Tom was too ill to get out of bed.

that

Tom was .... not get out of bed.

2 Although Sue did her best, she failed to win the race.

despite

Sue failed to win the race .... did her best.

3 That's the strangest game I've ever seen.

strange

I've .... game before!

4 A specialist is going to examine my knee next week.

have

I'm going to .... a specialist next week.

5 Her salary was so good she could afford a new car.

such

She earned .... she could afford a new car.

6 They have decided to reduce the number of phone calls they make.

down

They have decided .... the number of phone calls they make.

7 By the way, Tania and Tom both dislike eating meat.

nor

By the way, ... eating meat.

8 The weather was so bad they cancelled the open-air concert.

owing

The open-air concert .... the bad weather.

9 Pietro is taking Adrian's place in the tennis team.

replaced

In the tennis team, ... Pietro.

10 Is it necessary to wash this jumper before I wear it?

need

Does .... before I wear it?

Part 4: error correction

Read the text on the right and look carefully at each line. Some of the lines are correct, and some have a word which should not be there. If a line is correct, put a tick (✓) by the number. If a line has a word which should **not** be there, write the word in the space. There are two examples at the beginning (**0** and **00**).

CREATIVE WRITING COURSES

Despite the fact that very few books by new writers are being	0	✓
published, many of colleges offer courses in creative writing. I	00	of
used to wonder if there was any point in some such courses, when	1	
there was little hope of students getting to their work published.	2	
Nowadays, if a novel isn't been written by a celebrity, like a pop	3	
singer or a well-known writer who is always on TV, it has very	4	
little chance of selling. However, having just as finished studying	5	
as for a mature student on such a course, I believe they do have	6	
some use. Nobody can teach you to have too interesting ideas,	7	
but we were taught that, to make our stories commercial, they	8	
needed careful editing. This was due that to us trying to be so	9	
original that our stories were impossible to understand! We	10	
learnt that for people to enjoy of a story, it needs to be written	11	
in a clear style and have an exciting plot, so that people keep up	12	
reading. One of the my colleague's stories was a	13	
conversation between a supermarket trolley and a satellite dish,	14	
which it was certainly original, but who would want to read it?	15	

Exam reference

▶ See page 6 for Exam overview

Paper 1: Reading (1 hour 15 minutes)

There are four parts to this paper and a total of 35 questions. Questions in Parts 1, 2 and 3 carry two marks each. In Part 4 there are more questions, which carry one mark each.

Each part of the paper contains a text (or occasionally two or more shorter, related texts). These come from a variety of sources, including newspaper and magazine articles, stories and brochures.

Each text has a different type of task, which tests specific aspects of reading (e.g. understanding gist or finding specific information).

You can make notes on your question paper but the answers must be transferred to the answer paper before the end of the exam.

Part 1: multiple matching

▶ See pages 128–129 for an example.
This task requires you to match summary sentences or headings to each paragraph of the text. There is always an example, and an extra summary sentence or heading that doesn't fit anywhere.

This part of the paper tests your ability to identify the main information in each paragraph and separate it from the supporting detail. You need to find which of the options gives the same key information in different words.

Part 2: multiple-choice questions

▶ See pages 82–83 for an example.
There are questions on the text followed by four possible answers (A–D). You have to decide which answer is correct. The questions are in the same order as the information in the text.

This part tests detailed understanding of the text. Questions may include asking about opinions and attitudes expressed in the text, working out the meaning of vocabulary in context and understanding the relation between words and phrases (e.g. *What does 'it' refer to?*). There may also be a question which tests general understanding of the whole text (e.g. *Who was the text written for? Where does the text come from?*).

Part 3: gapped text

▶ See pages 158–159 for an example.
Either paragraphs or sentences have been taken out of the text, jumbled and put in a box after the text. The task is to decide where in the text each sentence or paragraph comes from. There is an example, and an extra sentence or paragraph which doesn't fit anywhere.

This task tests your understanding of how the text is structured. To do the task you have to be aware of the logical sequence of the text by looking for key words and ideas, and understand how grammatical and lexical devices are used to link sentences and paragraphs (e.g. *Having done that, she left*).

Part 4: multiple matching

▶ See pages 98–99 for an example.
The task is to match statements or questions to paragraphs (a group of different paragraphs related in theme, or a single text divided into paragraphs). Sometimes the information may be found in more than one section and you will be asked to provide two answers (in any order).

This part of the paper focuses on your ability to scan texts quickly in order to find specific information. Although the text may seem long, you do not need to read it in detail and the information required can usually be located quickly.

Paper 2: Writing (1 hour 30 minutes)

For this paper you have to write two texts of between 120 and 180 words. Both questions carry equal marks.

You are tested on your ability to achieve the task set. You must include all the necessary information, use a range of vocabulary and structures, organise your writing clearly, and use language which is appropriate for the person you are writing to. Any errors you make in grammar, spelling, punctuation, or paragraphing must not prevent adequate communication. Your handwriting must be legible.

Part 1: transactional letter

▶ See the Writing reference on page 207 for an example.
In Part 1 the task is compulsory. You are given a situation and some information to read (notes, illustrations, adverts, letters, notices, leaflets, etc.) and you have to write a formal or informal letter in response. Marks are based on a general impression in conjunction with how well you have achieved the task set, using the information given.

In order to achieve the task you must do the following.
- Carry out the instructions, using the information given.
- Include the information required from the input material, leaving out what is not relevant.
- Plan and organise your letter carefully, using suitable paragraphing and cohesive devices.
- Write in an appropriate style for whoever will be reading the letter.
- Use a variety of language to do whatever is required (e.g. complain, ask for or give information, etc.).

Part 2: writing task

▶ See the Writing reference on pages 209–215 for examples. You choose one of five options. Questions 2–4 always consist of three of these: an informal letter, a formal letter of application (e.g. for a job or scholarship), an article, a report, a story and a discursive composition. Question 5, which has two options, is always based on a 'set book' – the reading texts decided by the examination board.
You are told what kind of text to write (e.g. a story, a report, etc.) and given a context (e.g. who you are writing to and why you are writing). You have to decide what to include, how to organise your text and what kind of language to use.

Questions 2–5

Informal letter: this will be to a known reader, such as a pen friend. You are expected to write in a suitable informal style, and share your opinions, feelings or experiences, according to what the task requires.

Formal letter of application: this will be written to an individual or an organisation. You are expected to organise your letter and write in a suitable formal style.

Article: the context will be clear from the question or visual input. You are often expected to include a description of something/somebody or an anecdote. You should write in an appropriate style and engage the reader's interest.

Story: this is usually for a magazine, anthology or competition. You are given a sentence which you have to use, either at the beginning or the end. The aim is to interest the reader and write in a lively or dramatic style.

Report: you are expected to provide the reader (e.g. your boss, your teacher) with factual information in a neutral style and possibly to make suggestions or recommendations.

Discursive composition: this is usually written for a teacher. You usually need to discuss the good and bad points of a topic, and give your opinions and suggestions.

Set book: the questions are general enough for any of the set texts, and you may have to tell details of part of the story, describe the characters or a particular scene. The question might ask you to write a composition, a letter, an article, or a report and you are expected to discuss the question and not simply summarise the plot. You should imagine that your reader may be someone who has not read the book.

Paper 3: Use of English
(1 hour 15 minutes)

There are five parts to this paper and a total of 65 questions. Questions in Parts 1, 2, 4 and 5 carry one mark each. Part 3 carries two marks for each question. In this part of the exam, words must be spelt correctly. The question paper can be used for rough work but answers must be transferred to the answer sheet.

Part 1: lexical (multiple-choice) cloze

▶ See page 168 for an example.
To choose the correct word or phrase to fill the spaces in the text you have to:
- understand the context
- know the meaning of the 'missing' word
- know whether the 'missing' word would go with the other words in the context (e.g. Is it part of a fixed phrase? Which preposition follows it?).

You are tested on vocabulary: words and prepositions (e.g. *love of, succeed in*); prepositions and words/fixed phrases (e.g. *above average, do without*); phrasal verbs (e.g. *take after someone*); linking words (e.g. *although, in case*); adverbs (e.g. *particularly, nearly*); and sets of words with similar meanings (e.g. *travel, voyage, journey, excursion*).

Part 2: structural (open) cloze

▶ See page 152 for an example.
You have to fill in the spaces in a text with one appropriate word of your own choice so that it makes sense.
You are tested mainly on grammar, but you can also be tested on words and prepositions (e.g. *interested in, a way of*); fixed phrases (e.g. *on his way home, at least*); and phrasal verbs (e.g. *get on with someone*).
Grammar areas include: verb forms (e.g. auxiliaries, passives); pronouns (e.g. relatives – *who, which*, etc.); comparative forms (e.g. *more, less, than, as*); articles (*a, the*); determiners (e.g. *this, these*); possessives (e.g. *of*); conditionals; quantifiers (e.g. *one of*), time conjunctions (e.g. *before, while*); linking expressions (e.g. *because, but*); *neither/nor; it/there; make/do; whether or not; let/allow; as/like*, etc.

Part 3: key word transformation

▶ See page 167 for an example.
You are given the beginning and end of a sentence and you have to complete it so that it has a similar meaning to the sentence above it. There is a 'key' word, which you must use, and which you must not change in any way. Using the key word involves making more than one change to the original sentence. You have to use between two and five words including the key word. Contracted forms (e.g. *I'll*) count as two words.
You are tested on both grammar and vocabulary. Each question receives two marks; one mark may be given if there is a small error.
Grammar areas include: active and passive verb forms; comparatives and superlatives; indirect and reported speech; clauses of purpose and result (e.g. *so … that*); verbs + *-ing/to*; modals; *wish/it's time* + past; conditionals; verb + two objects; quantity (e.g. *hardly any*); adverbs; *it/there*; *make/let/allow*; *despite/in spite of*; *since/for*; *prefer/rather/had better*; *remember/forget*; *lend/borrow*; *in case*; *too/enough*; *so/such*.
Vocabulary areas include: words and preposition (e.g. *be good at*); phrasal verbs (e.g. *look forward to*); changing nouns to verbs; and expressions (e.g. *out of work*).

Part 4: error correction

▶ See page 120 for an example.
You read a text which contains an incorrect word in most of the lines. They are extra words that should not be there, not words that can be left out. Between three and five of the lines will be correct. There is no more than one incorrect word on each line, and if a word appears more than once on a line that word will not be incorrect.
You are tested mainly on grammar. Areas include: reflexives and possessives (e.g. *own, myself*); quantity (e.g. *some, lots, much*); verb forms; relatives; articles; *if/when* clauses; clauses of purpose; verbs + *-ing/to*; verbs with/without objects; clauses with question words; words with/without prepositions; *too/very/enough*; *so/such*; *all/both*; *either/or*; *instead/instead of*; *despite*; *rather/prefer*; and phrasal verbs.

Part 5: word formation

▶ See page 138 for an example.
You are given a short text and you have to change the form of a word at the end of each line to make it fit a space in the same line. For the word to make sense in context you may have to add a prefix (e.g. *un-*) or a suffix (e.g. *-able*), or both, to change it into a noun, adjective, verb form or adverb. You may need to make some words negative or plural according to the context; some verbs into participles (e.g. *write* ▶ *written*); and some

adjectives into superlatives (e.g. *big* ▶ *biggest*). You might have to make internal changes (e.g. *strong* ▶ *strength*) or compounds (e.g. *rain* ▶ *raindrop*). You don't need to make more than two changes to the original word.

Paper 4: Listening
(approximately 40 minutes)

This paper has four parts. Each part has one or more recorded texts and comprehension questions. There are a total of 30 questions. Each question carries one mark. Recordings can include interviews, conversations, talks and announcements, etc. The recordings might be a series of short extracts (of approximately 30 seconds) or longer extracts (of approximately 3 minutes). Each recording is played twice.
Each task focuses on a different aspect of listening (e.g. understanding the gist or main points, or identifying specific information).
You can make notes on your question sheet during the exam but at the end you are given 5 minutes to transfer your answers to the answer sheet provided.

Part 1: multiple choice (extracts)

▶ See page 89 for an example.
You will hear eight short unconnected recordings of one or two people speaking in different situations. Each extract lasts approximately 30 seconds and you hear each extract twice before you go on to the next one. In this part of the paper both the questions and the three options which go with each question are recorded, as well as being in your answer booklet, so that you have time to think about the recording coming up.
Each question requires you to 'tune in' and listen out for clues, so that you can understand a general situation (e.g. *What are the people talking about? How does the teacher feel? Who is speaking? Where are the children?* etc.). You are not being tested on the detail.

Part 2: note-taking/sentence completion

▶ See pages 118 and 164 for examples.
This is always a longer extract (approximately 3 minutes) with one or more people speaking. The questions require you to take notes or complete sentences, normally with a maximum of three words. The questions are in the same order as the text and all the words you have to write are on the recording. However, the words are not in the same order as on the recording – it is not a dictation.
The key is to listen for the information you need and ignore the rest. Your spelling must be understandable, though not necessarily perfect, and your handwriting must be clear.

Part 3: multiple matching

▶ See page 104 for an example.
You will hear five short related extracts, each with one or two speakers. You hear all the extracts together once, before you hear them all again a second time. The task is to match each extract to one of the six options on a list. One of the options is not used.

As in Part 1, this part of the paper tests your ability to listen for the general meaning; to pick up clues and get information about the context, ignoring irrelevant information.

Part 4: choosing from two or three answers

▶ See page 148 for an example
This is always a longer extract (approximately 3 minutes). It is often an interview, where people give their opinions. The task requires you to choose answers from two options (e.g. *Yes/No, True/False*) or three options (e.g. matching statements to three speakers).

As in Part 2, this part of the paper requires you to listen for specific information or detail.

Paper 5: Speaking
(approximately 14 minutes)

This paper is divided into four parts. Assessment is based on performance in the whole of the speaking test, based on the following criteria:

- how accurate and appropriate your vocabulary and grammar is
- the fluency and range of your language
- how comprehensible your pronunciation is
- how well you work with your partner or examiner to carry out the task.

There are always two examiners present. One of the examiners (the interlocutor) explains the tasks and asks the candidates questions, while the other (the assessor) assesses the candidates and gives marks. In Parts 1 and 2 the candidates speak mainly to the interlocutor and in Parts 3 and 4 with a partner (another candidate). You may or may not know your partner. You should speak as clearly and naturally as possible.

Part 1: interview

▶ See page 119 for an example.
The examiner will ask you personal information in an interview (approximately 3 minutes). You will have to use a range of social language and verb forms in order to talk about such things as: where you live, your family, what you do in your spare time and your future plans.

Part 2: individual long turn

▶ See page 149 for an example.
You have to speak without interruption for about a minute to compare and contrast two photos on a similar theme, and give your personal reaction to them. The examiner will tell you the subject of the photos and give you the task, which requires you to:

- talk about differences and similarities between the photos, and speculate on what they are about
- give your opinions on and reactions to something connected to the photos.

You also have to answer a question after your partner has spoken, so you need to look at his/her photos and listen to what he/she says, so that you can be prepared to comment.

Part 3: collaborative task

▶ See page 165 for an example.
You work with your partner for 3–4 minutes to complete a task, using the pictures or diagrams which the examiner gives you. The task may involve solving a problem, making a plan, putting things in order of priority or making a decision. There are no right or wrong answers and it is not necessary to agree with each other.

You are tested on your ability to cooperate and work together on a task: you are expected to take turns at speaking, sometimes lead the conversation, involve your partner and come to a conclusion. However, it is more important how you work towards the completion of a task than actually completing it.

Some of the language you need to use includes: asking for, giving and reacting to opinions and suggestions, speculating, interrupting, opening and closing the discussion.

Part 4: discussion

▶ See page 105 for an example.
You will be asked questions which develop ideas related to the topic in Part 3. The discussion will open up into more general areas.

This is an opportunity to show how much language you know. Although this part of the exam is led by the examiner, there must be a balance between giving your own opinions and listening to and involving your partner. The examiner will stop you after approximately 4 minutes.

Grammar reference

Contents

1 Articles

A The indefinite article

a/an: with singular countable nouns
(but *some* with plural or uncountable nouns and *one* when we want to emphasise the number)

1 When we introduce something new, unfamiliar or unexpected to another person:
*I need **a** new car.*
*It's **a** good opportunity to travel.*
*There's **an** old woman in the street.*

2 In descriptions and classifications (to say what kind of thing):
*It's **a** lovely day, isn't it? It's **a** big hotel. What **a** nice town!* (descriptions)
*My sister is **a** doctor.* (jobs)
*The play was **a** comedy.* (classifications)

3 Meaning all:
***An** orange has a lot of vitamin C.* (= all oranges)
(We also say: *Oranges have a lot of vitamin C.*)

4 Meaning *every* in expressions of time/quantity/speed:
*twice **a** week*
*two euros **a** kilo*

B The definite article

the: for singular and plural nouns.

1 When the other person knows who or what we are referring to:
*Where's **the** car?* (you know which car I mean)
*Do you know **the** people at that table?* (you can see them)
*There's a man and a woman outside. **The** woman says she's your sister.* (I have already mentioned the woman.)
***The** earth goes round **the** sun.* (it's the only one)

2 In certain fixed expressions:
*He joined **the** police/ **the** army/ **the** navy.*
*Let's go to **the** shops/**the** cinema/**the** theatre/**the** bank.*
*She plays **the** piano/**the** violin.*
*I went to **the** airport/**the** bus station.*

3 In some general statements:
*Who invented **the** telephone?* (inventions)
***The** tiger is in danger of extinction.* (species – but *Tigers are … is more common*)

4 The definite article is used with these proper nouns:
- oceans and seas (***the** Pacific ocean*)
- rivers (***the** Amazon*)
- groups of islands (***the** Bahamas*)
- mountain ranges (***the** Alps* but not individual mountains: ***Mount** Fuji*)
- deserts (***the** Sahara*)
- countries with plural nouns and political terms (***the** USA, **the** Netherlands, **the** Czech Republic*)
- groups of people (***the** Germans, **the** rich*)
- hotels/cinemas/theatres (***the** Ritz, **the** Variety Theatre*)
- newspapers (***the** Times*)
- political bodies (***the** Government, **the** Labour Party*)

C Zero (no article Ø)

Zero article before plural and uncountable nouns.

1 When we refer to something general or abstract:
*Ø **Houses** are getting much more expensive.*
*He's making Ø good **progress**.*
*He's got a lot of Ø **courage**.*
*He's studying Ø French **history**.* (but ***the** history **of** France*)

2 Before institutions, when someone is part of the institution:
*He's at Ø **university/school/church**.*
*She's in Ø **prison/hospital**.*
*I got to Ø **college** at 8:30.* (I'm a student there – part of the college)
BUT *I got to **the** college at 8:30.* (the building I was visiting)

3 Before:
- people: *My name's Ø **Brad Pitt**.*
- most countries: *He lives in Ø **Germany**.*
- continents: *Have you been to Ø **Asia**?*
- counties: *They come from Ø **Yorkshire**.*
- villages/towns/cities: *She works in Ø **London**.*

- parks: *We went for a walk in Ø **Hyde Park**.*
- streets: *I did some shopping in Ø **Oxford Street**.* BUT **the** High Street.
- languages: *I speak Ø **French**.*
- sports: *He plays Ø **golf**.*
- plural parts of the body: *He's got Ø big **ears**.*
- illnesses: *Bob's had Ø **appendicitis**.*
- gerunds: *We often go Ø **skating**.*

4 Before meals and in most expressions of time/dates/ seasons:
*at Ø **breakfast**, Ø **last week**, at Ø **5:30**, in Ø **June**, on Ø **time**, in Ø **autumn***

5 In certain fixed expressions:
*watch Ø **television** (but listen to **the** radio)*
*go to Ø **work/bed**, go Ø **home***
*go by Ø **bus/train/car***

2 Countable and uncountable

A Countable nouns

Most common nouns are countable. Countable nouns can be singular or plural. They refer to things we can count (e.g. *one car, two cars*). We can use *a/an* with singular countable nouns:
*I took **an** umbrella and **a** coat with me.*

B Uncountable nouns

Uncountable nouns (usually) have no plural. We can't count liquids (*water*), materials (*wool*) or abstract qualities (*progress, behaviour*). We use *some/any* (or no article) with uncountable nouns, not *a/an*:
some/any progress (NOT ~~a progress/two progresses~~)
Some common uncountable nouns are:
accommodation, advice, behaviour, bread, butter, electricity, fun, food, furniture, health, information, knowledge, luggage, money, music, news, research, salt, scenery, spaghetti, traffic, travel, trouble, weather, work

C Countable and uncountable nouns

1 Some nouns can be either countable or uncountable:

Countable	Uncountable
a chicken (the animal)	*some chicken* (the meat)
chocolate (the substance)	*chocolate* (a sweet or a drink)
two coffees (two cups of coffee)	*some coffee* (the substance)
a glass (of milk)	*glass* (the substance)
a hair (a single hair)	*my hair* (the hair on my head)
have a good time (experience)	*I haven't any time.*
a good cheese (a variety of cheese)	*I like cheese.* (in general)
a paper (a newspaper)	*Have you got any paper?* (the material)
There are four rooms/spaces.	*Is there any room/space?* (it's crowded)
He's got two businesses.	*do business* (buy and sell)

2 Some uncountable nouns can be limited by using a countable expression:
a piece/bit of (bread, news, information, advice)
a drop of (water/milk)
a slice of (bread/toast/cake)
an item of (news)

3 Some determiners go with countable nouns (e.g. *many*), some with uncountable (e.g. *much*) and some can go with both (e.g. *a lot of*).
Note: there is a difference in meaning between *few/a few* and *little/a little*:
Countable:
There are a few (= some) *people.*
There are few (= not many) *people.*
Uncountable:
There's a little (= some) *time.*
There's little (= not much) *time.*

▶ page 61 for examples of determiners that go with countable and uncountable nouns.
▶ page 192 for articles with countable and uncountable nouns.

3 Adjectives

A Form of adjectives

1 Most common adjectives have no special endings (e.g. *large, rich*).

2 Sometimes we add a suffix to a noun or verb to form an adjective, e.g.:
comfort (n.) > *comfort**able*** (adj.)
live (v.) > *live**ly*** (adj.)
Some common adjective suffixes include:
noun > adjective: *wood**en**, sens**ible**, child**ish**, fam**ous**, music**al***
verb > adjective: *act**ive**, care**ful**, help**less**, slee**py***

3 A number of adjectives end in *-ly* and look like adverbs e.g.: *lively, friendly, lovely, lonely, deadly*

4 Some adjectives have the form of the past or present participle.
- *-ed* (past participle) adjectives describe our reaction to something/someone:
  *I was very **bored** with/by the play.*
- *-ing* (present participle) adjectives describe the thing/ person/event/experience that causes the reaction:
  *The play was very **boring**.*
Other common pairs of participle adjectives include:
amused/amusing, annoyed/annoying, depressed/depressing, disappointed/disappointing, excited/exciting, interested/interesting, terrified/terrifying, tired/tiring

5 In two-part adjectives the second part is often a participle, e.g.:
well-known, beautifully-dressed, time-consuming

193

B Gradable and ungradable adjectives

1 An adjective which is gradable can be used in the comparative and superlative forms (e.g. *cold, colder, the coldest*). We can use an adverb of degree to make it stronger (e.g. **very** *cold*) or weaker (e.g. **fairly** *cold*).

2 Ungradable adjectives are extreme (e.g. *furious, awful*) or absolute e.g. (*dead, correct*). We can use an adverb which emphasises them, but not an adverb which makes them stronger or weaker:
absolutely *furious* (~~very~~ *furious*)
completely *wrong* (~~fairly~~ *wrong*)
totally *exhausted* (~~rather~~ *exhausted*)

3 Adjective word order
Normally, no more than three adjectives go before the noun. Adjectives go in a particular order according to what type of adjective they are.
The order of adjectives is:
opinion/judgement + size + age + shape + colour + pattern + nationality + material (+noun):

a **small**, **red**, **silk** scarf
  (size) (colour) (material)
a **lovely**, **old**, **Italian** car
  (opinion) (age) (nationality)
a **big**, **round**, **wooden** table
  (size) (shape) (material)

4 Adverbs

A Form of adverbs

1 In most cases, we add *-ly* to the adjective to form the adverb (e.g. *careful* > *careful***ly**).
If an adjective ends in *-ll*, we add *-y*, (e.g. *full* > *full***y**).
If an adjective ends in *-y*, the *-y* changes to *-i*, (e.g. *happy* > *happ***ily**).
In some cases other changes are needed:
fantastic > *fantastic***ally**, *remarkable* > *remarkab***ly**, *true* > *tru***ly**

2 *Good* is an exception and is irregular: *good* > *well*

3 Some adjectives have *-ly* endings (e.g. *friendly, lively, lonely, silly*). We cannot add *-ly* to make these into adverbs. Instead we use *in a … way/manner/fashion*:
*He smiled **in a friendly way**.*

4 Some adverbs have the same form as adjectives (e.g. *fast, hard, straight, far, early*):
*He works **hard**.* (adv.) *He's a **hard** worker.* (adj.)

5 Some adverbs have two forms with different meanings:
*I worked **hard** all morning.*
*He has **hardly** changed at all.* (almost not)

*The bus came ten minutes **late**.*
*I've been feeling ill **lately**.* (recently)

B Position of adverbs

1 Different types of adverbs and adverb phrases can be used in different positions in a sentence, but not always in every position. The most 'neutral' position for adverbs is at the end of the sentence, but they can go in front/mid position for emphasis:
Front: **Occasionally** *he misses the bus.*
Middle: *He **occasionally** misses the bus.*
End: *He misses the bus **occasionally**.*
But NOT: *He misses ~~occasionally~~ the bus.* (between verb and object)

2 Most frequency adverbs (e.g. *always, often, never*) go before the main verb, but after the verb *be*:
*He **always walks** to work.*
*He **is always** late.*

3 Frequency adverbials (e.g. *every week, twice a year*) can't go in mid position:
Front: **Every summer** *we go there.*
End: *We go there **every summer**.*
But NOT: *We ~~every summer~~ go there.*
We go ~~every summer~~ there.

C Adverbs of degree

We use adverbs of degree to make adjectives and adverbs stronger or weaker.

1 The adverbs *very* and *extremely* collocate with most gradable adjectives:
very/extremely *impressive, lively, beautiful*

2 The adverb *absolutely* collocates with most ungradable adjectives:
absolutely *wonderful, gorgeous, exhausted*

3 Other adverbs often tend to collocate with certain adjectives although these collocations are not exclusive:
utterly *useless, delightful, miserable*
highly *skilled, educated*
totally *crazy, exhausted*
completely *different, relaxed*

4 The adverbs *quite* and *rather* can have more than one meaning, depending on the adjective/adverb they are used with.
• *quite* + adjective (= *moderately, fairly*)
  *The book was **quite** good. It was **quite** a good book.*
  *I like him. He's **quite** nice.*
  (This use is not common in American English.)
• *quite* + ungradable adjective/adverb (= *completely/ absolutely*)
  *The news was **quite** extraordinary.*
  *He was **quite** right to make a complaint.*
• *rather* + negative adjective (= *moderately*)
  *He's **rather** a lazy student./He's **a rather** lazy student.*
• *rather* + positive adjective (= *very*)
  *She's **rather** good at maths.*

5 Comparatives and superlatives

A Types of comparison

1 We use the comparative form + *than*, or *as ... as* to compare two or more things:
*Chloe is a **better** swimmer **than** Hannah.* (to a higher degree)
*Harry is **as** good a mathematician **as** Ryan.* (to the same degree)
*Amy is **less** confident **than** Katie.* (to a lower degree)
*Amy is **not as** confident **as** Katie.* (to a lower degree)

2 We use the superlative form when we want to pick out one thing from all the others:
*Mount Everest is **the highest mountain** in the world.*

B Adjectives

1 Regular adjectives

		Comparative	Superlative
One syllable	*old*	*old**er***	*(the) old**est***
	large	*larg**er***	*(the) larg**est***
One syllable with one vowel + one consonant at the end	*big*	*big**ger***	*(the) big**gest***
One or two syllables with *-y* at the end	*happy*	*happ**ier***	*(the) happ**iest***
Two or more syllables	*careful*	***more** careful*	*(the) **most** careful*

2 Exceptions
- one syllable adjectives:
  *I feel **more ill** today than I did yesterday.*
  *I feel **colder** OR **more cold** today than I did yesterday.*
  *We got more and **more lost**.* (adjectives formed from past participles)
- some common two-syllable adjectives (e.g. *clever, gentle, simple, shallow, narrow, pleasant, cruel, polite, quiet, stupid*):
  *clever – clever**er** (OR **more** clever) – **(the)** clever**est** (OR **(the) most** clever)*
- two-syllable adjectives ending with *-y*:
  *He looks much **happier** (OR **more happy**) these days.*
- ungradable adjectives (e.g. *superior, unique, fundamental*) do not have a comparative form.

C Adverbs

1 We don't use *more/(the)most* with adverbs which have the same form as adjectives (e.g. *hard, fast, early, long, quick*):
*fast – fast**er** – (the) fast**est***
*early – earl**ier** – (the)earl**iest***

2 With most other adverbs we use *more/(the)most*:
***more** carefully/(the) **most** carefully*
Note: in informal English you will sometimes hear *-er/-est* adjectives instead of the more 'correct' *more/most* adverbs:
*He drove much **slower** than usual.* (instead of *much more slowly*)

D Irregular adjectives/adverbs

	Comparative	Superlative
good/well	*better*	*(the) best*
bad/badly	*worse*	*(the) worst*
much	*more*	*(the) most*
little	*less*	*(the) least*
far	*farther/further*	*(the) farthest/furthest*
old	*elder/older*	*(the) oldest/eldest*

E Sentence patterns

1 Comparative + *than*:
*The meat is more expensive **than** the fish.*
*He's taller **than me**.* (*than* + object pronoun)
*He's taller **than I am**.* (*than* + subject pronoun + verb)
Note: the *than* clause is sometimes not stated:
Fish is getting more expensive these days. (i.e. than it was before.)

2 *the* + superlative + *in/of*:
*The bathroom is **the** biggest room **in** the house.*
*She's **the** brightest student **in** the class.*
*Today is **the** shortest day **of** the year.*
Note: *the* is not always used with the superlative form:
Try your hardest!
Jack and Jessica were best.

3 *the* + superlative + clause:
*It's **the** fastest car **(that) I've ever driven**.*

4 *less/(the) least* (the opposite of *more/(the) most*):
*He's **the least intelligent person** (that) I know.*
*He's **less intelligent than** his sister.*
Note: more commonly used:
*He's **not as** intelligent **as** his sister.*

5 Comparing quantities
- We use *more/less/the most/the least* to compare quantities:
  *She spends **more/less** (money) than her brother does.*
  *She earns **the most/least** (money).*
- In formal style *fewer/fewest* is used before plural nouns:
  *There are **more/fewer** (of us) here each year.* (plural countable noun)
  *I spend **more/less** (of my) time on the golf course.* (uncountable noun)

6 Common modifiers ▶ page 16:
*The book was **a lot/much/far/a great (good) deal** more (less) interesting than I thought.* (a big difference)
*The film was **a bit/a little/slightly/rather** more (less) interesting than the book.* (a small difference)

7 Expressions:
*In the next few years the Internet will get **quicker and quicker**.* (to show an increase)
*It's getting **hotter and hotter**.*
*The **earlier we leave, the earlier** we get there.* (the two changes go together)
***The better the weather, the more crowded** the roads get.*
***The less** you earn, **the less** you have to spend.*
***The sooner, the better**.*

6 Clauses

A Identifying clauses in sentences

1 A clause has a subject and a verb, and it either forms a sentence:
I was walking home
or part of a sentence:
… when I met Pete.

2 There are many ways of joining clauses in sentences, e.g.:
words like *which* (relative clauses: ▶ page 196)
if (conditionals: ▶ pages 201–202)
than (comparatives and superlatives: ▶ page 195)
(said) that (reported speech: ▶ pages 203–204)
when (time: ▶ page 55)

B Clauses of reason, purpose, result and contrast

1 Clauses of reason (*Why?*):
*He couldn't see **because** he wasn't wearing his glasses.*
Other connecting words/expressions include:
because of/for/owing to/due to (+ noun)
as/since (+ subject + verb)
seeing/owing to the fact/due to the fact (that + subject + verb)

2 Clauses of purpose (*What for?*):
*I looked in the dictionary **to** check the meaning.*
Other connecting words/expressions include:
in order to/so as to (+ infinitive)
in order that/so that/in case, for fear (that) (+ subject + verb)
Note: we can also say:
*I looked in the dictionary **because** I wanted to check the meaning.*

3 Clauses of result:
*I feel **so** tired **that** I'm going to bed.*
Other connecting words/expressions include:
so much/so many … that and *such a … that* (+ subject + verb)

4 Clauses of contrast:
*I went to work **despite** the fact that I felt very tired.*
Other connecting words/expressions include:
• *in spite of/despite* (+ noun/present participle/perfect participle):
She fell asleep, in spite of the cold.
She stayed awake, despite being tired.
• *although/though/even though/even if/much as/whereas/ while/however/no matter how (much/many/badly)/in spite of the fact that* (+ subject + verb)
Note: *while* and *whereas* contrast ideas that don't contradict each other:
*Nurses' salaries have risen **while/whereas** doctors' salaries have fallen.*

C Participle clauses

▶ page 85 for participles used in reduced relative clauses.

In participle clauses the subject of the participle must be the same as the subject of the main clause.
Being a French teacher (= me), *I speak French very well.*

1 Present participles:
*I stayed awake all night, **thinking** about our life together.* (= and thought)
***After phoning** you, I realised my mistake.* (time: = After I phoned)
***In/On trying** to open the door, I broke my key.* (time: = While I was trying)
***Being** a pilot, I knew how to fly the plane.* (reason: = As I was a pilot)
***Having** a pilot's licence, I knew… .* (reason: = As I had …)
*I wrote **telling** her the news.* (purpose: = in order to tell her)
***Despite not feeling** well, I went into work* (contrast: = Despite the fact that I didn't feel well)
*The man **living** next door is an old friend of mine.* (relatives: = who lives)

2 Perfect participles:
***Having done** most of the course I want to finish it.* (reason: = Since I've done – active)
***Having been given** a pay rise, I decided to celebrate.* (time: = After I had been given – passive)

3 Past participles:
Past participles are used for passives and are found more in writing than conversation:
***Seen** from this distance, it looks quite attractive.* (= When it is seen)
***Although built** fairly recently, it looks quite old.* (= Although it was built)
*Cars **made** in Japan are very common in Europe.* (= which are made)

7 Relative clauses

A Relative pronouns in clauses

Relative clauses provide additional information about a noun, a clause or a sentence. They begin with a relative pronoun.

Noun	Relative pronouns
people	*who (whom, that)*
things (animals)	*that (which)*
time	*when*
place	*where (which* + preposition)
possession	*whose*

Note: the relative pronouns *what/who* can be used without a noun:
*They didn't know **what** (the thing) **I wanted/who** (the person) **I meant.***
***What** (the thing) **I saw** was amazing.*

B Defining relative clauses

1 Defining relative clauses (without commas) provide essential information:

*The man **who/that bought the jacket** is over there.* (people)
*That's the car **which/that won the race**.* (things)
*It was the moment **when I knew for sure**.* (time)
*He's the man **whose house is for sale**.* (possession)
*That's the house **where Sam lives**.* (places)

2 We usually place a preposition at the end of a relative clause:
*That's the house **which I used to live in**.* (places)
But we place a preposition before the relative pronoun in more formal English:
*The delivery date for your goods will depend on the postcode area **in which you live**.*
We also place a preposition before the relative pronoun when the relative clause is very long:
*This is the letter **in which** he said he was looking forward to coming home.*

3 The relative pronoun can be left out if is the object of the verb in the relative clause:
***The film** (which/that) **we saw** was three hours long.*

4 Participle clauses (see also page 85) and infinitives can sometimes replace relative clauses.
*People **buying** this product will be disappointed.* (= who buy)
*The car **parked** outside belongs to Tara.* (= which is parked)
*The last person **to leave** the office should switch the lights off.* (= who leaves)

C Non-defining relative clauses

1 Non-defining relative clauses are more common in written English than spoken English. They provide extra information (between commas) not essential to the sentence. The sentence would make sense without the clause:
*My mother, **who lives in Scotland**, is 94.*
*She was ill, **which was very unusual for her**.* (Here *which* refers to the whole main clause, not just the subject.)

2 After numbers and words like *some, many, most, neither*:
*There were a lot of people in the house, **some of whom** I'd met before.*
*I did German and Italian at university, **neither of which** I had learnt before.*

3 *That* is not used in non-defining clauses and object pronouns cannot be omitted:
*This book, **which** my father gave me, is over 50 years old.*
(NOT *This book, ~~that~~ my father gave me, …*)

8 Verb forms: the present

A Present habit

1 The present simple is used for:
- habits:
  *I **clean** my teeth every night.*
- permanent or long-term situations:
  *I **come** from Australia.*
  *They **live** near the sea.*
- permanent facts:
  *Ice **melts** in the heat.*

Typical time expressions used with the present simple include:
usually, always, never, hardly ever, as often as I can, twice a day, whenever I can

2 Present continuous (+ *always*) and *keep* (*on*) + *-ing* are used for surprising or annoying habits. (for things which happen very often/too often):
*Kate**'s always giving** me chocolates. I don't know why!*
*She**'s always saying** silly things. (It's annoying.)*
*She **keeps** (**on**) **saying** silly things.*

3 We use *tend to* for things that usually happen:
*He **tends to** interfere in other people's business.*
*Men **don't tend to/tend not to** live as long as women.*

4 We use *will* for:
- the typical way a person behaves:
  *My brother **will** sit for hours just reading a book.* (with a time expression e.g. *for hours*)
- stating what you think/assume is true:
  *That**'ll** be your sister on the phone. Can you answer it?*

B Present state

The present simple is used with certain verbs which describe a state rather than an action:
*I **like** college.*
*That cake **looks** good.*
*I **believe** you.*
These are 'state' verbs, such as verbs of:
- appearing: (e.g. *appear, seem, look*)
- thinking (e.g. *doubt, feel, gather, know, mean, remember, think, understand, expect*)
- feeling (e.g. *dislike, hate, love, want, wish, prefer*)
- sensing (e.g. *hear, see, smell, taste, sound*)
- owning (e.g. *belong, need, owe, own*)

These verbs are not normally used in the continuous, except when they describe a mental or physical action or process:
*I'm **thinking** of you all the time.* (mental action)
*He's **appearing** in a new film.* (physical action)

2 Other verbs for which we usually use the present simple include:
promise, refuse, agree, deny, depend, fit, mean, involve, matter

C Present event/situation

The present continuous is used for:
- something happening now: *I'm **watching** TV at the moment.*
- a temporary situation: *She's **studying** economics.*
- a changing/developing situation: *It's **getting** dark.*

Typical time expressions used with the present continuous include:
at present, currently, at the moment, for the time being, today

9 Verb forms: present perfect

A Present perfect simple

Form: *have* + past participle.

The present perfect simple is used to talk about past actions and situations in a time period that is unfinished:

*I've **lived** in China.* (in my life, which is unfinished)
*The taxi's **arrived**.* (it's here now)
*I've **lived** in this house for ten years.* (the ten-year period until now)

Note: *gone* and *been* are both used to make the present perfect of *go*, but with different meanings:

*He's **gone** to London* (he's in London now)
*He's **been** to London* (it's a past experience; he isn't in London now)

The uses of the present perfect simple include:

1   Experience:
    ***Have** you ever **met** a famous person?* (= at any time)
    *I've never **lived** abroad.* (= at no time)
    *He's **travelled** widely.*
    NOT ~~I have ever lived~~

2   Things (recently) completed in the past with a result now:
    *I've **hurt** my leg. I can't walk.* (past event – we are not thinking *when* it happened, but it's relevant now)
    *Look! The aircraft's **just** landed.* (= a short time ago)
    Note: *just* always goes before the main verb.

3   Things that have happened (or not happened) up to now:
    • *yet* (up to now – but we expect it to happen):
      *Have you read the letter **yet**?*
      *I haven't read it **yet**.* (NOT ~~I have read it yet.~~)
      Note: *yet* comes at the end of the sentence and is used only in questions and negative sentences.
    • *still* (up to now – but we expected it to happen by now):
      *They **still** haven't called me.*
      (NOT ~~They have **still** called me.~~)
    • *already* (before now)
      *Have you **already** seen this film?*
      *Yes, I've **already** seen it.*
      Note: *already* goes before the main verb or at the end of the sentence and is used in questions and positive sentences.
    Other adverbials used with the present perfect include *so far* and *up to now, recently*.

4   Unfinished actions or states which started in the past and continue now:
    *I've lived in this town **for five years**.*
    (NOT *I ~~live~~ in this town for…*)
    *She's been a teacher **since she left university**.*
    Note: to answer *How long…?* we use *for* and *since*:
    • *for* with a period of time: ***for** three weeks*
      (NOT ***during** three weeks*)
    • *since* with a point of time: ***since** 2000, **since** last week, **since** three weeks ago*

B Present perfect continuous

Form: *have* + *been* + *-ing*.

The present perfect continuous is used to talk about activities in a period of time that is unfinished. It places focus on the activity in progress, not the finished action.

1   Recent temporary activity:
    *I've **been reading** a good book.*

2   Recent repeated/extended activity:
    *Your brother **has been ringing**.*
    *She's **been playing** tennis all morning.*

3   Present perfect continuous/present perfect simple
    • the present perfect continuous focuses on the activity, not on whether the activity is finished or not. The present perfect simple can be used to focus on completion of an activity:
      *'Why are you so dirty?' 'I've **been cleaning** my room.'* (maybe the cleaning is finished, maybe not.)
      *I've **cleaned** my room. Do you want to see it?* (the cleaning is finished)
    • the present perfect continuous is also used for temporary situations which may change:
      *I've **been living** in this house for two years.* (I still live here but it's probably temporary.)
      *I've **lived** in this house for two years.* (I still live here and I probably won't move.)
    • *be, know* and other state verbs are not normally used in the continuous:
      *She's **been** a teacher since 1999.* (NOT *She's ~~been being~~ …*)
      ▶ page 197 for state verbs.

10 Verb forms: past time

A Past simple

Form: regular verb + *-ed* (*stay* > *stayed*); but there are many verbs with irregular forms (*see* > **saw**, *go* > **went**).

The past simple is usually used with a definite time expression (e.g. *last night, two years ago*) to talk about completed actions in past time.

1   Completed actions at a particular time in the past:
    *I **went** to Rome last Thursday.*

2   Completed situations over a definite period of time in the past:
    *I **worked** in a bank when I was younger.*

3   Repeated actions/situations in the past:
    *We **went** to the beach every summer.* (past habit)

4   Actions which happen quickly one after the other:
    *When I **arrived** they **turned** off the television and **started** cooking.*

Note: the past simple is also used in reported speech (▶ page 203) and to talk about unreal situations (▶ pages 201–202 for Conditionals and 205 for *wish*).

B Past continuous

Form: *was/were* + *-ing* (e.g. *was living*).
The past continuous is used in the following ways.

1 At a particular time in the past when we were in the middle of a (temporary) action/situation:
*On Friday night we **were listening** to a CD.*
Sometimes the action/situation is interrupted by a shorter event (in the past simple):
*We **were listening** to a CD when the telephone **rang**.*
Sometimes other people are doing things at the same time:
*We **were listening** to a CD while my brother **was reading** a book.*

2 Background descriptions:
*(We went out into the street.) It **was raining** hard and people **were carrying** umbrellas.*

3 Describing typical behaviour with *always*:
*She **was always smoking** in the house.*

4 To talk about planned events that did not happen:
*We **were meeting** Jane the next day but she didn't come.*
Notes:
● we use the past continuous to focus on the activity or its effect on us. We are not saying whether or not the action is completed. With the past simple, the action is always completed.
● with state verbs such as *have, seem, know*, etc. we usually use the past simple not the past continuous:
(*I **knew** him well.* NOT *I **was knowing** him well.*)
  ▶ page 197 for state verbs.

C Past perfect simple

Form: *had* + past participle (*had visited*).
The past perfect simple is used when we talk about actions or events before a past time:
*When we got to the airport the plane **had** already **left**.*
However, if the order of events is clear, we often prefer the past simple:
*The plane left before we **got** there.*
Note: the past perfect simple is also used in reported speech.
  ▶ pages 203–204 to talk about unreal situations.
  ▶ pages 201–202 for Conditionals and 205 for *wish*.

D Past perfect continuous

Form: *had* + *been* + *-ing* (e.g. *had been working*)
We use the past perfect continuous for an activity over a period of time up to a specific time/event in the past:
*Before I came to London I **had been working** in Paris.*
*They **had been waiting** for an hour when the bus finally arrived.*
Notes:
● we use the past perfect continuous to focus on the activity or its effect on us, not the completed action.
● with state verbs (*seem, know, understand*, etc.) we usually use the past perfect simple not the past perfect continuous (▶ page 197 for state verbs):
*It **had seemed** difficult to do.* (NOT *It **had been seeming**…*)

E Past habit

1 Past simple + adverb of frequency can be used for past habits:
*Every day I **got up** at 7 a.m. and **went** to work by bus.*

2 *Used to* for states/habits which are no longer true:
*I **used to** live in Edinburgh.* (state)
*I **used to** go out every Friday.* (habit)

3 We can use *would* for habits – but NOT states – which are no longer true:
*When I was younger, I **would** go out every Friday.*
(but NOT *When I was younger I **would** live in London.*)

4 We can use *kept (on)* to suggest criticism of a habit:
*He **kept (on)** talking while I was trying to sleep.*

11 Verb forms: the future

A Future forms

A variety of forms can be used to talk about the future:
● *be going to* + infinitive
● present continuous (▶ page 197)
● *shall/will* + infinitive
● present simple (▶ page 197)
● *be to* + infinitive
● *be due to/be about to* + infinitive
● *be on the point of* + *-ing*
● future continuous (*will/shall/going to* + *be* + *-ing*)
● future perfect (*will/going to* + *have* + past participle)
● future perfect continuous (*will* + *have* + *been* + *-ing*)

B Future meanings

1 Planned events
● we use *going to* for things we've already decided/intentions:
I'm going to buy a new suitcase. My old one broke last week.
● present continuous (+ a time expression) is used for arrangements:
I'm taking my driving test tomorrow. I applied a few weeks ago.
● we use the future continuous for a planned/routine action without personal intention – polite:
***Will** you **be going** to the meeting tomorrow? If so, could you give my apologies?*
Note: state verbs like *feel, know*, etc. are not normally used in the continuous. ▶ page 197 for State verbs.

2 Fixed events
● present simple (+ a time expression) is used for public timetables and programmes:
*The bus **leaves** in half an hour.*
*My French classes **finish** next week.*
● *is/are to* for formal official arrangements:
*The Queen **is to visit** Australia next year.*

3 Unplanned events
We use *will/shall* for events decided more or less at the moment of speaking (e.g. offers, promises, requests, refusals, decisions):

*That looks heavy. **Shall** I help you?/I'll help you.*
*It's cold in here. **Will** you close the door?* (request)
*I **won't** lend her any money. She never pays it back.*

4 Predictions
  - *be going to* is used when we notice something in the present which will make something happen:
    *I feel ill. I think **I'm going to** be sick.*
    *It's very cloudy. I'm sure it's **going to** rain.*
  - we use *will/'ll* when we expect something to happen – it is our opinion based on experience/knowledge:
    *We'll be there/We **won't** be there before midnight.*
    *The sun **will** rise at 6:30 a.m. tomorrow.*
  - To show how sure we are about something we use phrases like:
    I expect/I'm sure/I think/I don't think (we'll be late).
    or modals (▶ page 106):
    *We **may/might/could** be there before midnight.*

5 For events close to happening we can use *about to* or *on the point of*:
  *She's **about to** burst into tears.*
  *She's **on the point of** bursting into tears*
  We can use *due to* for more planned events:
  *The bus **is due to** arrive at nine o'clock tomorrow.*

6 The future continuous is used for action in progress at a fixed time in the future:
  *I'll **be lying** on a beach when you get this card.*

7 The future perfect is used for something completed before a specific time in the future:
  *We'll **have finished** before you get back.*
  (OR *We **may** have finished … if it is less sure.*)

8 We use the future perfect continuous for something that may not be completed/may be ongoing at a specific time in the future:
  *I'll **have been learning** English for five years by the time I take the exam.*

9 Future in the past: sometimes when we are talking about the past, we want to refer to something that was in the future at that point in the past. We use the same structures that we use for talking about the future, but change the verb forms:
  *I **was going to** come but I changed my mind.*
  *We arrived at the building where the interview **was to** take place.*

10 The present simple is used in time clauses with future meaning and Type 1 conditional clauses:
  *When you **see** Tom, give him a big kiss for me.* (time clause)
  *If the Beach Café **is** full, we'll go to Maxim's instead.* (Type 1 conditional)

12 Modals

Modals express our attitudes and emotions to an event or situation. The modal auxiliary verbs are: *can, could, may, might, must, will, would, shall, should, ought to* and *need*.

There are other non-modal verbs and expressions (e.g. *be able to, have to, allow*) which we can sometimes use instead of modal verbs.

A Form

Present time:			Past time:			
	modal	+ infinitive		modal	+ *have*	+ past participle
You	can	go.	You	could	have	gone.

Notes:
  - *he/she/it can go* (there is no change in the third person)
  - modal verbs have no infinitive form

B Permission

1 *Can, could* and *may* are used to talk about permission:
  - *can*:
    ***Can** I go out? Is that all right?* (asking for permission)
    *He **can** go to the cinema on his own. That's OK.* (giving permission)
  - *could*:
    ***Could I** borrow some money?* (asking for permission – more polite than *Can I…?*)
    *She said that I **could** go to the party.* (reporting permission)
  - *may*:
    ***May I** leave class early today? I've got a job interview.* (asking for permission – for more formal situations)

2 Other non-modal verbs and expressions can be used to talk about permission:
  - *let* + object + infinitive
    *My parents **let me go** to concerts with my friends.*
    Note: *let* does not have a passive form.
  - *allow (to)*
    *They **allow her to watch** TV.* (*allow* + object + *to-*infinitive)
    *I **was allowed to leave** class early today.* (passive + *to-*infinitive)
    Note: in a sentence like this, where the permission resulted in an action, we can't use *could* (NOT *I ~~could~~ leave the class early today*).
  - *permit (to)*
    *You **are permitted to smoke** only in the designated areas.*
    *Smoking **is permitted** only in the designated areas.* (rules made by someone else – more formal than *allow*)

C Prohibition

1 *Can't, couldn't, mustn't* and *may not* are used to talk about prohibition:
  - *can't*:
    *He **can't** go to a nightclub. He's too young.* (prohibition)
  - *couldn't* (past form of *can*):
    *He said I **couldn't** use it.* (he refused permission)
  - *mustn't*:
    *You **mustn't** talk in the library. Please be quiet!* (direct order)
    Note: the past form of this sentence is :
    *I **wasn't allowed to** talk in the library.*

- *may not*:
  Candidates **may not** leave the room during the exam. (prohibition)

2 Other non-modal expressions can be used to talk about prohibition and rules that are made by someone else:
   - *not supposed (to)*
     You're **not supposed to** park here.
   - *allow (to)*
     My manager **won't allow me to take** the day off.
     You're **not allowed to take** photographs here.
   - *permit (to)*
     You **are not permitted to smoke** in here.
     Smoking **is not permitted** here. (more formal than *allow*)
   - *forbid/ban*
     Cars are **forbidden/banned** in the town centre. (prohibition – very strong)
     Note: *forbid* is more likely to be used in formal notices than when speaking.

D Obligation and necessity

1 We use *must/mustn't* to express strong obligation or necessity:
   - *must* (stronger than *should/had better*):
     I **must** post the letter straightaway. (I, personally, feel it is necessary)
     Note: For the future of *must* we use *will/'ll have to* and for the past we use *had to*:
     I'**ll have to** hurry or I'll miss the last bus.
     She **had to** go home because she felt ill.
   - *mustn't* (stronger than *shouldn't*):
     You **mustn't** forget your keys. (an obligation NOT to do something)

2 Other non-modal verbs can be used to talk about strong obligation and necessity:
   - *have (got) to* is used when the situation or someone else (not the speaker) makes it necessary:
     I **have to** work late tonight. My boss says so.
     We'll **have to** invite my mother next time. (the situation makes it necessary)
     I **had to** go to the doctor's yesterday. (past time – it was necessary)
   - *make* is used for a strong obligation imposed by someone else:
     Her parents **make** her wash the dishes. (*make* + object + infinitive)
     She **is made to** wash the dishes. (passive + *to*-infinitive)

3 *Should/shouldn't, ought to/ought not to* are used to express a slightly less strong obligation or a duty/responsibility:
   You **should/ought to** phone and let them know you'll be late.
   They **shouldn't** leave without permission.

4 *Should have/ought to have* is used when something was the right thing to do, but you didn't do it:
   You **should have/ought to have** had an early night last night. You look tired. (you didn't go to bed early)
   Note: *shouldn't have* is commonly used, but *ought not to have* is rare.

5 *Supposed to* is a non-modal expression we use to talk about our responsibilities and the correct way of doing things:
   What time **are we supposed to** be at the office?

E Lack of obligation/necessity

1 We use *don't have to/haven't got to, needn't/don't need to, needn't have* and *didn't need to* to express lack of obligation or necessity:
   - *don't have to/haven't got to*
     You **don't have to** wash those dishes. They're clean. (it's not necessary)
     Note: *have got to* is more informal than *have to*.
     We use *didn't have to* as the past form of both *don't have to* and *haven't got to*:
     I **didn't have to** go to the doctor's yesterday. (it wasn't necessary)
   - *needn't/don't need to*
     You **needn't/don't need to** wash those dishes. They're clean. (it's not necessary)
     Note: *need* can be a modal verb (negative = *needn't*) or an ordinary verb (negative = *don't need*).
   - We use both *needn't have* (modal verb) and *didn't need to* (ordinary verb) when we talk about past time, but they have different meanings:
     There were plenty of seats on the train. We **didn't need to** stand. (It wasn't necessary.)
     There were plenty of seats on the train. We **needn't have** stood. (It wasn't necessary, but we did stand.)

F Advice and recommendation

1 *Should(n't)/should have, ought to/ought to have* are used to give advice and recommendations. (*Ought to* is less commonly used than *should*.)
   You **should** see it – it's a great film. (recommendation)
   You **shouldn't/ought not to** go to work today – you really don't look well. (advice)
   Note: the past forms *should have/shouldn't have* suggest criticism:
   You **should have** told me you weren't coming. I waited for ages.
   He **shouldn't have** shouted at me.

2 The non-modal expression *had better (not)* is stronger than *should/shouldn't*:
   It's cold. You'**d better** wear a coat. (it's the best thing to do)
   Hurry up! We'**d better not** be late.

▶ page 106 for modals of speculation and deduction.
▶ page 121 for modals of ability.

13 Conditionals

We can categorise conditionals into three main groups:
- likely or real events/situations:
  If you go out later, can you please turn out the light?
- unlikely (or imaginary) events/situations:
  If I had four million euros, I'd buy a big house in Spain.
- unreal events/situations in the past
  If I'd arrived late again, my boss would have been furious.

Notes:

- the main clause can come before the *if* clause in conditional sentences, but the punctuation is different:
  If it rains, we won't have a picnic. (a comma comes after the *if* clause)
  We won't have a picnic if it rains. (there is no comma between the clauses)

A Likely/real conditionals (Type 1 and zero)

1 Type 1 conditionals are used for events/situations that are likely to happen:
  - present + modal (with present/future meaning)
    If there's a good film on TV, I'll watch it. (possible/likely situation + result)

*If you **need** a ticket,*	*I **can** get you one.* (offer)
	I'll get you one. (promise)
	*I **might** be able to get you one.* (possibility)

  - present + *going to*
    *If there's a good film on TV, I'm definitely **going to** watch it.*
  - present + imperative
    *If the phone **rings**, please **answer** it.* (instruction – for a possible event)
  - other conjunctions can be used to introduce conditions (e.g. *as long as, provided that, even if, unless*):
    *I'll kill you **unless** you turn that music down!* (= if you don't)
    *She won't go, **even if** she's invited.* (= whether or not)
    *I'll cook dinner, **as long as** you do the washing-up.* (= only if)

Notes:

- If we are sure something will happen, we use *when*:
  ***When** I leave school, I'm going to become a teacher.* (NOT ~~If I leave...~~)

2 A 'zero conditional' is used for facts that are always true. We use a zero conditional when both events happen and *if* means *when*:
  - present + present:
    *If/When you **press** this switch, the television **comes** on.* (always true/normal event/fact)
  - past + past:
    *If/When the weather **was** bad, we always **stayed** indoors.* (past habits)

3 There are other possible patterns for situations/events which are likely or possible:
  - modal + modal/imperative:
    If you'll just wait a moment, I'll see what I can do. (request)
    *If you **should** get lost, **go** into the Tourist Office.* (less likely, but possible)
    *If it'll help you to sleep, **open** the window.* (result)
  - present continuous + modal/imperative:
    *If you're expecting someone, I **can** leave.*
  - present perfect + modal/imperative:
    *If you've finished your work, we **can** go.*

B Unlikely/imaginary conditionals (Type 2)

1 Type 2 conditionals are used for unlikely or imaginary events/situations in the present or future. In Type 2 conditionals:
  - past + *would/could/might* + infinitive:
    *If you **went** abroad, you **might learn** something about foreign cultures.* (unlikely that you will go, but possible)
    *If you **were driving** to London, which way **would** you **go**?* (imaginary – you're not driving)
    *If he **didn't have** a car, he'd **find** it difficult to get to work.* (imaginary – he has a car)
  - both *was* and *were* can be used with *If I/he/she/it …* :
    *If I **were** rich, I wouldn't work.*
    *If I **was** rich, I wouldn't work.* (not normally used in formal English)
  - *were* can start the sentence and replace *if* in formal English:
    ***Were** you really ill, I'd look after you, but you're perfectly OK.*
  - *should* is sometimes used instead of *would* after *I* and *we* in more formal contexts (e.g. formal letters):
    *I **should** be grateful if you would contact me … .*

2 We can use Type 2 conditionals for offers, suggestions, advice and requests:
  *I **wouldn't do** it if I **were** you.* (advice)
  ***Would** you **mind** if I **used** your phone?* (request)
  An offer can be made more or less direct, depending on the type of conditional used:
  Type 1: *If you **need** the key, I **can** probably find it.* (direct)
  Type 2: *If you **needed** the key, I **could** probably find it.* (less direct/I'm less sure you need the key)
  Type 3: *If you **were to need** the key, I **could** probably find it.* (even more tentative, polite)
  Note: polite requests can also be made using *If you would …* :
  *If you **would** take your seats, ladies and gentlemen, we'll **start** the meeting.*

C Unreal/imaginary conditionals in the past (Type 3)

1 Type 3 conditionals are used for unreal or imaginary events/situations in the past. They are often used to express regret or criticism:
  - past perfect + *would/could/might* + *have* + past participle:
    *If I **had heard** the alarm, I **would have** woken up on time.* (but I didn't hear it so I overslept.)
    *I **would have** helped her if she had asked me.* (but she didn't, so I didn't help.)
  - *had* at the start of the sentence can replace *if* (formal):
    ***Had** you been ill, I would have looked after you.*

2 It is possible to mix conditionals Type 2 and 3, particularly when a past event has an effect in the present:
  *I **would be married** now if I'd **had** the courage to propose to her.*
  *If you **were** more intelligent, you **would have thought** about that before.*

▶ page 205 for *wish/if only*.

14 Passives

In passive sentences, the action, event or process is more important than who or what does the action:
*Fruit **is picked** in the autumn.*
If we want to mention the 'person doing the action', we use *by*:
*I **was robbed** last night **by** a man in a dark jacket.*

A Forms

		to be	+ past participle
present simple		*is*	
present continuous		*is being*	
past simple		*was*	
past continuous		*was being*	
present perfect		*has been*	
past perfect	*It*	*had been*	*made in Taiwan.*
be going to		*is going to be*	
will		*will be*	
future perfect		*will have been*	
present/future modal		*may be*	
past modal		*must have been*	

Negative: *It **wasn't made** in Europe.*
Question: ***Was** it **made** in Taiwan?*
Note: verbs that do not take an object (e.g. *arrive*) do not have a passive form: (NOT *She ~~was arrived~~*.)

B Sentence structure

1 In an active sentence the subject is the person/thing that does the action. In a passive sentence the subject is the person/thing to which something happens:

Active:	subject	active verb	object
	Tracey Emin	*won*	*the prize.*
Passive:	subject	passive verb	agent
	The prize	*was won*	*by Tracey Emin.*

2 In a sentence with two objects there are two possible sentence structures, but usually we make the person the subject of the passive sentence:

Active:	subject	active verb	indirect object	+ direct object
	He	*gave*	*Sue*	*a CD.*

Passive: *Sue was given a CD.*
(*A CD was given to Sue* is possible but less likely.)

3 We can use the passive with 'reporting verbs' (e.g. *say, expect, suppose, agree, know, think, understand, claim*) to talk about an opinion held by some people/a lot of people/experts, etc. The following patterns can be used:

- subject + passive + *to*-infinitive:

Our team	*was expected*	*to do well.*
It	*is supposed*	*to be a fine day tomorrow.*

- *It* + passive + *that*

It	*has been agreed*	*that we have to make improvements.*

4 Some verbs (*see, hear, make, help, know*) are followed by an infinitive (without *to*) when they are active, but a *to*-infinitive when passive:
*They **heard** him **shout**. > He **was heard to shout**.*

C Use of passives

1 Passives are more often used in written language (e.g. newspapers, reports, scientific writing, notices and announcements). They can often sound formal and impersonal:
*Customers **are requested** not to leave their bags unattended.*

2 Passives can be used to take personal responsibility away from the speaker:
*Income tax **will be increased** next year.*

3 We sometimes use passives to continue the theme of what is being talked about. In the following sentence the new information – Beethoven – is put at the end for emphasis:
*This is a marvellous symphony. It **was written** by Beethoven.*

4 Passives are also used when information about who does something is expressed in a long phrase:
*He **was given** a box of chocolates by a woman wearing a dark coat and black boots.*

5 In informal English we can sometimes use *get* + past participle with a passive meaning, for things that happen by accident or unexpectedly:
*The postman **got bitten** by a dog.* (= was bitten)
*How **did** your car **get damaged**?* (= who/what was it damaged by?)

15 Reported speech

'I want to give you something,' he said. (direct speech)
*He **said** (that) he **wanted** to give me something.* (reported speech.)

A Reporting statements

1 To report something said in the past, we normally change forms one step back in time. This is sometimes called 'backshift':

Direct speech		**Reported speech**
Present:		
*I **don't like** you.*	>	*She said she **didn't like** me.*
*What **are** you **doing**?*	>	*He wanted to know what I **was doing**.*
Present perfect:		
*I've never **been** to China.*	>	*He said he **had** never **been** to China.*
Past:		
*I **saw** him.*	>	*He said he **had seen** him.*
*I **was having** lunch.*	>	*He said he**'d been having** lunch.*
Future:		
*I**'ll help** you.*	>	*She said she **would help** me.*
*We**'re going** out.*	>	*They said they **were** going out.*
Some modals:		
*I **can't** read it.*	>	*He said he **couldn't** read it.*
*We **must** go.*	>	*They said they **had to** go.*
*I **may** be late.*	>	*She said she **might** be late.*

2   No backshift is needed with:
  • past perfect:
    I **had seen** him. > He said he **had seen** him.
  • modals: would, should, might, could, ought to:
    We **might** go out for meal. > They said they **might** go out for a meal.

3   Sometimes backshift is needed with other forms, depending on the context:
    He **said** he **wanted** to give me something. (reporting the past)
    He **said** he **wants** to give me something. (we are emphasising it is still true)
    He **said** he **had wanted** to give me something. (to emphasise one thing happened before the other)
    He **had said** he **had wanted** to give me something but he changed his mind. (said/wanted happened before changed his mind)

4   Some changes in common time and place words are:

Direct speech		Reported speech
today	>	that day
tomorrow	>	the next day/the following day
next (week)	>	the following (week)
yesterday	>	the day before, the previous day
last (year)	>	the (year) before/the previous (year)
this	>	that
here	>	there
come	>	go
bring	>	take

B Reporting questions

To report questions:
  • we use a reporting verb (e.g. ask, want to know, wonder) and the same word order as in statements:
    'Do you like science fiction films?' > He asked **if I liked** science fiction films.
  • Yes/No questions – use if or whether:
    'Are you coming with us?' > He asked **if** I was going with them.
    'Do you want tea or coffee?' > She asked me **whether** I wanted tea or coffee.
  • Wh- questions – use the wh- question word:
    'When is she leaving?' > He wanted to know **when she was leaving**.
  • in questions with modals, only can and may change:
    '**Can** you tell me the way?' > She asked if I **could** tell her the way.
    '**Could** you tell me the way?' > She asked if I **could** tell her the way.
    '**May** I interrupt for a moment?' > I asked if I **might** interrupt for a moment.

C Reporting requests/commands

To report requests/commands we use the reporting verbs: ask, tell:
  • verb + object + to-infinitive:
    'Come here, please!' > He **asked me to go** there.
  • for negative requests/commands use not + to-infinitive:
    'Please don't speak so quickly.' > He **told me not to speak** so quickly.

D Reporting verbs

Some reporting verbs simply report the speaker's words (e.g. say, tell, state, answer, reply). Other reporting verbs tell us something about the speaker's intention. The choice of verb sometimes depends on how we interpret what the person was saying:
He **persuaded** me that he wanted to give me something.
This group of verbs includes:
admit, advise, claim, convince, feel, insist, persuade, suggest, think, urge, warn

E Verb patterns

1   Verb + to-infinitive:
    agree/ask/offer/promise/refuse/threaten (+ **to see her**):
    He **refused to see** her.

2   Verb + object + to-infinitive:
    tell/advise/ask/invite/order/persuade/remind (+ **her to come**):
    I **told her to come**. (NOT I told to her to come.)

3   Verb + -ing:
    admit/deny/report (+ **being/having been there**)
    He **denied having been** there.
    suggest/recommend (+ **doing something**):
    They **suggested trying** the new Chinese restaurant.

4   Verb + object + that:
    tell/advise/convince/persuade/promise/remind + **me that** …
    They **told me that** I should come back later.
    (NOT They told to me that …)

5   Verb + object + preposition + -ing:
    congratulate + **him on passing** the exam
    accuse + **her of cheating**
    blame + **us for breaking** it
    discourage + **you from going** to the concert
    Note also:
    • apologise **to** + object + for + -ing:
      I **apologised to her for being** late.
    • insist **on** + -ing:
      We **insisted on seeing** the manager.

6   Verb (+ preposition + object) + that:
    say/admit/complain/explain/mention/suggest + **(to him) that** …
    With these verbs the hearer is not the direct object:
    Ann **said (to him) that** she felt tired.
    (NOT Ann said him that …)

▶ pages 204–205 for verbs + -ing forms and infinitives.

16 Verbs + *-ing* forms and infinitives

I haven't **finished reading** the newspaper. (verb + -ing)
I **hope to see** you soon. (verb + to-infinitive)
I saw him **leave**. (verb + infinitive)

A Verbs followed by *-ing*:

admit, adore, appreciate, avoid, can't face, can't help, can't stand, can't resist, carry on, consider, delay, deny, detest, dislike, don't mind, enjoy, fancy, feel like, finish, give up, imagine, involve, keep (= continue), mention, mind, miss, postpone, practise, put off, resent, risk, suggest, understand

B Verbs followed by *to*-infinitive

afford, agree, aim, appear, arrange, ask, attempt, can't afford, can't wait, choose, claim, decide, demand, deserve, expect, fail, guarantee, happen, help, hope, learn, manage, mean, offer, plan, prefer, prepare, pretend, promise, refuse, seem, swear, tend, threaten, turn out, want, wish
Note: many verbs followed by *to*-infinitive express a concern for the future (e.g. *arrange, expect, hope, intend, plan*).

C Verbs followed by *-ing* OR *to*-infinitive

1 Verbs with a small or no change in meaning:
 - *begin, can't bear, bother, can't stand, continue, hate, intend, like, love, prefer, propose, start*:
 I **started watching/to watch** television. (no difference in meaning)
 Don't **bother washing/to wash** the floor.
 - *-ing* sometimes suggests a general statement (and acts like a noun) and the *to*-infinitive suggests a specific action in the future:
 I **prefer cycling** to swimming.
 (general activity NOT ~~I'd prefer to cycle to to swim~~)
 I **prefer to go** by bike but you can walk. (specific action)
 I'**d love to come** to the cinema with you. (specific activity after *would*)

2 Verbs with a change in meaning:
 forget, go on, mean, need, regret, remember, stop, try:
 - I'll never **forget seeing** you looking so miserable. (a past event)
 Don't **forget to post** the letter! (in the future)
 - I **remember locking** the door. (in the past)
 Please **remember to write** to me. (in the future)
 - He **went on talking** and talking. (continued)
 He **went on to ask** me how old I was. (changed the activity/subject)
 - Being a good piano player **means doing** a lot of practice. (involves)
 Did you **mean to leave** the house unlocked? (intend)
 - I **need to have** a bath. (I must – it's important)
 This room **needs painting**. (somebody needs to do it – passive meaning)
 - I **regret telling** you my secrets. (in the past)
 I **regret to have to tell** you that I no longer love you. (I'm telling you now)
 - **Stop worrying!** (no longer do something)
 She **stopped to talk** to me. (stopped and changed activity)
 - **Try changing** the bulb. (to see what happens – experiment)
 I **tried to phone** you last night. (made an effort)

D Verbs followed by infinitive

1 modal verb + infinitive
 I **might go** to the meeting, but I **can't stay** long.
 Note: the exception is *ought*:
 You **ought to tell** him the truth.

2 *make/let* + object + infinitive
 The teacher **made us do** the exercise again.
 My boss **let me go** home early, because I wasn't feeling well.
 Note: the passive form of this structure is:
 We **were made to** do the exercise again. (passive + *to*-infinitive)
 (▶ See also pages 200–201 for *make* and *let*.)

3 Certain expressions (e.g. *I'd rather, You'd better*) are followed by the infinitive (without *to*):
 I'**d better go** now, or I'll be late.

E Verbs followed by *-ing*/infinitive

Some verbs of the senses (e.g. *see, hear, feel*) can be followed by either *-ing* or an infinitive:
 - I **heard** her **sing** a lovely song. (I heard the whole song)
 I **heard** her **singing** a lovely song. (I heard part of it)
 - He **saw** the book **fall off** the shelf. Then he picked it up.
 He **saw** the book **falling off** the shelf and caught it.

17 *wish*

A Regret (present situation)

wish + past
(when we are sorry about a present situation and want it to be different):
I **wish** we **had** a lot more money. (but we haven't)
I **wish** I **was** a bit slimmer. (OR *I wish I were* … in formal style)
I **wish** we **weren't sitting** in a classroom right now.
I **wish** I **could** swim. (but I can't)

B Imaginary situations/events in the future

1 *wish + could*
 (when we wish for a change in the future that will probably not happen):
 I **wish** I **could** see her. (I want it to happen but it won't)
 Note: *hope* + present:
 I **hope** I **pass** my driving test. (this future event IS possible)

2 *wish* + other person/thing + *would*
 (often when we are annoyed with something):
 I **wish** you **would stop** biting your nails. (I want you to stop)
 I **wish** it **would** stop raining. (I want it to happen)

C Regret (past situation)

wish + past perfect
(when we are sorry about a past situation, but it is impossible to change it now):
I **wish** I **had worked** harder at school. (but I didn't work hard)
▶ pages 201–202 for Conditionals.

Writing reference

Contents

Introduction

This Writing reference is here to help you with your writing in preparation for Paper 2 of the FCE exam.

First, there is a checklist, which you should use every time you complete a piece of writing.

Then, for each type of writing that might come up in the exam, there is an example question (Question 1), a 'model answer' to that question, with notes to help you see the important points, and another exam question (Question 2).

If you are working on your own with this Writing reference, read Question 1 and the model answer carefully. Refer back to the pages in the main units for more information and help. Then answer Question 2, following the guidelines here and in the main units.

If you are working with a teacher, he/she will tell you when and how to use the Writing reference.

Writing checklist

Content and style

- Is your answer the right length? You will lose marks if it is under 120 words, and the examiner may not read more than 180 words.
- Have you answered all parts of the question? You will lose marks if you don't include all the required content points.
- Is your answer interesting to read?
- Have you communicated clearly?
- Is your style appropriate for the question (e.g. a formal or informal letter, a lively article)?
- Is your style consistent (e.g. no informal words in a formal letter)?
- Will your writing have the effect you want on your reader?

Organisation

- Have you divided your answer into paragraphs?
- Does each paragraph have ONE main idea, which is appropriate to what you are writing?
- Are the paragraphs in a logical order?
- Have you used linking expressions to connect ideas between paragraphs (e.g. *However, On the other hand*)?

Language

- Have you included a range of grammatical structures (e.g. in a story: past simple, past continuous, past perfect)?
- Is there a good range of vocabulary (e.g. in a story, adverbs to bring it to life: *He stopped suddenly, absolutely horrified.*)?
- Is your vocabulary specific, not general (e.g. *a hot, sunny day* not *a nice day, an enjoyable meal* not *a good meal*)?
- Have you used a range of appropriate linking expressions (e.g. *but, so, after, because* within a sentence, and *Finally, What's more,* to connect ideas in two sentences)?
- Have you used time expressions appropriately (e.g. *when, after, as soon as*)?
- Is your handwriting easy to read?
- Are your spelling and punctuation correct? You will not automatically lose marks for poor spelling, punctuation and handwriting, but it will affect the examiner's general impression mark.
- Have you checked for grammar mistakes, in particular the ones you know you often make?

Part 1: Transactional letter

▶ See pages 42–43, 72–73, 102–103, 132–133, 162–163 for work on transactional letters.

Question 1

You want to visit the Paris Fashion Show and your pen friend Danielle, who lives in Paris, has agreed to put you up in her flat. Read the information about the show and the train timetable she has sent you. You need some more information. Using the notes below that you have made, write a letter to Danielle.

PARIS FASHION SHOW

Spring collection

Saturday 4 May 09:30–18:30

London–Paris

FRIDAY
Depart London
14:00
16:00
18:00
Journey time approx. 3 hrs.

NOTES
Prefer last train Fri. – OK/too late?
Flat near station? Directions?
Show – first time – what clothes to wear?
Weather/clothes?
Sun. – park? River cruise? Or...?

Write a **letter** of between **120** and **180** words in an appropriate style. Do not write any postal addresses.

Question 2

You would like to learn Russian and you see this advertisement in a newspaper. You would like to know more. Read the advertisement and the notes you have made. Write a letter to the school asking for more information.

NEVA SCHOOL OF LANGUAGES

LEARN RUSSIAN IN ST. PETERSBURG   beginners?

Come and learn Russian with us on the banks of the River Neva.

hrs per week?————Two-week courses throughout the year.
    – cost?

                    Small groups.———— 6? 12?

close to school?———— Family accommodation available.

            Study centre for evening and weekend study.———times?

Write a **letter** of between **120** and **180** words in an appropriate style. Do not write any postal addresses.

Model answer (Question 1)

Set the context (mention something the other person has sent you, or give a reason for writing.)

Only include necessary information – but ALL the information necessary to answer the question. Don't repeat whole phrases from the input.

Keep the style consistent (informal).

Start a new paragraph for different subject matter.

Finish by referring to what will happen next.

Make sure the ending is in the same style.

Dear Danielle,

Thanks for the information you sent me about the Fashion Show. It should be a great event.

I'm trying to decide which train to get. Personally, I'd prefer to get the last one from London but it doesn't get to Paris until about nine o'clock. Will that be OK, or is it too late for you? Also, I don't know how to get to your flat. Is it near the station? Perhaps you could send me directions.

I've never been to a fashion show before. What kind of clothes do you think I should wear? And what's the weather like at the moment? Will I need to bring some warm clothes?

By the way, what shall we do on Sunday? How about going for a walk in the park, or going on a river cruise? Or maybe you've got some other ideas.

Anyway, I can't wait! Looking forward to hearing from you. See you soon.

Love,

Ivana

(167 words)

Part 2: Informal letter

▶ See pages 12–13 for work on informal letters.

Question 1

Last week, you organised a surprise birthday party for someone in your family, and your pen friend wants to hear about it. Write a letter to your pen friend, describing what kind of party you organised, who you invited and how it went.

Write your **letter**. Do not write any postal addresses. (Write your answer in **120–180** words in an appropriate style.)

Model answer

You will usually need to use a first name. Invent a name if necessary. Don't write *Dear friend*.

Start with a fixed phrase showing the situation with the reader.

Possibly add a general comment.

Start a new paragraph, as the topic has changed slightly. Use an informal linking expression.

Good to use a range of appropriate vocabulary and informal expressions.

Make sure you finish with an informal phrase.

Dear Sarah,

Good to you hear from you again. I hope you're still enjoying your job.

Do you remember in your letter you asked about the party I was organising for my mother's birthday? Well, it was a fantastic success. I told mother we were taking her out for a quiet meal at a local restaurant, but in fact I'd hired a large room in a hotel and invited all her old friends!

Anyway, I picked mother up and told her I'd changed my mind. We were going to have a meal in a hotel. You should have seen her face when she walked into the room and everyone cheered! She just couldn't believe it and burst into tears. Then the party got going, and it didn't finish until four in the morning. We were absolutely exhausted but mother had had a wonderful time.

Must dash now, I've got to go to college. Hope to hear from you soon.

Love,

Tania

Ask a question directly.

Use some exclamation marks (but not too many) to express emotions. Use contractions.

Short sentences are acceptable.

When you close, make an excuse to finish and/or refer to the current situation with the reader again.

(167 words)

Question 2

You have decided to go on holiday in the country where your English friend lives. Write a letter to your friend, explaining why you have not written for a while, and asking for advice on where to visit, what to see and the best way of travelling round the country.

Write your **letter**. Do not write any postal addresses. (Write your answer in **120–180** words in an appropriate style.)

Part 2: Formal letter

▶ See pages 26–27 for work on formal letters.

Question 1

You want to attend a course in English and American Studies in an English-speaking country and you see this section in a college prospectus:

SCHOLARSHIPS

Every year, two scholarships are offered to candidates from overseas who can show how our one-year course would help their career.
Scholarships cover fees, accommodation and food, but not transport or personal spending money.
Apply in writing, explaining why you think you deserve a scholarship.

Write your **letter**. Do not include any postal addresses. (Write your answer in **120–180** words in an appropriate style.)

Model answer

Say why you are writing and what you are responding to (e.g. an advert, a prospectus).

Use a formal, neutral style. (Remember: no contractions, no colloquial language, no direct questions, no informal punctuation such as exclamation marks.)

Be polite and positive, but not too much!

Use a formal ending.

Sign your name and then print your name clearly underneath.

If you know the name of the person, begin *Dear Mr Smith/Dear Ms Jones*, etc.

In one paragraph, briefly describe you/your situation.

In the next paragraph, make it clear why you are applying for a scholarship and why you would be a suitable candidate. Make sure you cover all the points in the question.

Dear Sir/Madam,

I would like to apply for one of the scholarships I saw advertised in your prospectus.

At present I am training to be a secondary school teacher of English and I finish my course at the end of June. However, I feel I still have a lot to learn about the language and culture of the English-speaking world and would benefit considerably from a course in an English-speaking country.

The reason I am applying for a scholarship is that I cannot afford the cost of studying abroad. I have no income except for my student grant, so if I am fortunate enough to be given a scholarship, I would have to work part-time to save some personal spending money. My parents will borrow some money for my airfare if I am successful.

I would appreciate being given the opportunity to study at your college and would be very grateful if you would consider my application.

Yours sincerely,

Marco Prodi

MARCO PRODI

(162 words)

Question 2

You see this advertisement in an international newspaper. You are interested in applying for the job.

WINTER IN THE ROCKIES?

We are looking for young people to work in our ski shop this winter. If you are interested, write to us saying why you might be a good person.
Reasonable salary, and we provide help with accommodation. Free ski pass included. Flexible hours. Apply in writing.

Write your **letter**. Do not include any postal addresses. (Write your answer in **120–180** words in an appropriate style.)

Part 2: Story

▶ See pages 56–57 for work on stories.

Question 1

> You have decided to enter a short story competition in a student magazine. The story must **end** with these words:
>
> *'I'm very glad that's over!' said Katie as we made the long drive back home.*
>
> Write your **story**. (Write your answer in **120–180** words in an appropriate style.)

Model answer

If you have to invent an opening line, make sure it is dramatic enough to attract the readers' interest and stimulate their imagination.

Use adverbs to make the action more vivid.

You can create suspense and excitement by writing short sentences.

Remember to convey the feelings of the characters.

Create atmosphere when setting the scene. You might need to use the past continuous or past perfect continuous.

Make sure you make the sequence of actions clear.

Use vivid adjectives to bring what you are describing to life.

Use the words given in the question, without changing anything. Notice that direct speech can be used in a story for variety and interest.

The city was deserted that night, as Katie and I wandered through the narrow streets. It had been raining earlier and the full moon shone brightly on the wet stones.

Suddenly we heard the sound of running footsteps. Then there was a cry and the footsteps stopped. Nervously, we walked back. Perhaps someone had been killed, or kidnapped in the street.

As we were turning the corner, we saw a crazy-looking man lying in the street, holding his ankle. He had obviously slipped on the wet stones and he was screaming at us to stay away.

To our relief, at that moment the police appeared. The man was in too much pain to move and they were easily able to force him into their car. They told us he was an extremely dangerous criminal and we had had a lucky escape. 'I'm very glad that's over!' said Katie as we made the long drive back home.

(168 words)

Question 2

> You have been invited to write a short story for a young person's magazine. The story must **begin** with these words:
>
> *Jack was asleep in the chair, dreaming, when the phone rang.*
>
> Write your **story**. (Write your answer in **120–180** words in an appropriate style.)

Part 2: Article

▶ See pages 86–87 for work on articles.

Question 1

You see this competition in an international magazine.

COMPETITION

Imagine you were on a desert island. What would you miss most?
Write an article briefly describing an important object, person or
place in your life and give reasons for your choice. The best article
will be published and the writer will receive £500.

Write your **article**. (Write your answer in **120–180** words in an appropriate style.)

Model answer

Introduce the topic. Although you don't know your readers personally, you can address them directly and ask them a question.

Note the question says the description should be 'brief'.

Your style will not be formal. This article has a personal style; others might have a more neutral style.

Life away from home

How would you feel about living on a desert island? I can't imagine anything worse. I would miss a lot of things, but most of all I would miss my home.

My home is a small house on the outskirts of a city. It was built about fifty years ago and has a small garden. In the summer our country gets very hot but our house is always cool.

You would probably think our house is nothing special, but I have lived there all my life and all my friends live nearby. It is a happy place, where I feel completely safe. Whenever I go away, I look forward to coming back, lying on my bed, reading a book and listening to my brother and sister arguing downstairs!

I love travelling and meeting new people, but if I were on a desert island I would be away from the place I love most – my home – and I would hate that.

(164 words)

Think of a title that will catch the reader's attention.

Give specific examples to bring your article to life.

Finish with a sentence which summarises what you have said.

Question 2

You see this advertisement in an international youth magazine.

Technology – how do you get on with it?

We are looking for short articles describing people's experiences – good or bad – of technology. Write and tell us how you have used technology and whether you have got on well with it.
We will publish the best articles in this magazine.

Write your **article**. (Write your answer in **120–180** words in an appropriate style.)

Part 2: Discursive composition

▶ See pages 116–117 for work on discursive compositions.

Question 1

You have recently had a class project on animal welfare and vegetarianism. Now your teacher has asked you to write a composition, giving your opinions on the following statement.

Some people believe that humans should not eat meat. Do you agree?

Write your **composition**. (Write your answer in **120–180** words in an appropriate style.)

Model answer

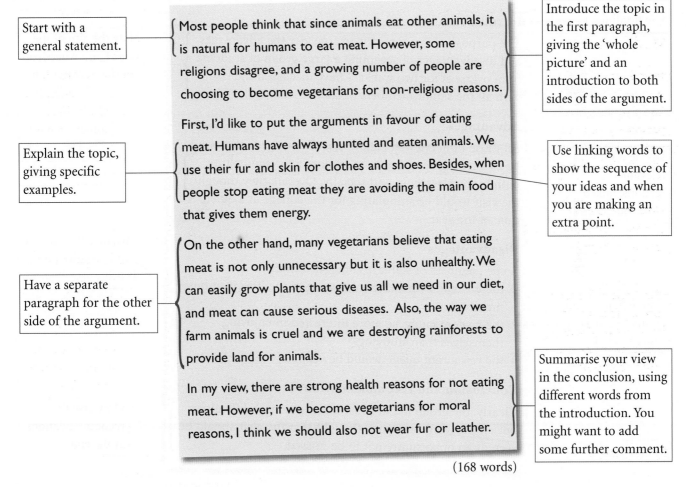

Start with a general statement.

Most people think that since animals eat other animals, it is natural for humans to eat meat. However, some religions disagree, and a growing number of people are choosing to become vegetarians for non-religious reasons.

Introduce the topic in the first paragraph, giving the 'whole picture' and an introduction to both sides of the argument.

Explain the topic, giving specific examples.

First, I'd like to put the arguments in favour of eating meat. Humans have always hunted and eaten animals. We use their fur and skin for clothes and shoes. Besides, when people stop eating meat they are avoiding the main food that gives them energy.

Use linking words to show the sequence of your ideas and when you are making an extra point.

Have a separate paragraph for the other side of the argument.

On the other hand, many vegetarians believe that eating meat is not only unnecessary but it is also unhealthy. We can easily grow plants that give us all we need in our diet, and meat can cause serious diseases. Also, the way we farm animals is cruel and we are destroying rainforests to provide land for animals.

In my view, there are strong health reasons for not eating meat. However, if we become vegetarians for moral reasons, I think we should also not wear fur or leather.

Summarise your view in the conclusion, using different words from the introduction. You might want to add some further comment.

(168 words)

Question 2

You recently had a class discussion about television. Now your teacher has asked you to write a composition.

Young children watch too much television. Do you agree?

Write your **composition**. (Write your answer in **120–180** words in an appropriate style.)

Part 2: Report

▶ See pages 146–147 for work on reports.

Question 1

Your college has been asked to accept a group of 50 students from another country for two weeks. You have been asked by your principal to find out what the advantages and disadvantages would be of accepting this group. Is it a good idea?

Write your **report** to the principal. (Write your answer in **120–180** words in an appropriate style.)

Model answer

Use headings.

Divide it into relevant sections, linked to the question.

Listing/Numbering points can make it easier to read.

Generalise.

State the aim of the report and where you got the information.

Quote in an impersonal way

Use a clear, neutral style.

Balance the positive and negative points fairly.

Only give the recommendations at the end.

Report on Proposed Visit by 50 Overseas Students

Introduction

The purpose of this report is to consider the advantages and disadvantages of accepting a large group of students from overseas for two weeks. I have discussed the issue with all the senior members of college staff.

Advantages

All those I interviewed believe that for students this would be an exciting opportunity to explore a foreign culture, both in the classroom and socially. Overall, they thought the visit would be stimulating for the college at a quiet time of the year.

Disadvantages

Some members of staff are concerned that:
1 there would be insufficient seating in the library at busy times.
2 the visitors might be more interested in enjoying themselves than studying.
3 the restaurant queue would be very slow at lunchtime.

Conclusion and recommendation

Clearly, the group might cause some practical difficulties but on the whole everyone thought that the visit should be seen as an opportunity not to be missed.

(162 words)

Question 2

You work for a travel agent in an English-speaking country. You have been asked to write a report for your boss, recommending the best time of year to arrange leisure tours to your country. You have been asked to comment on such things as the weather, special attractions and festivities.

Write your **report**. (Write your answer in **120–180** words in an appropriate style.)

Part 2: Descriptive composition (set book)

▶ See pages 176–177 for work on descriptive compositions.

Question 1

> Which is the most memorable character in the book you have read? Write a composition for your teacher describing what part the character plays in the story, and why the character is so memorable. Give reasons for your choice.
>
> Write your **composition**. (Write your answer in **120–180** words in an appropriate style.)

Model answer

The most memorable character for me in *Animal Farm* is Napoleon. After the animals on Mr Jones' farm revolt against their masters, the pigs become their leaders and Napoleon is their chief.

> In the question, you are asked to describe the character's part in the story.

Give specific examples.

At first, Napoleon seems to be a good leader of the revolution. He and Snowball (another pig) organise the animals and introduce them to the Seven Commandments, which aim to make everyone equal. However, we see that Napoleon might be dishonest when he tells the other animals there are more important things to worry about than milk, and then the milk disappears. I think he takes it for himself.

Napoleon and Snowball argue a lot and eventually Napoleon gets the dogs to drive Snowball off the farm. One by one the commandments are broken, and Napoleon becomes a cruel dictator. He kills many of the animals for plotting against him and he even hires a pig to taste his food in case someone tries to poison him.

> Show the character at a different stage of the novel and link your answer to the question.

Summarise your opinion in a simple conclusion.

I believe Napoleon is memorable because he is a very good example of how easily power corrupts.

(176 words)

Question 2

> Which do you think is the most dramatic scene in the book you have read? Write a composition for your teacher briefly describing the scene you have chosen, and how it fits in with the rest of the story. Give your reasons.
>
> Write your **composition**. (Write your answer in **120–180** words in an appropriate style.)

Spelling

1 Words ending in one -e
- Remove e before -ing:
  love ▶ loving
  (but **not** words with -ee: agree ▶ agreeing)
- Keep e before -ly:
  fortunate ▶ fortunately
  (but **not** -le adjectives: probable ▶ probably)
- Keep e before -ment:
  advertise ▶ advertisement

2 Verbs ending in -ie
Change -ie to -y:
lie ▶ lying

3 Words ending in consonant + -y
Change -y to -ie:
try ▶ tries, tried
baby ▶ babies
happy ▶ happier, happiest

4 Words ending in vowel +-y
Keep y:
play ▶ plays, played.
But note:
day ▶ daily
lay ▶ laid; say ▶ said; pay ▶ paid

5 Words ending in -c before -ed/-ing
Change -c to -ck before -ed/-ing:
picnic ▶ picnicking
panic ▶ panicked

6 Words ending in one consonant
Double the final consonant before -ing, -ed, -er, -est for:
- one-syllable words with 1 vowel + 1 consonant:
  stop ▶ stopping, stopped
  hot ▶ hotter, hottest
- two- or three-syllable words with the final syllable stressed:
  be'gin ▶ be'ginning
Do not double the final consonant of:
- words with 2 vowels before the final consonant:
  rain ▶ raining
  look ▶ looked
  cheap ▶ cheaper
- words with 2 final consonants:
  start ▶ started
  rich ▶ richer

- two- or three-syllable words with the final syllable **not** stressed:
  'enter ▶ 'entering
  But note in British English: double final -l after one vowel:
  'travel ▶ 'travelling
- words ending in -y or -w:
  stay ▶ stayed
  slow ▶ slower

7 Nouns ending in -o
Add -es in the plural:
potato ▶ potatoes
tomato ▶ tomatoes

8 Nouns ending in -our
Remove u in the adjective:
humour ▶ humorous

9 Endings often misspelt:
- Adjectives (see also Unit 4):
  -ible/-able: sensible, responsible; comfortable, suitable
  -ful: beautiful, hopeful
  -ent: independent, convenient, excellent
  -ous: anxious, conscious, delicious, famous, various
- Nouns (see also Unit 10):
  -al/-le: arrival, refusal, principal / principle
  -er/-or: actor, operator, visitor but driver, employer, writer
  -ent/-ant: excitement, employment but assistant, servant
  -ness: happiness, weakness
- Verbs (see also Unit 18):
  -ise/-ize: surprise, exercise
  British English usually: realise, modernise, recognise
  American English: realize, modernize, recognize

10 Some useful rules
- isc (verb)/ -icc (noun):
  advise/advice, practise/practice
- i before e except after c:
  niece/relieve; deceive/ceiling
  (Exception: foreign)

Some commonly misspelt words:

accommodation address affect (v.)/effect (n.) bicycle
business busy committee disappoint embarrass
Europe familiar guilty heard heart immediate
juice loose /luːs/ (adj.)/lose /luːz/(v.) medicine
necessary pronunciation recommend separate
similar until

Punctuation

Name		Uses	Examples
Apostrophe	'	To show someone owns something.	*Tom's car*
		To indicate a contraction.	*He isn't here.*
Capital letter	B	To begin sentences, for the pronoun *I*, names, countries, cities, days of the week and months (not seasons) of the year.	*Graham and I play tennis on Saturdays in June.*
Colon	:	To introduce a list.	*There are three possibilities: first we could ...*
		In formal writing, before a phrase that gives more information about the main clause.	*The house was small: it had a kitchen and one bedroom.*
Comma	,	To divide a sentence into sections to make it easier to understand:	
		Before and after a non-defining relative clause.	*Another man, who looked a lot younger, was drinking coffee.*
		To separate items in a list.	*The man was wearing black trousers, a white shirt and a blue tie.*
		To separate a tag question from the sentence.	*It's hot, isn't it?*
		To separate an introductory word or phrase from the rest of the sentence.	*By the way, how are you?*
		Before or after 'he said' (when writing conversation).	*'I'm tired,' she said.*
Dash	–	To separate a statement that is extra to the main idea.	*I love pasta – particularly spaghetti – and other Italian food.*
Exclamation mark	!	To express emotional emphasis in informal writing.	*What a lovely day!*
Full stop/point/ period	.	To show the end of a sentence.	*That's very clear.*
		In abbreviations.	*e.g. etc.*
Question mark	?	At the end of a direct question.	*Are you tired?*
Semi-colon	;	To separate two main clauses that have a link in meaning.	*It was late; it was getting dark.*
Speech marks (quotation marks/inverted commas)	"..." '...'	When we write down the exact words someone says. (They can be double or single.)	*"I'll help you," she said.* *'I'll help you,' she said.*

Speaking material/Keys

Unit 6: Speaking (Paper 5 Part 2) (p.45)
Individual long turn: Exercise 4

STUDENT B:

Unit 6: Use of English 1 (p.46)
Answer key: Lead-in: Exercise 1a

1 True. (Although cats distinguish some colours better than others, they don't generally distinguish colours very well.)
2 True. (It is estimated to be anywhere between 100 and a million times better.)
3 True. (They have a very large brain and live for a long time. They particularly remember extremes of kindness and cruelty on the part of humans.)
4 True. (The snowy tree cricket (*Occanthus fultoni*) is popularly known as the 'thermometer cricket' because the approximate temperature (Fahrenheit) can be estimated by counting the number of chirps in 15 seconds and adding 40.)
5 True. (It is believed they sense changes of air pressure in their digestive system.)

Unit 8: Speaking (Paper 5 Part 3) (p.59)
Collaborative task: Exercise 3

STUDENT 1: **You are the examiner. Read the instructions below to Candidates A and B. Stop the discussion after three minutes.**

Instructions:
Now, I'd like you to talk about something together for about three minutes. I'm just going to listen. Here are some pictures which show people doing different sports. (*Point to the photos on pages 58–59.*)
First, talk to each other about the advantages and disadvantages of taking up each of these sports. Then decide which one is most suitable for someone who doesn't have much spare time.
You have only about three minutes for this, so don't worry if I stop you. Please speak so that we can hear you. All right?

Unit 12: Speaking (Paper 5 Part 2) (p.88)
Individual long turn: Exercise 4a, Task 2

STUDENT B: Compare and contrast the photographs, and say why you think people enjoy concerts like this.

STUDENT A: Listen to student B without interrupting. Stop him/her after one minute, and say briefly which concert you would prefer to go to.

Unit 14: Speaking (Paper 5 Part 3) (p.105)
Collaborative task: Exercise 2a

STUDENT 1: You are the examiner. Read the instructions below to students 2 and 3. Stop the discussion after three minutes.

Instructions:
Now, I'd like you to talk about something together for about three minutes. I'm just going to listen.
Here are some photographs which show different styles of clothes. (*Point to the photos on pages 104–105.*)
First, talk to each other about which of the clothes you would wear and which you would not wear. Then decide which would be best to wear at a friend's birthday party. You have only about three minutes for this, so don't worry if I stop you. Please speak so that we can hear you. All right?

Unit 16: Listening (p.118)
Answer key: Before you listen: Exercise 1b

Jarvis Cocker – bird-watching; Rod Stewart – model trains; Julia Roberts – knitting; Kate Moss – jigsaws

Unit 18: Speaking (Paper 5 Part 2) (p.134)
Individual long turn: Exercise 3, Task 1

STUDENT 1: You are the examiner. Read out the instructions below to Candidates A and B and point to the photos on page 134 (Unit 18, Speaking). Stop Candidate A after one minute.

Instructions:
To Candidate A: [Name], here are your two photographs. They show two different ways of shopping. *(Point to the photos on page 134.)* I'd like you to compare and contrast these photographs, saying which you think is a better way to shop. You only have about a minute for this, so don't worry if I interrupt you. All right? *(Stop Candidate A after one minute.)*
To Candidate B: [Name], which way do you prefer to shop?

Unit 20: Speaking (Paper 5 Part 2) (p.149)
Individual long turn: Exercise 2b, Task 2

STUDENT 2: You are the examiner. Read out the instructions below to Candidates A and B and point to the photos on page 221. Stop Candidate A after one minute.

Instructions:
To Candidates A and B: I'm going to give each of you two different photographs and I'd like you to talk about them.
To Candidate A: [Name], here are your two photographs. They show two different types of dancing. *(Point to the two photos on page 221.)* I'd like you to compare and contrast these photographs, and say which one you think is more popular. You only have about a minute for this, so don't worry if I interrupt you. All right? *(Stop Candidate A after one minute.)*
To Candidate B: [Name], do you like dancing?

Unit 20: Speaking (Paper 5 Part 2) (p.149)
Individual long turn: Exercise 2a, Task 1

STUDENT 1: You are the examiner. Read out the instructions below to Candidates A and B and point to the photos on page 149 (Unit 20, Speaking). Stop Candidate A after one minute.

Instructions:
To Candidates A and B: I'm going to give each of you two different photographs and I'd like you to talk about them. *To Candidate A:* [Name], here are your two photographs. They show two different ways of spending an evening. *(Point to the photos on page 149.)* I'd like you to compare and contrast these photographs, and say which people you think are enjoying themselves more. You only have about a minute for this, so don't worry if I interrupt you. All right? *(Stop Candidate A after one minute.)*
To Candidate B: [Name], what kind of films do you like watching?

Unit 18: Speaking (Paper 5 Part 2) (p.134)
Individual long turn: Exercise 3, Task 2

STUDENT 2: You are the examiner. Read out the instructions below to Candidates A and B and point to the photos on page 220. Stop Candidate A after one minute.

Instructions:
To Candidate A: [Name], here are your two photographs. They show different places to buy food. *(Point to the two photos on page 220.)* I'd like you to compare and contrast these photographs, saying which you think is a better place to buy food. You only have about a minute for this, so don't worry if I interrupt you. All right? *(Stop Candidate A after one minute.)*
To Candidate B: [Name], do you like shopping for food?

Unit 24: Speaking (Paper 5 Part 2) (p.179)

Individual long turn: Exercise 2b

Unit 24: Speaking (Paper 5 Part 3) (p.179)

Collaborative task: Exercise 3b

Unit 22: Speaking (Paper 5 Part 3) (p.165)

Collaborative task: Exercise 2

STUDENT 1: **You are the examiner. Read out the instructions below to Candidates A and B and point to the pictures on pages 164–165 (Unit 22, Speaking). Stop the discussion after three minutes.**

Instructions:

Now, I'd like you to talk about something together for about three minutes. I'm just going to listen.

Here are some pictures which show ways of keeping healthy. *(Point to the pictures on pages 164–165.)* First, talk to each other about how each of these things can help. Then decide which you would recommend to somebody who wanted to get healthy quickly.

You have only about three minutes for this, so don't worry if I stop you. Please speak so that we can hear you. All right?

Unit 24: Speaking (Paper 5 Part 1) (p.179)

Interview: Exercise 1

Home town

Where are you from?
How long have you lived there?
What do you like about living there?

Family and home

Could you tell us something about your family?
And what about your home? What's it like?

Work/Education

Do you work or study?
(if working):
What does your work involve?
What do you enjoy most about your job?
(if studying):
What are you studying at the moment?
Why did you decide to study *(candidate's subject)*?
What sort of job are you hoping to do in the future?

Free time/Leisure

What do you like doing in your free time?
What do you enjoy most about *(what candidate does in his/her free time)*?

Likes and dislikes

Music
What sort of music do you like?
Do you like going to concerts or listening to music at home? Why?
Films
How often do you go to the cinema?
What sort of films do you enjoy?
Sport
Are there any sports you enjoy doing? *(if yes)*: What do you like about it/them?
What sports do you enjoy watching on television?

Functions reference

1 Adding information

Yes, and as well as that … .
Apart from that … .
Not only that … .
And there's another thing … .
I hadn't thought of that. We could also … .

2 Agreeing and disagreeing

Yes, that's true.
So do I.
Neither do I.
I couldn't agree more.
I suppose so.
I agree up to a point, but … .
Yes, but (what about) … ?
Do you think so?
But don't you think that … ?
Actually, I think it's more important … .

3 Checking you understand

I'm not quite sure what we have to do first.
So you want me to … ?
Sorry, do you mean we have to … ?

4 Comparing and contrasting

They both show … .
They both seem to be … .
Both of … are … .
Both of these people look as if … .
There are … in both photos.
In this one … and this one … .
Neither of them … .
The one on the right shows … while/whereas in the other one there's … .
One thing which is different (in this one) is … .
The main difference is that the top one seems to be … while the bottom one … .
The main difference between … and … is … .
This one is … whereas … is … .

5 Correcting yourself

What I meant was … .
Sorry, I meant to say … .
I mean … .

6 Expressing advantages and disadvantages

The good thing about … is … . On the other hand … .
One disadvantage about … is … . Having said that, … .

7 Expressing likes, dislikes and preferences

I would like … but … .
I wouldn't mind … but on the other hand … .
Although … I'd like … because … .
I think I'd prefer … as … .
I'm not really very interested in … .
If I had to choose … .
I prefer … .
I think I would say … .
To be honest, I haven't thought much about it.

8 Expressing opinions

I think … .
For me, one of the most important … is … .
I don't think it matters … .
I just don't think it's … .
Personally, I … .
It's very hard to say, but … .

9 Giving and asking for suggestions

Why don't we start by … ?
Shall we … first?
Let's begin with … .
We could start by talking about … .
Let's decide which … .
Shall we make a decision?
Do you agree?
What would you say?
Do you think we should … ?

10 Interrupting

Can I just say … ?
Sorry to interrupt, but … .

11 Paraphrasing

It's something you need when … .
It's when you … .
You use it to … .
It's like a … .
It's a … where/that/who … you (+ verb).
It's a kind of … .

12 Speculating

It could be/could have been … .
It can't be/can't have been … .
It might be/might have been … .
It must have/must have had … .
I get the impression that … .